D0875379

prevention
in
family
services

NEW PERSPECTIVES ON FAMILY

Published in cooperation with **(ncfr)** National Council on Family Relations

Series Editor: **John Scanzoni**
Family Research Center
University of North Carolina, Greensboro

Books appearing in New Perspectives on Family are either single- or multiple-authored volumes or concisely edited books of original articles on focused topics within the broad field of marriage and family. Books can be reports of significant research, innovations in methodology, treatises on family theory, or syntheses of current knowledge in a subfield of the discipline. Each volume meets the highest academic standards and makes a substantial contribution to our knowledge of marriage and family.

Other volumes currently available from Sage and sponsored by NCFR:

THE VIOLENT HOME: A Study of Physical Aggression Between Husbands and Wives, *Richard J. Gelles*

ROLE STRUCTURE AND ANALYSIS OF FAMILY, *F. Ivan Nye*

SONS OR DAUGHTERS: A Cross-Cultural Survey of Parental Preferences, *Nancy Williamson*

CONFLICT AND POWER IN MARRIAGE: Expecting the First Child, *Ralph LaRossa*

THE AMERICAN FAMILY: A Demographic History, *Rudy Ray Seward*

THE SOCIAL WORLD OF OLD WOMEN: Management of Self-Identity, *Sarah H. Matthews*

FAMILIES AGAINST SOCIETY: A Study of Reactions to Children with Birth Defects, *Rosalyn Benjamin Darling*

ASSESSING MARRIAGE: New Behavioral Approaches, *Erik E. Filsinger and Robert A. Lewis, eds.*

SEX & PREGNANCY IN ADOLESCENCE, *Melvin Zelnick, John F. Kantner, and Kathleen Ford*

SINGLES: Myths and Realities, *Leonard Cargan and Matthew Melko*

THE CHILDBEARING DECISION: Fertility Attitudes and Behavior, *Greer Litton Fox, ed.*

FAMILY ALLOCATION OF WORK, *Michael Geerken and Walter R. Gove*

PREVENTION IN FAMILY SERVICES: Approaches to Family Wellness, *David R. Mace, ed.*

prevention
in
family
services

approaches to
family wellness

edited by
DAVID R. MACE

Published in cooperation with
the National Council on Family Relations

 SAGE PUBLICATIONS Beverly Hills / London / New Delhi

For information address:

SAGE Publications, Inc.
275 South Beverly Drive
Beverly Hills, California 90212

SAGE Publications India Pvt. Ltd.
C-236 Defence Colony
New Delhi 110 024, India

SAGE Publications Ltd
28 Banner Street
London EC1Y 8QE, England

Printed in the United States of America

Library of Congress Cataloging in Publication Data

Mace, David Robert.
   Prevention in family services.

   (New perspectives on family)
   "Published in cooperation with the National Council on Family Relations."
   1. Family—United States—Congresses. 2. Family Social work—United States—Congresses. 3. Marriage—United States—Congresses. 4. Parenting—United States—Congresses. I. Title. II. Series.
HQ536.M23 1983   306.8'5'0973   83-17854
ISBN 0-8039-2154-3
ISBN 0-8039-2155-1 (pbk.)

THIRD PRINTING, 1985

Contents

circled = did not read

List of Tables
and Diagrams

TO CLARK VINCENT

Whose clear vision and sound judgment pointed to the future need to reorient our services to families toward a new focus on prevention.

Series Editor's Foreword

The National Council on Family Relations is composed of persons from a wide variety of disciplines—research and theory, social policy, clinical and therapeutic projects, and education. Education, taken in its broadest sense, is a mutual concern for most all of us. No matter what field we specialize in, it is our goal to share research information and clinical insights for the benefit of individuals, families, and the society. With that goal in mind, David R. Mace and his colleagues have prepared this book on what they term "family wellness." Through detailed descriptions of many different strategies and programs, they offer a positive and practical approach to the challenges facing marriages and families today. We welcome these distinguished authors to the growing NCFR-Sage Series.

—John Scanzoni

Prologue

David R. Mace

In October, 1981, a national conference was held in Milwaukee under the title "Toward Family Wellness: Our Need for Effective Preventive Programs." It was jointly organized by the Association of Couples for Marriage Enrichment (ACME) and The National Council on Family Relations (NCFR), and given strong support from the Aid Association for Lutherans (AAL) which has its headquarters in Wisconsin and had at that time a section on family health.

The project was developed because some of us had become interested in a change we had begun to observe in the kinds of services which are now being offered to families. This took the form of a shift in emphasis from an almost total preoccupation with remedial services to a new goal of matching our remedial services with corresponding preventive services. This was particularly evident in the development of the marriage and family enrichment movement.

The purpose of the conference was to seek out people across the country who were experimenting with the new preventive approaches, and to bring some of them together to exchange views and experiences.

A program was planned, and invitations were sent out to persons selected as possible speakers and leaders of workshops. Their interest may be judged by the fact that all of them accepted our invitation, and came at their own expense. Other participants in the conference were mainly members of the sponsoring organizations.

The conference went very well indeed. Those who participated were excited and enthusiastic. It became clear to us all that "family wellness," the term we coined to describe what we had come to discuss, represented a new approach which was not only greatly needed but was already being promoted here and there and seemed likely to become what someone called "the wave of the future."

[11]

The planning group made an important decision—to prepare a book which would try to make the message of the conference more widely known and understood. Putting this book together became my responsibility, and I now have the pleasant task of introducing it to its readers.

I should explain that the chapters do not reproduce exactly the material that was presented at the conference. Some chapters do so, others go beyond what was covered in Milwaukee, and some of the writers had not even been present. However, the aim of the book is exactly the same as that of the conference—to present what we believe are very promising new approaches to the services we are currently offering to North American families.

The title of the book perhaps requires some explanation. "Wellness" is a new and unfamiliar word. It will not even be found yet in some dictionaries.

That is exacty why we chose it—both for the conference and for the book. "Healthy families" might have seemed a more obvious choice, but unfortunately the word "health" had come to be associated in many of its uses with illness. You can be in a state of either good health or bad health. The word can be qualified positively—vigorous, robust, or even perfect health—but it can also be qualified negatively—poor, indifferent, or even miserable health. Wellness can also be qualified positively, but not negatively. Wellness is unequivocally a term describing a good and desirable state, and that was what we were looking for. We think the term "family wellness" will catch on, but of course only the future can tell.

I wish to express here my gratitude to all the writers who took the time to put their chapters together and, by doing so, made the book possible. My opinion may be biased; but I think we have come up with a good and timely publication. And I hope, dear reader, that you will find it so.

I have decided to dedicate this book to Clark Vincent. His many friends will agree that he is one of the most brilliant behavioral scientists of his generation. It was my privilege to work with him at the Behavioral Sciences Center attached to the Bowman Gray School of Medicine in Winston-Salem from 1967 to 1977. Unfortunately a serious breakdown in health forced his early retirement. Otherwise, he might well have been editing this book. We who know him recognize him as an outstanding pioneer in the promoting of the cause of preventive services to families, and we believe that the vision he shared with us will one day, and hopefully soon, be translated into action.

Part I

Theory, Research, and Policy

The meaning of the term "family wellness" is explained, and the need for a shift in our professional services from a remedial to a preventive emphasis is advocated. New information and new attitudes supporting this change in approach are reported. The possibilities of such a change in policy are assessed at the professional level.

1

What This Book Is About

David R. Mace

"As every good chairperson should know, you must define your terms."

That is the purpose of this chapter, We are embarking on an investigation of something that is relatively new. A vast literature exists on what are called "family problems"—the events that lead to trouble and stress, to conflict and crisis, to disorder and disruption, to maladjustment and dysfunction, to misunderstandings and misdemeanors, to quarrels and hassles, to breakdowns and break-ups, and to divorce and dissolution. We have a rich and varied vocabulary to describe families failing to fulfill our hopes, expectations, and ideals. Books have been written that describe every conceivable disaster that can befall a family and prescribing the appropriate remedy—whom to call in, where to go for help, what to do until help arrives, and what the chances are for recovery.

In this extensive literature, the assumption seems to be that family problems just happen and represent a fact of life. Consequently, it is implied, we need to provide a whole network of "services" which will be in constant readiness to deal with every kind of crisis. In recent years, these services have been undergoing a vast expansion, and they now offer an impressive army of "experts" whose dedication and skill are not to be questioned. However, their cost in time and money is becoming so great that we may soon have to consider whether the issue might not be approached from a different angle. Would it not be possible to cut down the flow of pathology which is making such heavy demands in terms of *remedial* services, by supplementing these services beforehand with *preventive* services? As one college counselor expressed it: "I've spent the last ten years fishing troubled youngsters out of the river. Now I'm beginning to ask why they got into the river in the first place, and whether something might be done at the other end."

The logic behind this statement is clear and convincing. Consider two of our major remedial services—one very old, the other relatively new.

First, consider the field of *medicine*. According to Charles Dull, who represents a major life insurance company (the AID Association for Lutherans), over 96% of health care costs in the United States today are spent for diagnosis and treatment and less than 4% for prevention.

This was dramatized in a report in the *New England Journal of Medicine* (summarized in the September 1980 issue of Reader's Digest, page 9) that described a survey of 2.238 patients who, in the course of a year, were treated by six Boston hospitals. It was found that 13% of these patients taxed the hospitals' resources as much as the remaining 87%. Since only 10% of Americans enter a hospital in the course of any given year, this suggests that half of our total hospital resources are being consumed by 1.3% of the population. What was significant was that these particular patients proved to have high incidences of smoking, drinking, and overeating—all considered bad habits from a health point of view, and all of which are preventable.

A similar situation was described by the Surgeon General in his 1979 report on *Health Promotion and Disease Prevention:* "Perhaps as much as half of U.S. mortality in 1979 was due to unhealthy behavior or life-styles, 20% to environmental factors, 20% to human biological factors, and only 10% to inadequacies in health care."

These facts illustrate how far medicine will have to travel in order to develop effective preventive services. Alex Comfort has declared that "the United States has a sickness industry, not a health service" (*Psychology Today,* December 1981, page 112). Many physicians are aware of this and are eager to do more in the the area of prevention.

Second, consider the field of *mental health*. It will be sufficient to quote George W. Albee, an authority in the field, from a lecture at the University of Minnesota on May 21, 1980:

Whereas widespread mental and emotional disorders that affect large numbers of people are never eliminated or brought under control by attempts at treating each individual afflicted, and whereas widespread emotional disorders *have* been shown to be controllable by successful efforts at prevention, *therefore* it is startling that practically all of our current efforts in mental health go into individual therapy and almost nothing goes into the support of efforts at prevention. For example, the budget of the National Institute of Mental Health, using the broadest possible definition of prevention, shows that no more than 2% is spent currently for prevention!

It is not our purpose here to explore these fields. They do however serve as typical examples of our general attitude to dealing with crisis situations. As Albee went on to say, "it is difficult to give up immediate rewards for long-term gain, especially when short-term sacrifice may mean . . . loss of political popularity . . . . Prevention philosophy runs counter to the search for immediate gratification."

Another assessment brings home the lack of wisdom in our present policy. In a book on emotionally handicapped children, Eli Bower (1960) recounts the following story:

Luther Woodward, at a meeting of the American Orthopsychiatric Association, described an ancient Cornish test on insanity as follows: The subject to be tested was placed in a room in which there was a pail of water directly under a water faucet. The water was turned on and the subject given a ladle and asked to bail the water from the pail. If he first turned off the faucet before beginning to bail, he was considered sane. If he continued to bail with the water still running into the pail, he was declared insane [p. 16].

WHAT *IS* PREVENTION?

The old adage tells us that prevention is better than cure. I have never met anyone who was prepared to contest this. But when we begin to talk about prevention *in practice*, it is surprising how confused the issue can become. So let us try to define this word, in the sense in which we shall be using it in the following pages.

The American Heritage Dictionary defines the word "prevent" as follows: "To keep from happening, as by some prior action." It goes on to say that the word "strongly implies decisive counteraction to stop something from happening." In the medical context, this means "thwarting or warding off illness or disease." John F. Dempsey gives us a very obvious illustration: "Although families are clamoring for more control over their lives, they are not exercising the controls they now have. If people voluntarily controlled their tobacco, drug, and alcohol use, the preventive benefits to families would be enormous" (Dempsey, 1981: 135).

We are to think, then, of a logical sequence of events. If it is known that behavior A leads in most instances to undesirable later consequences whereas behavior B usually results in the avoidance of these consequences, then a successful effort to persuade people to choose B rather thatn A will have good results for all concerned. If we are to make life good for people, therefore, we must if possible arrange accordingly. Some may not respond; but it is obviously our plain duty to make the issue clear and to give them the option.

As a matter of fact, this is already happening. Our lives are filled with preventive restraints which most of us accept without even thinking about them. The electrical system in your home is installed with all kinds of safeguards to prevent you from getting shocks. Railroad tracks are enclosed by fences to prevent people from getting run over. Traffic lights at street junctions prevent collisions. Regular visits to the dentist prevent you from losing your teeth prematurely. Your life insurance policy will hopefully prevent you from finding yourself penniless in your later years. You can think of plenty of others—the list is endless. The intellectual superiority of human beings has enabled them to make life rewarding by creating all kinds of preventive systems.

THREE LEVELS OF PREVENTION

When we look at the troubles which can afflict families and consider how they can be prevented, we find that it can be done at three levels:

Primary prevention. This is obviously the best approach. It means using positive early intervention to enable the family to avoid the kinds of trouble that might otherwise be very damaging. For example, if husband and wife could clearly understand and use, from their very first meeting, the principles of effective couple communication as it can now be taught, they would be able to avoid all kinds of misunderstandings from which other couples tend to suffer; in addition, they would naturally teach their children to use the same effective means of communication. It is already clear that some day this should happen universally.

Secondary prevention. We are now considering a situation in which it is too late for primary prevention. The family members are already in trouble. As a result of poor communication, misunderstandings are causing prejudiced judgments and alienation, and tensions are building up. However, the situation has not yet reached crisis proportions. Concerned about what is happening, the mother reads about a course on communication that is being offered to family members. She attends, learns a great deal, starts to read books she had never heard of, and begins to practice the new approaches at home. Her husband and the children get interested, and soon they are all working together at their communication system, with or without outside help. A lasting improvement in relationships results. This is secondary prevention—catching trouble early, so that it doesn't reach serious proportions.

Tertiary prevention. This applies to a situation where the family is already in serious trouble. A major crisis has developed and there is real danger of a break-up. At the eleventh hour, the parents are directed to professional help and after a period of therapy, the tensions die down and the family system begins to function positively. It becomes clear that a major factor in the diagnostic picture was the inability of the members to communicate effectively with each other, and it becomes a focal element in the therapy to provide now the communication training they didn't have before and which might have spared them the pain and distress they have suffered. This is tertiary prevention—providing reeducation to ensure if possible that the family will not again suffer a major crisis based on ineffective communication.

To some extent these preventive processes overlap, and cannot be precisely distinguished from each other. What is important is to provide families, as early as possible, with the knowledge, the tools, and the skills that are necessary if they are to fulfill reasonable hopes and expectations for their relationships. The programs described in this book cover all three levels of prevention, although all would agree that primary prevention represents the ideal.

SOME PREVENTIVE APPROACHES

The overall preventive task can include a number of different components. It will be sufficient here to refer to three of them:

(1) Giving information. Many of the new resources we can offer families today are based on knowledge that has come to us recently from the behavioral sciences. It might be supposed that this material could be presented in a classroom setting and that this information would be applied in the lives of the students, either then or at some later time. That was the supposition on which the traditional forms of "family life education" were based. However, the value of this approach is now being widely questioned. Knowing about family relationships is unfortunately no guarantee that what is known will be put into practice. One must go through a succession of stages—from information to stored knowledge, from knowledge to insight, from insight to experimental action, and from experimental action to behavioral change—before what has been learned is translated into action. It is important to note that since we are talking about relationships, each stage must be covered by two or more of the persons involved in a family system. True, we must begin with the the assimilation of the appropriate knowledge, but there is a long way to travel before it really gets into action.

(2) Marriage and family enrichment. This is the term now being used for what might also be called "experiental education." It means the application of our new knowledge to actual life situations following the succession of stages just described. It means a life-changing process in which new and different ways of behaving are learned by family members and learned *in practice*, usually by participation in a continuing group situation where couples help couples and families help families. Sometimes this is called "skill training" to emphasize that it involves (it *must* involve) behavioral changes in the interacting persons. These are very new approaches that until recently were

neither clearly understood nor widely practiced but which hold out great promise.

(3) Social and environmental change. Although the programs described in this book are carried out in the context of our present culture, those who are developing them are well aware that the environment is often lacking in support of, and is even hostile to, what we are trying to bring about. The hope is, therefore, that as the real needs of families are better understood, our society will come to see that it must be more actively supportive of family goals.

Some awareness of this emerged in the 1980 White House Conference on American Families which had a good deal to say about preventive action, mainly in the form of supports for programs which would improve the family environment and for restraints upon civic and political actions that have negative impact on family well being. Another interesting example of this approach is the concept of "family advocacy" developed by the Family Service Association of America, which Clark Blackburn has described thus:

> Our knowledge base comes from our work with thousands of individual families, our skill is in helping them to mobilize their own strengths. Both our knowledge and our skill are essential to effective advocacy . . . Your reports . . . have given you and us new insights into the causes of many family problems—the external pressure points that are destroying families. Advocacy is doing something about those causes [Manser, 1973: 61].

The task of prevention, therefore, in its totality, includes these three components: learning more about families through study and research and spreading that information; training family members in what Nelson Foote called "interpersonal competence;" and changing the cultural environment to provide social supports for families as they are the foundation of our national life.

WHAT *IS* FAMILY?

Having attempted to define what we mean by prevention, our remaining task in this chapter is to define what we mean by families, and by family wellness.

Earlier in this century, almost any group of people who were discussing families would have had much the same image in their minds. They would probably have been aware that some variations of patterns were to be found among the major human cultures and even greater variations among primitive peoples, but the average Western family followed a uniform pattern. Based on the "nuclear" family of father, mother, and children, the picture could expand to the "extended" family by including other members related either by blood or by marriage (consanguinity and affinity, in legal terminology). Here and there an adopted child might be included but that was the limit to which a family might be extended.

Since then, the picture has become greatly confused. With the phenomenal increase in divorce rates, all kinds of new situations have emerged—for example, children with six or more grandparents, and lots of stepbrothers and stepsisters. With the emergence in the 1960s of "alternative lifestyles" and now the rapid spread of cohabitation, families today may consist of people totally unrelated to each other in terms of the old standards.

The dictionaries have tried valiantly to keep up with the new concepts. The American Heritage offers nine different definitions of the word "family." One of them even says that a family can be a local unit of the Mafia—in other words, a bunch of crooks can be a family! So we had better be careful!

I was closely involved in the early planning of the 1980 White House Conference, and was the scheduled speaker at one of its sessions. It soon became clear, however, that the failure to define closely what was meant by the word "family" opened up the discussion to all kinds of issues—social, political, and legal—which had been no part of the original intention. At times the conference became almost a battleground for a host of peripheral yet highly controversial issues.

Since it is almost impossible today to set limits to the scope of family *structure*, it seems better to focus on family *function*. Our task then becomes much easier because there are only two *major* functions fulfilled by families:

(1) *Families exist to produce children and to transmit human culture from one generation to the next.* Because our days on earth are numbered, we must have some effective means of passing on the torch to others who will take our place. Because there is death, there must also be birth. If in just one generation no children were produced, the

human race would perish. And if in one generation those destined to die were unable to pass on to their successors the cultural values which they had inherited, human civilization could come to an abrupt end.

That, and nothing less than that, is the primary function of the family. Its task is to produce babies—to love and nurture them, to teach and guide them, to equip them in every possible way to become good family members as well as good citizens in the next generation. Achieving this is worth every effort and any sacrifice. I would call families that do this *reproducing families*.

(2) *The second purpose of families is to carry out a socialization function.* Of course, this is included in the reproducing function. It is a vital part of the task of parents in raising their children. A child becomes an adult by copying the significant others in its life who serve as models. so the socializing function is also an integral part of the reproducing function.

However, this socializing function by itself can be widely extended in many directions. There are people who never get involved in the reproductive task, but need the love, companionship, and support that families provide. Of course the reproductive task doesn't cover the whole of the lifespan; yet most of us continue to need a small, secure social unit in which we can share the more private areas of our lives and be supported when the going gets rough.

MAJOR FUNCTIONS OF THE FAMILY

If we focus on these two major functions, it is not difficult to define the goals that successful families should meet. Indeed, they are not essentially different. The first, obviously, is that the family should provide a setting in which children have the maximum possible chance of developing their highest personal potential and growing up to be mature, responsible adults. This is the original and fundamental purpose of a family. Apart from this, families as we have known them thoughout human history would have had no reason to exist because the socializing function could have been met in other ways.

The second function of the family is to provide people of all ages and conditions with the opportunity to find emotional and social security through close relationships in which they can live together in mutual love and trust. The word "love" is capable of wide interpretation, and whole books have been written in the attempt to define it. We shall have to be content with the following definition attributed to Harry Stack Sullivan, a well-known psychiatrist: "When the health and well-being of another person is an important to me as my own health and well-being, the state of love exists." The ideal, obviously, is for this state of affairs to be mutual and continuous. When this happens, a condition of trust and openness is built up. Over time this generates a state in which each person can feel confident that he or she is fully known and, at the same time, deeply loved. This represents a situation, and I believe the ideal situation, in which a person may achieve a secure sense of identity.

Of course many familes, indeed most families, fall far short of this ideal. Nevertheless, I would suggest that it does represent the goal toward which all families should strive. This state of untrammeled mutual confidence fulfills both of the family's major functions—to provide both the developing child and also the developing adult with a secure sense of emotional security and self-worth.

WHAT IS FAMILY WELLNESS?

Our final task is to define family wellness. In fact, we have already done so. It is the state of relationship, experienced as far as possible by all family members, that we have just defined. It represents people moving toward the appropriation of their full relational potential. It is not a static condition because people are always growing and changing and static relationships would mean an end to growth. It is a continuous and creative adaptation to the ever-changing world, within and without, in which persons live and move and have their being. It can be gained, and lost, and then regained. It represents the dictum of Robert Louis Stevenson, who said that the true goal of human life is not to arrive, but to travel hopefully.

It is, of course, a state of *health*. We could have used that term by speaking of "family health," but unfortunately the images conjured up by the word "health" tend to be of physicians in white coats, ambulances, and hospitals. We could have talked of "family growth," of "family enrichment," or of "family enhancement"—all would have been acceptable. But we chose the word "wellness" because it is not yet a term in general use and is not yet in many dictionaries. For us, its associations are entirely positive, and our hope is that this may remain so. If a person says that he or she is "well," that means an entirely good and desirable state. If a task can be called "well done," we assume that it has been creditably accomplished. Likewise, when we talk of "family wellness," we are thinking of a condition that would represent the highest ideal we could entertain for our own family and the summit of achievement we could wish for in any other family.

So this book represents a quest for ways and means to make family wellness available to many families, and a belief that the best way to do so is to learn how to provide effective preventive services. It has been written by a varied group of people who are all dedicated to the pursuit of that high goal.

REFERENCES

ALBEE, G. W. (1918) *Social Science and Social Change; The Primary Prevention of Disturbance in Youth.* Third Annual Gisela Konopha Lecture; May 21: Center for Youth Development, University of Minnesota.

BOWER, E. M. (1960) *Early Identification of Emotionally Handicapped Children in School.* Springfield, IL: Charles C. Thomas.

DEMPSEY, J. J. (1981) *The Family and Public Policy.* Baltimore: Brookes Publishing.

COMFORT, A. (1981) *Psychology Today,* December: 112.

MANSER, E. [ed.] (1973) *Family Advocacy: A Manual for Action.* New York: Family Service Association of America.

2

Strong Families

A PORTRAIT

Nicholas Stinnett

The quest for self-fulfillment during the twentieth century has developed into a major goal in American culture (Yankelovich, 1981). However, in our preoccupation with this objective we have neglected the family and lost sight of the fact that so much of the foundation necessary to facilitate the life-long process of individual self-fulfillment (such as the development of interpersonal competence, self-confidence, self-esteem, respect for self and others, and the vision and knowledge that life can be enriched) is developed within strong, healthy families.

We have considerable evidence that the quality of family life is extremely important to our emotional well-being, our happiness, and our mental health as individuals. We know that poor relationships within the famiy are very closely related to many problems in society (such as juvenile delinquency and domestic abuse).

As we look back in history we see that the quality of family life is very important to the strength of nations. There is a pattern in the rise and fall of great societies such as ancient Rome, Greece, and Egypt. When these societies were at the peak of their power and prosperity, the family was strong and highly valued. When family life became weak in these societies, when the family was not valued—when goals became extemely individualistic—the society began to deteriorate and eventually fell.

Obviously, it is to our benefit to do what we can to strengthen family life; this should be one of our nation's top priorities, but unfortunately it has not been.

So much of what is written about families has focused on problems and pathology. On the newsstand we see many books and magazine articles about what's wrong with families and the problems that families have. There are those who like to predict that the family will soon disappear and that it no longer meets our needs.

Certainly we need information about positive family models and what strong familes are like. We need to learn how to strengthen families. We don't learn how to do anything by looking only at what *shouldn't* be done. We learn most effectively by examining how to do something correctly and studying a positive model. We have not had this positive model as much as we need it in the area of family life. Understanding what a strong family is provides educators, counselors, and families with a positive model. Getting this knowledge first-hand from those who have created a successful family situation gives us a good picture of how families become strong.

We have many strong families throughout this nation and the world. There has been little written about them because there has been very little research focusing on family strengths. It was with this in mind that we launched the Family Strengths Research Project, a search that has taken us throughout our nation as well as to other parts of the world. This research was inspired in part by the pioneer work in family strengths of Otto (1962, 1964).

Our search began in Oklahoma where we studied 130 families identified as strong. More recently we have completed a national study of strong families representing all regions of the nation, an investigation of strong Russian immigrant families, a study of strong black families, and an examination of strong families from various countries in South America.

The research method varied. For example, one approach was represented by the Oklahoma study. In this project we had the assistance of the Cooperative Extension Service to help identify the strong families. We asked the Home Economics Extension Agent in each of the counties of Oklahoma to recommend a few families that the agent considered particularly strong. The Home Economics Extension Agents were suited to this task for three reasons—their background training in family life, their concern for improving family life as part of their work, and the great amount of contact they have with families in the community. Also, we gave the agents some guidelines for selecting the families. The guidelines were that the families demonstrated a high degree of marital happiness, a high degree of parent-child satisfaction as perceived by the Extension Agent, and that the family members appeared to meet each other's needs to a high degree.

For purposes of this study, all the families were intact with husband, wife, and at least one child living at home. The first requirement for inclusion in this sample of strong families was the recommendation of the Extension Agent. The second requirement was that the families rate themselves very high in terms of marriage satisfaction and parent-child relationship satisfaction. The 130 families that met these two conditions were included in the sample. Both urban and rural families were represented in the sample, although there were more families from small cities, towns, and rural areas than from large urban areas. In most instances, we found very little difference between the urban and rural families.

A second research technique was demonstrated by the national study. The strong families in this study responded to an article sent to various daily and weekly papers across the nation. The 41 newspapers asked to run the article were selected to ensure a sample from all regions of the country, and from both rural and urban areas. The news release described the national study and asked families who felt they qualified as strong families to send their names and addresses to the researchers. The philosophy behind this approach can be debated almost endlessly. In short, we believed that rather than we as professionals defining what a strong family is, we would let families make the decision themselves.

The response to the news release was tremendous. Each family that responded was sent copies of the Family Strengths Inventory for the husband and wife. Many families also sent elaborate stories describing their family and its characteristics and activities in detail. The inventory focused on both the husband-wife and parent-child relationships and collected demographic information. Only families that rated themselves very high on marriage happiness and parent-child satisfaction were included in the final sample. This was similar to the screening procedure used in the Oklahoma study. The final sample size for the national study was 350 families.

In summary, we researched 130 families in the Oklahoma study, 350 families in the National Project, and 180 families in the South American study. In addition, smaller studies of Russian immigrant families and black families have been completed. In all of these research projects the families completed questionnaires and later a few of them were interviewed. Our question covered a broad range of factors concerning their relationship patterns. For example, we asked how they deal with conflict, about communication patterns, and about power structure. When we analyzed the vast quantity of information, we found six qualities that stood out among these strong families. Six qualities they had in common seemed to play a very important role in their strength and their happiness. It is interesting that the same six qualities were found to characterize strong families in all of the research studies we conducted.

THE SIX QUALITIES OF THE STRONG FAMILIES

Appreciation

The first quality of the strong families was certainly one of the most important. It emerged from many different questions and in many ways that we were not expecting. The results were permeated by this characteristic. That quality is appreciation. The members of these families expressed a great deal of appreciation for each other. They built each other up psychologically, they gave each other many positive psychological strokes; everyone was to feel good about themselves.

All of us like to be with people who make us feel good about ourselves; we don't like to be with people who make us feel bad. One of the tasks of family counselors who are working with family members who make each other feel terrible is to get them out of that pattern of interaction and into a pattern where they can make each another feel good. William James, considered by many people to be the greatest psychologist our country has every produced, wrote a book on human needs. Some years after that book was published he remarked that he had forgotten to include the most important need of all—the need to be appreciated. There are so many things that we do for which we receive no reward other than appreciation; perhaps we all need to work on our ability to express appreciation. One difficulty in this is that we sometimes fear that people will think we're not sincere or that it's empty flattery. This need not be a concern. We *can* be sincere.

Every person has many good qualities, many strengths. All we have to do is look for them, and be aware of them.

There are many ways in which we can develop the ability to express appreciation and thus make our human relationships better and certainly improve the quality of our family life. One widely used technique is one that Dr. Herbert Otto, Chairman of the National Center for Exploration of Human Potential, has used and written about a great deal. It has also been a tool for many counselors and is now being used by families on their own. This is called the "strength bombardment" technique. Here is the way it operates: The entire family comes together. There may be a group leader or counselor, or some member of the family can act as a leader. One person in the family is designated as the target person. For example, the mother may begin as target person. She is asked to list the strengths that she feels she has as a person. If she lists only two or three because she's modest, the leader can urge her to list others. After she has finished the list, her husband is asked to add to her list of strengths. Or he may elaborate on the strengths that she has already listed. When he has finished, each of the children is asked to add to mother's list of strengths. When this process is finished, the husband becomes the target person. The same procedure is repeated for him. Then each of the children becomes the target person.

The "strengths bombardment" technique is very simple, but the results have been amazing. When families do this exercise, they become more aware of each other's strengths, and more aware of their strengths as a family. They get into a pattern of looking for each other's good qualities and they also get into the habit of expressing appreciation. The result of this with so many families is that it makes their interaction with each other more positive. Some follow-up studies done with families who have gone through this activity show that the increased level of positive interaction is maintained for a period of time after the exercise has been completed. Many families are now using this technique periodically on their own.

Spending Time Together

A second quality found among strong families is that they did a lot of things together. It was not a "false" togetherness; nor a "smothering" type of togetherness—they genuinely enjoyed being together. Another important point here is that these families structured their life-styles so that they could spend time together. It did not "just happen," they *made* it happen. And this togetherness was in all areas of their lives—eating meals, recreation, and work.

One interesting pattern which has emerged from our research is the high frequency with which the strong families participate in outdoor activities together such as walking, jogging, bird watching, camping, canoeing, horseback riding, and outdoor games. While there are many strong families who are not particularly fond of outdoor activities, the finding in our research that so many strong families employed this as an important source of enjoyment and of their strength as a family raises the question of how the participation in outdoor activities as a family might contribute to family strengths. One logical possibility is that when families are particiapting in outdoor activities together they have fewer distractions—the family members are away from the telephone and the never-ending array of household tasks—and can concentrate more upon each other, thus encouraging a good communication experience. Another possibility is that physical exercise is often one benefit of participation in outdoor activities and the exercise itself contributes to personal feeling of well-being, health, and vitality.

Commitment

A third quality of these strong families was a high degree of commitment. These families were deeply committed to promoting each other's happiness and welfare. They were also very committed to the family group, as was reflected by the fact that they invested much of their time and energies in it. We have not had very much research on commitment, and perhaps in recent years it has not been fashionable to talk about it. Yet, Yankelovich (1981) observes that our society is now in the process of leaving behind an excessive self-centered orientation and moving toward a new "ethic of commitment" with emphasis upon new rules of living that support self-fulfillment through deeper personal relationships. Also, as David and Vera Mace (1980) have noted, only if you have produced a commitment to behavior change have you done anything to improve the life of a person or the life of a marriage or family.

Some of the best research on commitment has been done in communes. Some communes have been successful and others have not.

One of the main differences found between the two groups is commitment. Those communes that are the most successful, that last the longest and that are the most satisfying in terms of the relationships, are those in which there is a great deal of commitment—among individuals and to the group. Again, commitment in the communes was reflected in the amount of time the members spent together. The same was true with the strong families.

All of us are busy and we sometimes feel that we have so many things to do that we are pulled in a thousand different directions at the same time. Strong families experience the same problem. One interesting action that these families expressed was that when life got too hectic—to the extent that they were not spending as much time with their families as they wanted—they would sit down and make a list of the different activites in which they were involved. They would go over that list critically and inevitably there were some things that they really did not want to be doing, or that did not give much happiness, or that really were not very important to them. So they would scratch those activities and involvements off their lists. This would free time for their families and would relieve some of the pressure. As a result they were happier with their lives in general and more satisfied with their family relationships.

This sounds very simple, but how many of us do it? We get involved too often and it's not always because we want to be. We act so often as if we cannot change the situation. We *do* have a choice. An important point about these families is that they took the initiative in structuring their life style in a way that enhanced the quality of their family relationships and their satisfaction. They were on the "offensive." We may have talked too much about families as simply reactors in society, being at the mercy of the environment. In fact, there is a great deal that families can do to make life more enjoyable. These strong families exercised that ability.

Good Communication Patterns

The fourth quality was not a surprise. Strong families have very good communication patterns. They spend time talking with each other. This is closely related to the fact that they spend a lot of time together. It's hard for people to communicate unless they spend time with each other. One of the big problems facing families today is not spending enough time together. Dr. Virginia Satir, a prominent family therapist, has stated that often families are so fragmented, so busy, and spend so little time together that they only communicate with each other through rumor. Unfortunately, too often that is exactly what happens.

Another important aspect of communication is that these families also listen well. They reported that their family members were good listeners and that this was important to them. The fact that family members listen to one another communicates a very important message—respect. They are saying to one another, "You respect me enough to listen to what I have to say. I'm interested enough to listen too."

Another factor related to communication is that these families do fight. They get mad at each other, but they get conflict out in the open and they are able to talk it over, to discuss the problem. They share their feeling about alternative ways to deal with the problem and in selecting a solution that is best for everybody. These strong families have learned to do what David and Vera Mace (1980) have reported to be essential for a successful marriage—making creative use of conflict.

High Degree of Religious Orientation

The fifth quality that these families expressed was a high degree of religious orientation. This agrees with research from the past 40 years, that shows a positive relationship of religion to marriage happiness and successful family relationships. Of course, we know that there are persons who are not religious who have very happy marriages and good family relationships. Nevertheless a positive relationship between marriage happiness and religion exists according to the research of many years. These strong families went to church together often and they participated in religious activities together. Most of them, although not all of them, were members of organized churches. All of them were very religious.

There are indications that this religious quality went deeper than going to church or participating in religious activities together. It could most appropriately be called a commitment to a spiritual life style. Words are inadequate to communicate this, but what many of these families said was that they had an awareness of God or a higher power that gave them a sense of purpose and gave their family a sense of support and strength. The awareness of this higher power in their lives helped them to be more patient with each other, more forgiving, quicker to get over anger, more positive, and more supportive in their relationships. Many of the values emphasized by religion, when put into action, can certainly enhance the quality of human relationships. Dr. Herbert Otto has observed that we could spend more time looking at the spiritual aspect of developing human potential, and perhaps we could benefit by exploring more about the spiritual aspects of developing family strengths. For these strong families, religion played a major role.

Ability to Deal with Crises in a Positive Manner

The final quality that these families had was the ability to deal with crises and problems in a positive way. Not that they enjoyed crises, but they were able to deal with them constructively. They managed, even in the darkest of situations, to see some positive element, no matter how tiny, and to focus on it. It may have been, for example, that in a particular crisis they simply had to rely to a greater extent on each other and a developed trust that they had in each other. They were able to unite in dealing with the crisis instead of being fragmented by it. They dealt with the problem and were supportive of each other.

CONCLUSIONS AND RECOMMENDATIONS

The qualities that characterized the strong families in our research coincide with what other researchers examining healthy families have reported (Otto, 1964; Lewis et al., 1976; Lewis, 1979; Nelson and Banonis, 1981). It is interesting that most of these qualities that we found to characterize strong families have been found to be lacking in families that are having severe relationship problems and in families broken by divorce. This fact supports the validity of the finding and suggests the importance of these qualities in building family strength. How can we translate this information into practical help to strengthen families? What kind of recommendations can we make? What can we do?

(1) One recommendation is that we help families develop some of these skills, such as the ability to express appreciation and good communication patterns. If we were able to do that, relationships and the quality of family life could be improved. This can be done—in fact, it is being done. One example is the research project we instituted at the University of Nebraska, the Family Strengths Enrichment Program. This was an eight-week program in which couples were assisted in developing skills and competencies found to be characteristic of strong families. Pre- and posttests were administered to the couples. The results indicated significant, positive increases in marriage and family satisfaction. Substantial positive change was found in the ability of the couples to communicate, to deal effectively with conflict, and to express genuine appreciation.

Also, considering the emphasis by these strong families on outdoor activities, recreational areas could be expanded and developed more for family units. For example, having special family days and outdoor seminars specifically for families might encourage them to do more as a unit.

(2) Communities, in order to be strong and healthy, must have strong and healthy families. Threfore, we need to devise more research projects which relate family strengths to community needs. We then need to follow though to help the communities use the information we obtain through the research. An example can be found in Lincoln, Nebraska, where a very interesting demonstration project called the Willard Community Family Strengths Project was established. The project was developed in response to a pressing community need. This particular section of Lincoln—the old Willard School District—had a disturbingly high vandalism and deliquency rate. It was the imaginative thesis of Lela Watts, a Ph.D. student at the University of Nebraska, that the most effective way to meet the delinquency problem was a total family approach. So a program beginning in 1980, was conducted to build the strengths and skills of the families of the youth in the neighborhood. Building self-esteem, communication skills, and expanding the scope of activities which the entire family enjoyed were among the areas of focus for the Willard Family Strengths Program. Some excellent research data were collected, but most importantly the delinquency and vandalism rates were reduced by 83% within a six-month period. This program is ongoing and at the time of this writing the deliquency and vandalism rates had been reduced almost to the point of elimination.

(3) Another recommendation that we could make is to have a comprehensive human relationships education program incorporated at the preschool, elementary, secondary, and college levels. Isn't it amazing that we have not already done that? Good human relationships are basic and vital to our happiness, our well-being and our mental health.

(4) Also, if we are truly serious about strengthening family life, we might make more of a concerted effort to improve the image of family life. Perhaps we need to make commitment more fashionable as we are so much influenced by it. Some psychologists have stated that if we are really serious about strengthening family life, we are going to have to build much more prestige into being a family member, in being a good father, mother, wife, or husband. We are influenced tremendously by what we think we are rewarded for.

Perhaps we could improve the image of family life through some television spots like public service announcements. The Mormon Church, for example, has done an excellent job of this. They have some very effective television spots. These short announcements could communicate messages about the importance of expressing appreciation or the importance of parents listening to their children for example.

(5) Another thing that we are going to have to do is reorder our values and priorites. We will have to make family life and human relationships a top priority, and apply this commitment in terms of the way we spend our time and our energy.

(6) Finally, in order to build stronger families in the future we must match our remedial services with preventive services, as David and Vera Mace (1980) have urged. We must turn from our preoccupation with pathology and the commonly accepted practice of spending all our energies doing "patchwork" and "picking up the wrecks." This approach is more expensive—both financially and in terms of human suffering. In order to be most effective we must make preventive services and programs available early in the lives of individuals and families to provide them with skills, knowledge, motivation, and positive models that can help develop family strengths. Just one example of how this might be done is through more family life education and enrichment programs in the community, which could be organized through such groups as churches, schools, YMCA, YWCA, and local Family Service Association Organizations. Secondary and primary schools could place more emphasis on family life education in the

curriculum and encourage, if not require, all students to participate. College curriculum could also be improved by placing more emphasis on family strength in marriage and family classes and designing whole courses specifically for teaching ways to develop family strengths.

Strong families are the roots of our well-being as individuals and as a society. The dream of facilitating strong families that produce emotionally and socially healthy individuals can be realized. The positive potential for the family is great.

REFERENCES

MACE, D. and V. Mace (1980) "Enriching marriages: the foundation stone of family strength," in N. Stinnett et al. (eds.) Family Strengths: Positive Models for Family Life. Lincoln: Univ. of Nebraska Press.

NELSON, P. T. and B. BANONIS (1981) "Family concerns and strengths identified in Delaware's White House Conference on families," in N. Stinnett et al. (eds.) Family Strengths 3: Roots of Well-Being. Lincoln: Univ. of Nebraska Press.

LEWIS, J. M. (1979) How's Your Family? New York: Brunner/Mazel.

———R. W. BEAVERS, J. T. GOSSET, and V. A. PHILLIPS (1976) No Single Thread: Psychological Health in Family Systems. New York: Brunner/Mazel.

OTTO, H. A. (1964) "The personal and family strength research projects: some implications for the therapist." Mental Hygiene 48: 439-450.

———(1962) "The personal and family resource development programs: a preliminary report." Int. J. of Social Psychiatry 8: 185-195.

YANKELOVICH, D. (1981) New Rules: Searching for Fulfillment in a World Turned Upside Down. New York: Random House.

3

Promoting Family Wellness

IMPLICATIONS AND ISSUES

Ted W. Bowman

Today, the goal of strengthening families is rapidly being transformed from a deep-felt hunger of the heart to a realistic and achievable possibility. Until recently, our knowledge about family wellness was limited. We relied on our intuition, on informal conclusions, and on folklore more than on research about what the families themselves had found strengthening. That no longer need be the case; a growing body of information about indicators of health in families is becoming available for use by families themselves, and by persons working with families.

The implications are profound. Families can begin to work deliberately toward some of the goals that foster wellness. Specific programs can be developed that reflect more of a health focus. Policies at national, state, and local levels can be evaluated in the light of family health awareness. Churches, schools, and community agencies can become more proactive in their pursuit of supports for families.

It is to these ends that this chapter is addressed. It will be divided into three sections. First, a rationale for family wellness will be presented. That will be followed by a sampling of indicators of family wellness, drawn from many sources. Finally, some implications and issues posed by a posture of family wellness will be explored.

A RATIONALE FOR FAMILY WELLNESS

In 1953, 30 years ago, the Family Service Association of America addressed health in families through a pamphlet entitled "What Makes for Strong Family Life." That document closed with this paragraph:

> The family is important because it shapes us. More than any other force, it determines the kind of people we are and the kind of people tomorrow's citizens will be . . . the family . . . will be the most powerful influence in the development of people's personality and character [p. 14].

Similarly, Hope Leichter, in a more recent article, wrote that it is within the family that the whole range of human experience takes place. Everything from welfare, love, hate, tenderness, deception, ownership, communal sharing, hierarchies, and decision making happens in families. Indeed, much of the experience of families and most of the writing about families has supported the unique power and influence of family interaction. The Minnesota Council of Family Relations in a "Position Statement on Strengthening Families" put it in this way:

> We believe that in every person there is potential for growth and change and that too often this potential is unrecognized, untapped or underutilized.

> We further believe that one of the most significant forces for growth of and change in persons can be a supportive, nurturing group. Through interaction with persons whom we trust, we are able to explore better ways of doing things.

> And we believe that the family is a group that *more than any other group* determines the kind of people we are.

Experientially, families (like marriages) have operated by what Clark Vincent (1973: 258-260) called the "myth of naturalism"—

the belief that persons "naturally" know how to be good spouses, parents, or relatives. We have assumed that persons, just by growing up and reaching a certain age, are ready to be spouses and parents. The concept of family wellness challenges this assumption, saying with Elizabeth Kubler-Ross (1975: 165) that humankind will survive only through the commitment and involvement of individuals in their own and in other's growth and development as human beings.

The issue, then, is one of tapping the power and influence of families. David Mace has often used the image of a gold mine for the potential of couples and families. In the gold mine, much of the potential and power is unseen and is waiting to be discovered. so it is with families. Family wellness indicators may be one of the critical resources useful in enhancing potential.

SOME FAMILY HEALTH INDICATORS

The amount of available information about family wellness has expanded greatly in the last seven years. Some of the new data have been drawn from interviews with family members who have been asked to identify the attributes and activities that have been sustaining and nurturing for them. Nick Stinnett has reported some of that information (see Chapter 2). Other reports have come from professionals who, after years of working with families, are now reflecting on "the growth dimension" that they have discovered in persons and families with whom they have had contact. Results from several different studies are presented here so that similarities and differences can easily be noted. While not an exhaustive list, these do represent perspectives for our consideration and use.

Comparison of the resources is difficult because of differences of purpose, length, language, and methodology in gathering results. Three of the reports—Stinnett, Lewis et al., and Hill—are reseach studies. Satir and Whitaker are noted family therapists who have reflected on their years of work with families around the world. The research of Robert Hill is exclusively with black families. Even with these differences, however, important similarities can be noted. Indeed, the fact that these studies or observations are drawn from such a wide cross-section of persons adds to their credibility as common indicators of health. To aid readers in making comparisons, lists of indicators in the authors' own language are presented, followed by a table showing similar findings. This table summarizes the major indicators of family wellness that are shared by these investigators.

Six Qualities of Strong Families (Stinnett, 1979)

(1) Members express a great deal of appreciation for one another.
(2) Family members make the effort to structure their lifestyles so that they have time to spend together.
(3) Direct communication.
(4) Promotion of each other's happiness and well-being.
(5) Commitment to a spiritual life-style (religious orientation).
(6) An ability to cope with crisis.

Four Key Factors (Satir, 1972)

(1) Promotion of positive self-worth.
(2) Open communication system.
(3) Clarity as to family rules and expectations (motivation emerging from self-initiative, not from a sense of obligation).
(4) Link to the wider society—commitment beyond the family.

Eight Descriptive Characteristics of Healthy Families (Lewis et al., 1976)

(1) An affiliative rather than an oppositional attitude about human encounters.
(2) A respect for one's own and the subjective world views of others.
(3) Openness in communication.
(4) A firm parental coalition.
(5) An understanding of varied and complex human motivations rather than a simplistic, linear, or controlling orientation.
(6) Spontaneity rather than rigid stereotyped interactions.
(7) High levels of initiative rather than passivity.
(8) The encouragement of the unique rather than bland human characteristics.

Five Characteristics that Have Been Functional for the Survival, Development, and Stability of Family Members (Hill, 1971)

(1) Strong kinship bonds.
(2) Strong work orientation.
(3) Adaptability of family roles.
(4) Strong achievement orientation.
(5) Strong religious orientation.

Characteristics of a Self-Actualizing Family, A Family That Grows (Carl Whitaker, in a workshop in Minneapolis, September 8, 1980)

(1) A family "with everybody in it"—a sense of the whole.
(2) An ability to understand time and space—the members see their family moving.
(3) Availability of all roles to all people.
(4) Flexible family relationships.
(5) Freedom to join and to separate.
(6) Presence of an intrapsychic family—verbal history, mythologies, and stories.
(7) Open system—available for contact with the networks around them.
(8) A family where any member can be worked on.

Framework of Family Strengths (Otto, 1975)

(1) The ability to provide for the physical, emotional, and spiritual needs of a family.
(2) The ability to "give and take" in the area of child-rearing practices and discipline.
(3) The ability to communicate effectively.
(4) The ability to provide support, security, and encouragement.
(5) The ability to initiate and maintain growth-producing relationships and experiences within and without the family.
(6) The capacity to maintain and create constructive and responsible community relationships in the neighborhood, town, school, and so on.

(7)   The ability to grow with and through children.
(8)   An ability for self-help, and the ability to accept help when appropriate.
(9)   An ability to perform family functions and roles flexibly.
(10) Mutual respect for the individuality of family members.
(11) The ability to use a crisis or a seemingly injurious experience as a means of growth.
(12) A concern for family unity, loyalty, and intra-family cooperation.

SOME IMPLICATIONS AND ISSUES

Our increasing information about those factors that foster family wellness should serve to challenge all of us to devote more time and effort to the goal of strengthening families. No longer must we rely exclusively on our intuition, on good will, and on trial and error in our efforts to promote strong families. Those assets can now be blended with information, gathered from our own families and others, to be used in achieving our hopes and wishes. the implications of family wellness indicators are profound because the lives of families can be dramatically influenced by this information. However, there are also issues which deserve sensitive response and handling. Let us consider some of these:

(1) *Many of the indicators of health are skill-related.* This provides us with cause for hope, inasmuch as skills are teachable and learnable. Communication, conflict resolution, appreciation, giving and receiving, and goal-setting skills are identified as sources of strength in many of the reports. Skill-based programs for couples, parents, and families have been developed and are now widely available. Many have been tested and have been shown to be useful and practical for family members. Support for such programs, and support for their use in the early stages of human life, can contribute much to family and community wellness.

(2) *The importance attached to spiritual and religious dimensions.* This challenges the common assumption that spiritual values should be separated from emotional or family issues and that such

TABLE 3.1 Family Wellness Indicators Identified by Three or More Sources

	Stinnett	Satir	Lewis et al.	Hill	Whitaker	Otto
Communication (direct and/or open)	x	x	x		x	x
Appreciation, respect for one another	x	x	x			x
Spiritual, religious commitment	x	x		x		x
Adaptability, flexibility			x	x	x	x
Clarity of family rules		x	x			x

matters should be handled exclusively by the clergy. The evidence shows that religious dimensions represent an important variable for many families and that they should therefore be considered as a part of therapeutic or educational intervention. This would provide a more wholistic picture of the forces and factors influencing family interaction and family decision making.

(3) *Proper use of wellness information.* One of the potential dangers of family wellness indicators lies in their possible misuse. A choice must be made between opportunity or obligation, assistance or burden, challenge or demand. There is a danger that family wellness indicators will be shared with or interpreted by families as a new "should," one more rule they must follow in order to be successful. The indicators could become yet another check-list or criterion by which we rate or grade ourselves or other families.

In contrast to these attitudes is that of seeing the indicators as information useful to us as a "check-up" or as a challenge to us to talk more with family members about those forces and factors that they believe to be strengthening. Rather than being imposed from outside, hopes and wishes can then emerge from within.

(4) *Interdependence between families and outside resources.* One of the more crucial implications for family wellness is the creative tension between self-reliance and effective utilization of community resources. Unfortunately, some recent articles and books have pictured these two as in opposition. The dangers of dominance by professionals, of looking to the "experts" for answers, of failure to recognize intuitive or learned abilites and skills—these have been points well-made by many writers. Advocacy on behalf of helping families to help themselves has become a clarion call for family and/ or parents' rights.

My interpretation of the family wellness reports suggests a creative tension, an interdependence between families and family-serving professionals. Timely use of professional assistance can aid families in coping with crises or in developing skills within a framework of fostering self-reliance. To achieve this, professionals need to more adequately explain their services to consumers including explanation of credentials, methodology, costs, time expectations, and undergirding principles or beliefs about persons and families. Similarly, consumers should request and require adequate information before making a decision about participation. Too often human service consumers ask fewer question of a therapist or educator than they would ask an auto mechanic.

(5) *The cause of family wellness is nonideological.* We cannot allow it to be captured by the right or the left, by the conservatives or the liberals. All of us must join together in promoting, supporting, and sustaining all opportunites and services that really strengthen families.

CONCLUSION

The cause of preventive services has long been advocated. Sages and politicians, consumers and academics, children and adults have spoken or written in support of health-promoting services. Yet the record of human services clearly shows, to an almost incredible extent, more programs and many more dollars in the areas of crisis or remedial services.

One of the arguments used in attacking primary prevention has been what George Albee (1980: 14) calls "the fuzziness of the concepts." To the extent that such an argument has been convincing in the past, the growing body of information about health in families now provides persuasive answers. Specific data collected from families about what strengthens them has profound implications for all persons working with families. Fuzziness or lack of information can no longer be used as an excuse. Family members themselves, by identifying the nurturing, sustaining forces in their lives, challenge all of us. We must meet that challenge.

REFERENCES

ALBEE, G. W. (1980) "Social science and social change: the primary prevention of disturbance in youth." Occasional Paper #2, Center of Youth Development and Research, University of Minnesota.
HILL, R. B. (1971) *The Strengths of Black Families.* New York: Emerson Hall.
KUBLER-ROSS, E. (1975) *Death: The Final Stage of Growth.* Englewood Cliffs, New Jersey: Prentice-Hall.

LEICHTER, H. J. (1974) "The family as educator." *Teachers College Board* 76 (December): 175.

LEWIS, J. M., W. R. BEAVERS, J. T. GOSSETT and V. A. PHILLIPS (1976) *No Single Thread: Psychological Health in Family Systems.* New York: Brunner/ Mazel.

OTTO, H. A. (1975) *The Use of Family Strength Concepts and Methods in Family Life Education.* Beverly Hills: Holistic Press.

SATIR, V. *Peoplemaking.* (1972) Palo Alto, CA: Science and Behavior Books.

STINNETT, N. (1979) "In search of families," in N. Stinnett et al. (eds.) *Building Family Strengths.* Lincoln: Univ. of Nebraska Press.

VINCENT, C. E. (1973) *Sexual and Marital Health.* New York: McGraw-Hill.

4

Prevention as a Profession

TOWARD A NEW CONCEPTUAL FRAME OF REFERENCE

Luciano L'Abate

Following what has gone before, the purpose of this chapter will be to examine the professional services we are currently offering to families, and to consider how they might be improved.

Most of our present services are *remedial.* Following the medical model, we wait until families are in serious trouble before we offer any "intervention." Then, we move in with all our resources with the intention of reversing the destructive processes which have been alienating the family members from each other, often for years.

We were able to justify this approach as long as families in trouble appeared to represent only a very small percentage of all families. But now the number of malfunctioning families has reached such proportions that a change of policy is urgently needed. Referring back to the test of sanity described in the first chapter, the only change of policy that can make sense is to go to the faucet and see if we can cut down the flow of pathology at its source. The name of this particular approach is *primary prevention.*

My purpose in this chapter is to consider briefly the following questions:

(1) What exactly *is* prevention, as it applies to families in trouble?
(2) Is it really better than cure? In other words, can we do it effectively?
(3) How might professionals go about setting up preventive programs in the family field?

FORMS OF PRIMARY PREVENTION

Price et al. (1981) equated prevention with community mental health. Both from a historical and cultural viewpoint, this is open to question. A great deal of preventive work has originated outside the field of community mental health—in Social Skills Training (SST) for example (L'Abate, 1980, 1981). In fact, the community mental health movement has failed rather dismally to generate preventive programs, and has rather stagnated at the level of evaluation, with little or no effort at prevention. In spite of this, Price et al. have dealt helpfully with conceptual, organizational, political, and operational issues of importance to preventers. One of these is the assertion that both health promotion and competence-building activities will automatically have preventive effects, even if they are not labeled as such. This concept is basic to the whole field of skill building for families (L'Abate, 1977; L'Abate-Rapp, 1981). "Whether or not a particular health promotion activity actually prevents any disorder from occurring must be demonstrated empirically and claims of prevention should be greeted with the proper skepticism and empirical scrutiny" (Price at al. 1981: 1).

Catalano and Dooley (1980) made useful additions to the definition of primary prevention by distinguishing between *proactive* services (those which prevent the occurrence of risk factors) and *reactive* services (those which improve the response to risk factors). Obviously both are relevant because it is at least difficult if not impossible to avoid stressors altogether. Catalano and Dooley (1980) also distinguish between macro and micro levels of prevention—major programs for large organizations and even for society in general, and more limited efforts to control family and psychobiological factors. In dealing with family wellness, we are mainly in the field of micro-reactive prevention.

THE CASE FOR PREVENTION

"An ounce of prevention," it has often been said, "is worth a pound of cure." We have tended to accept this uncritically. However, we need to look at the hard facts and see what evidence can be cited to support this positiion. Here are some arguments worthy of consideration:

(1) *Prevention is cheaper.* Can it be demonstrated that this is so? Cummings (1977), investigating the field of National Health Insurance, showed that one psychotherapeutic interview decreased considerably and significantly the number of medical visits made by patients compared to patients who had not had such an interview. He calculated that the savings related to that one interview were in the region of thousands of dollars. These data have been used as strong support for the use of psychotherapy over medicinal treatment.

However, it is not customary to view psychotherapy as a preventive measure. If it is so, we may need to ask: "Can we prevent prevention?" Can we intervene so that people will not *need* psychotherapy? Perhaps we can. Wildman (1977) in his doctoral dissertation showed how distressed couples could profit by enrichment at the hands of first-year graduate students. Their gains were equal to those of a sample of equally distressed couples who received therapy by therapists with an average span of experience of 12 years.

Does that mean that we should do away with psychotherapy? Certainly not; but it may mean that we can make it unnecessary for *some* people to need psychotherapy because we are able to offer them other options. There is always going to be a need for professional psychotherapists, but their services are expensive and are available (both in private and in public services) to only a very small percentage of the population.

Widespread family wellness would clearly lead to a desirable reduction of the nation's economic burdens. The interest of the Federal Government is demonstrated by a series of publications dealing with strengthening the family (Corfman, 1979a), family violence and child abuse (Corfman, 1979c), and mental illness in the family (Corfman, 1979c). This suggests that our message may not fall on deaf ears! In this excellent collection one will find articles from the best representatives of family interests in the country. The volume on strengthening the family would be of particular interest to preventers.

(2) *Prevention is innovative.* Garfield (1981) reviewed the field of psychotherapy in its historical development and assessed the variations over its course since its inception. He concluded that "it is also clear that no real breakthroughs have occurred during the last forty years and that despite claims to the contrary, the innovations and modifications developed have not produced truly remarkable results."

I beg to differ from Garfield's conclusion. I do believe that a real breakthrough has taken place in the development of skill-oriented, preventive programs (L'Abate, 1980; 1981) that will in some ways overlap with psychotherapy, but which in many other ways will deal with populations that psychotherapy cannot reach or touch.

(3) *Prevention is easier.* No human endeavor is easy and preventive efforts are not going to be easier to apply and to deliver. However, working with functional families should inevitably be less difficult to the extent that resistances, psychological defenses, and entrenched patterns of relating should be less extensive and less rigid. This, of course, does not mean that problems will not be present. It does mean that they will respond to different ways of being handled.

(4) *Prevention is happier.* Lewis et al. (1976) in their classic study of normal families found that what characterized most of the functional families was a *joie de vivre* and a spontaneity that was not present in more average families. We know from our experience of enriching all sorts of families (L'Abate, 1977) that most functional families can be identified on one simple and single dimension: plenty of laughter. These families have an unusual ability to enjoy life, hence working with such families would seem to produce more fun. Even enrichment becomes fun because to some of these families living is enjoyable.

(5) *Prevention is cleaner.* In working with more functional families we usually do not get involved in "messes"—such as agencies, courts, lawyers, police, schools, and so forth. Hence, energy and time can be applied where they really count: to the family itself and to its processes of growth. There are fewer irrelevancies and distrac-

tions to deal with and it is easier to see movement and change than in more dysfunctional couples.

Assuming for the time being that the arguments, as stated above, are valid (and this still needs to be demonstrated) we may try now to summarize the case for prevention. If we can deal with and remove incipient dysfunctional behavior patterns and help to avoid their recurrence in the future, this in and of itself might seem to be a sufficient rationale. Yet it is not enough. We have to make our argument sound very convincing if we are going to sway those who do not want to hear.

Let us therefore state the case, as clearly as possible, for all the three levels of prevention—primary, secondary, and tertiary.

(1) *Before it happens.* We know that dysfunctional patterns are transmitted across the generations, from parents to children. All of us can say that we are products of the preceding generation. This is not to put the "blame" on our predecessors, it is simply a matter of sequence. Dysfunction and psychopathology develop *over time* for a multiplicity of reasons.

Prevention means cutting in on this sequence and changing whatever might change the downward direction of existing trends and substitute for these an upward spiral. By downward, I mean disruptive and destructive; by upward I mean constructive and enhancing. This represents the process of primary prevention.

(2) *Before it gets worse.* If a dysfunctional pattern has already developed, there is always a hope that it could correct itself or even terminate. In fact, however, this is highly unlikely apart from external intervention: we know that dysfunctional family systems do not have sufficient negative feedback loops to change the system upward (Lewis et al., 1976). On the contrary, most dysfunctional family systems tend either to stay the same (homeostasis) or to get worse. Getting worse may mean such crises as divorce, suicide, hospitalization, or psychotherapy.

(3) *Before it is too late.* Even if the oucome becomes less life-threatening than suicide or homicide, it is still an unfortunate fact that may fail to reach people in need. Hence we need to help prevent dysfunction, before it reaches the breakdown point, because then it may be *too late!*

No matter how much we would want to argue in favor of prevention, we need to remember that mental health workers, both public and private, do not have a stake in it. I am arguing that professionals do not want to be trained in enrichment or in any other type of preventive approach (L'Abate, 1980, 1981). I am not the only one to take this position; among others, Goldston makes it very clear (1977). He noted in his early review of preventive programs that "the barrier of professional values is in my view the most important of all. So long as public health values are regarded by mental health workers as inferior to clinical values, primary prevention efforts will lag." Goldston defined a program as a planned effort to approach various aspects of an identified major field by means of a series of interrelated projects; a single, isolated, one-shot project is *not* a program (1977: 35). In addition, a program contains and connotes a "sustained commitment" consistent with planned social change. Hence, we need to look elsewhere for future development that may bid well for prevention.

DO WE NEED A NEW PROFESSION?

It must by now be very clear that established mental health professions (psychiatry, psychology, social work, psychiatric nursing, and counseling) are not going to help the preventive movement. Professionals do not want to be trained in preventive approaches for at least four reasons:

(1) *Prevention doesn't pay.* When was the last time you or I heard of a salaried position open or available for prevention? What portions of the budget of the federal, state, or county governments are allocated to prevention? Who receives pay—or even part of a paycheck—for preventive activities? Where are job descriptions at any level of civic service for preventive work? Do we need to ask more? Some preventers I know have been private entrepreneurs who have done well in marketing their approaches (PET, CCP, ACME), or they are college teachers whose connections and practices are tied up to their teaching and research activities.

(2) *Prevention is not glamorous enough.* How about the excitement of helping a suicidal patient, or calling oneself a therapist, the one who heals? What higher calling can one have than that? Dealing

with dysfunction gives one a feeling of importance and status; and as indicated above, you can earn a good living. Therapy is a very seductive activity. I am a therapist, and so I should know what I am talking about! But for every couple or every family I may help, I think of those whom I cannot reach or help. Thus, no matter how exciting therapy may be (and it is) I cannot help feeling the need to reach out to many others! This has been one of the themes of my professional career (L'Abate, 1973).

What is exciting or glamorous about prevention? Do we know? Can you be excited by prevention in the way we are excited by therapy? Where is the status? Prevention must appear to be as important as or even more important than therapy if we want others to follow in our footsteps.

(3) *Prevention stifles creativity.* Often our graduate students, eager to become instant therapists, either resent taking enrichment coursework; or, if they take it (because they have to!) they do as little as they can. As soon as possible, they want to go to therapy. Enrichment and other preventive approaches have by necessity a structure—that is, they have a definite content and usually they are tied to a definite period of time. How boring, and how restrictive! Why should a bright, highly selected graduate student do that?

(4) *Prevention is too limited.* Prevention, because of its structure, may appear limiting to persons who see themselves as creative and value themselves as free agents (as most psychotherapists do). The values are different, the goals and expectations are different, and the pay-offs may be different. Hence, we cannot rely on established mental health professions to become concerned with prevention. These prejudicial attitudes toward prevention even extend to the specialized field of marriage and family therapy. This is discussed further by Claude Guldner in this volume (see Chapter 18).

SOME PROMISING POSSIBILITIES

As I see it, we must either create a new profession that would be willing to take prevention seriously, or we must use individuals who cannot become professionals because of their limited education and credentials but who may receive on-the-job training. I have explored at least five different possibilities in this regard:

(1) *Social Skills Training (SST)*. This new movement (L'Abate, 1980, 1981) includes most of the researchers and leaders in the preventive area. Although a heterogeneous group professionally, it does include mostly psychologists and educators interested in a variety of topics including effectiveness training, fair fighting, problem solving, and sexuality.

(2) *Applied Developmental Psychology*. Recently I was lucky enough to participate in the First National Convention on Applied Developmental Psychology, at which a list of 150 applied psychology programs that are either in the course of development or are already on the board was presented. These are not clinical programs, mind you; they are *applied*. Their major orientation is toward groups and research. They are all working toward innovative, different approaches to dealing with the many problems that beset us. In fact, it seems to me that this is a new profession in search of a mission! If even half of these programs were to adopt a preventive stance in their training and services, we would have something shaping up. Prevention is a mission in search of a profession, and applied developmental psychology is a burgeoning profession in search of a mission.

Another possible source of personnel might be the counseling profession (Lewis and Lewis, 1981). However, I doubt very seriously that this profession is going to become involved in prevention. How are we going to keep them in the field of prevention once they have seen psychotherapy?

(3) *Applied Undergraduate Instruction*. Another possibility is to train a few selected undergraduates as marriage and family enrichers. We started this in 1981 at Georgia State University and we hope to continue (L'Abate et al., 1980). The crucial issue here will be whether we can help them find jobs after they graduate:

(4) *Volunteers*. I have been a strong believer in the enormous potential, as yet untapped, of using volunteers (L'Abate, 1967). I

believe that here we can find an appropriate and exciting source of new personnel power that deserves our attention. Jim Kacholka and Hillary Buzas have been involved with me in training volunteers affiliated with the Link Counseling Center in Sandy Springs, Atlanta. If we are able to demonstrate that enrichment programs can be delivered by these volunteers successfully, responsibly, and at minimum cost, we will have demonstrated that prevention can take place as part of the mission of two different social agencies. If these agencies can do it, why not others?

(5) *Family Studies.* As I have kept in touch with many family studies programs in Home Economics around the country, I have become aware of their increasing interest in enrichment and other preventive measures. Some of the interst, to be frank, is expressed more by the students than by faculty members. Yet, I am hopeful that these expressions may eventually result in definite coursework and eventual curricula (L'Abate, 1980). If these programs will not take the leadership, who will? To obtain such an outcome we must recognize our own importance and also be recognized by external sources—institutions, the public, and by the consumers themselves. The process will not be easy, and it will take time. We will need to adopt new priorities in finding public health programs at all levels of government; new conceptual references in publications, coursework, curricula, practica, and internships. We will need not only to carry out preventive programs, but also to show that (a) they work, (b) they work better than "cures," (c) they are cheaper than "cures," and (d) they are just as exciting as "cures."

TOWARD A SYNERGETIC MODEL OF PREVENTION

The major need for the field of prevention is to work on a mutually synergetic model above and beyond petty interprofessional rivalries and tedious guild territorialities. This synergetic model will need to relate various areas with each other—and that envisages an ideal world where people can work and collaborate rather than compete with each other. It is based on the assumption that change (synthesis) derives from the integration of dialectically linked opposites.

Let us consider some possibilities:

(1) *Research with service.* The traditional dichotomy between researchers and clinicians has been evident in spite of the claim of psychologists that they have been training scientist-practitioners for the last 30 years. In spite of such emphasis (even among psychologists) this dichotomy is even present as a human characteristic. Professionals in general are more interested in service, and only those in academic careers have an interest in research as well. This unfortunate disparity is still evident in the enrichment field, as Hof and Miller (1981) commented:

> We wonder why the helping professions have been so slow to accept the viability of a marital or marriage enrichment approach to dyadic inter-actions and relationships. Part of the answer may lie in the failure of many proponents of marriage enrichment to have been seriously concerned with appropriate research and theoretical consultations [pp. 65-66].

Hof and Miller go on to wonder further why mental health professionals have failed to heed the enrichment movements, hoping that further research will move these professionals to "learn and develop specific skills in preventive marital health and marriage enrichment in order to help couples develop their potential for effective relationships."

I think that Hof and Miller had failed to get the message I have already received over years of experience—that *most mental health practitioners are not interested either in research or in prevention!*

Therefore it will be up to us to join *both* activities together and set up research as a prerequisite for credentialing and certification. Instead of looking at the professional pedigree, accrediting agencies or committees should start asking for *evidence of effectiveness* as demonstrated by one or more research projects conducted by the practitioner. If we think that research is crucial to the future of prevention, why not set it up as a criterion of accreditation?

Without research it is doubtful whether family wellness programs are going to amount to much more than family life education, which is a great deal to do about nothing because no one thus far has been able to prove that family life education has any significant impact on families (L'Abate and Rapp, 1981). Repetition of the same error (bypassing the research and evaluation component) will only repeat the past errors of family life education.

(2) *Evaluation with intervention.* Most practitioners are interested in (and paid for!) intervening, not for evaluating. Our society is geared to rewarding activity (no matter how random and aimless!) rather than reflection. Reflection is a luxurious activity that receives few rewards. Rushing in to help is what makes us feel good and is what we are paid for—in spite of questionable results!

When we are talking about research, we are really talking (but not exclusively) about evaluation. And when we talk about evaluation, we are talking about (a) pre- and postintervention and follow-up; and (b) the process of intervention. These two are the critical areas. Can't we at least require our students, if not practitioners, to present *one*, just *one*, study with a pretreatment and posttreatment evaluation? And any evaluation of treatment would be based on consideration of posttreatment changes and immediate outcome plus long-range (six months to a year) follow-up. This should be a minimum requirement. Why do we look at credentials and letters of recommendation (which are secondary indications of professional competence) and not require one single case study with the foregoing criteria of evaluation?

I believe that the lack of social and medical clout of the mental health profession is due in part to our failure to document our effectiveness—or lack of it—with actual accounting. This inadequacy in accountability has been responsible for questionable standards of professional competence and effectiveness.

(3) *Theory with practice.* Practitioners are pragmatists. They are interested in what works, and to hell with theory! Who cares about abstractions and irrelevant speculations? Give me what I can use and leave theory to those who can afford it! Naturally, if research and evaluation receive short shrift from a profession, theory will receive the same treatment. The practitioner is concerned with short-sighted pay-offs—"Will my client get better or feel better?" Researchers, evaluators, and theorists are interested in long-term results. The question is, which of these two approaches will produce more effective treatment?

We should therefore demand "real" criteria rather than paper credentials of everyone who wants to practice in the field of prevention. I would even insist that unless such criteria are used, the area of prevention is doomed from the start. If we create a profession without standards of accountability, we shall merely follow in the footsteps of the mental health enterprise where such standards are not required. I know that in asking this I am setting myself up to be a minority of one against the main stream. It will not be the first time that this has happened, and it will not be the last!

(4) *Prevention with intervention.* In a perfect world, prevention should take place in the very same agencies that practice intervention. Different specialists should practice different skills, unlike what is happening now in the mental health field where everybody, regardless of degree, training, experience, and constitutional make-up, practices psychotherapy. We cannot distinguish any more how a psychiatrist differs from a social worker, and how both differ from a psychologist or mental health nurse. This, I submit, is due to the *lack of standards for accountability,* where skills are no longer proprietary for a specific discipline and everyone can perform (supposedly) the job of another professional from a different discipline.

The most fortunate thing that could happen to the field of prevention is that many existing professionals will not be interested in it. Therefore, prevention will become the province of *new* professionals who hopefully may learn from the errors of predecessors in another field. Preventers have now the opportunity to set up their own criteria for evaluation of professional practice and of effectiveness. I sincerely hope that such standards will not be abandoned or forgotten so that, as far as standards are concerned, there will be a clear separating line between preventers and interveners. Prevention is a field much too important for us to omit standards of accountability and effectiveness!

(5) *Professionals with nonprofessionals.* The job is too big to be done by professionals alone. For a long time I have been advocating (L'Abate, 1973) a hierarchial professional structure where various types and levels of clerical, technical, advanced technical, and professional expertise can be identified, labeled, and allowed to

flourish under clearly established guidelines. Instead of a situation of professionals versus nonprofessionals, which I find repugnant, I am advocating a career lattice of different types and levels of expertise in prevention in which various professionals and nonprofessionals will collaborate creatively in striving for a common goal.

My hope is that eventually we may succeed in producing new identities whose main personal and professional objectives will be to prevent rather than to "cure" and whose calling will be as honored, respected, and valued as any other healing profession. I hold prevention to be the highest form of healing that exists.

NOTE

1. For further information on this conference, please consult my paper entitled "Issues in applied developmental psychology: reflections on the first Mailman Conference" which as been submitted for publication.

REFERENCES

CARLSON, B. E. and L. V. DAVID (1980) "Prevention of domestic violence," pp. 41-62 In R. H. Price et al. (eds.) Prevention in Mental Health: Research, Policy and Practice. Beverly Hills, CA: Sage.

CATALANO, R. and P. DOOLEY (1980) "Economic change in primary prevention," pp. 21-40 in R. H. Price et al. (eds.) Prevention in Mental Health: Research, Policy and Practice. Beverly Hills, CA: Sage.

CORFMAN, E. [ed.] (1979a) Strengthening the Family. Rockville, MD: NIMH.— (1979b) Family Violence and Child Abuse. Rockville, MD: NIMH.—(1979c) Mental Illness in the Family. Rockville, MD: NIMH.

CUMMINGS, N. A. (1979) "The anatomy of psychotherapy under national health insurance." Amer. Psychologist 32:711-718.

FELNER, R. D., S. S. FARBER, and R. PRIMAVERA, (1980) "Children of divorce, stressful life events, and transitions: a framework for preventive efforts," pp. 81-108 in R. H. Price et al., Prevention In Mental Health: Research, Policy and Practice. Beverly Hills, CA: Sage.

GARBARINO, J. (1980) "Preventing child maltreatment," pp. 63-79 In R. H. Price et al., Health: Research, Policy and Practice. Beverly Hills, CA: Sage.

GARFIELD, S. L. (1981) "Psychotherapy: a 40-year appraisal. Amer. Psychologist 36: 174-183.

GOLDSTON, S. E. (1977) "An overview of primary prevention programming," pp. 23-40 in D. C. Klein and S. E. Goldston (eds.) Primary Prevention: An Idea Whose Time Has Come. Rockville, MD: NIMH.

HOF, L., and W. R. MILLER (1981) Marriage Enrichment: Philosophy, Process and Program. Englewood Cliffs, NJ: Prentice-Hall.

L'ABATE, L. (1981) "Skill training programs for couples and families," pp. 631-661 in A. S. Gurman and D. P. Kniskern (eds.) Handbood of Family Therapy. New York: Brunner/Mazel.—"Toward a theory and technology for Social Skills Training: suggestions for curriculum development." Academic Psychology Bull. 2: 218-230.—(1977) Enrichment Structured Interventions for Couples, Families and Groups. Washington, DC: University Press of America, 1977.—(1973) "The laboratory method in clinical child psychology: three applications," J. of Clinical Child Psychology 2: 8-10.—(1967) "The personality of volunteer housewives and Candy-Stripers. Volunteer Administrations 1: 29-36.—and G. RAPP (1981) Enrichment: Skill Training for Family Life. Washington, DC: University Press of America.

L'ABATE, L., L. BURGE-CALLAWAY, R. CHATLOS, C. HOLLAND, and M. MILAN (1980) "Applied undergraduate instruction: report of committee." Psychology Department, Georgia State University, July.

LEWIS, J. M., W. R. BEAVERS, M. T. GORSETT, and V. A. PHILLIPS (1976) No Single Thread: Psychological Health in Family Systems. New York: Brunner/Mazel.

PRICE, R. H., R. F. KETTERER, B. C. BADER, and J. MONOHAN [eds.] (1981) Prevention in Mental Health: Research, Policy, and Practice. Beverly Hills, CA: Sage.

WILDMAN, R. W. III (1977) "Structured Versus Unstructured Marital Intervention, pp. 154-183 in L. L'Abate (ed.) Enrichment: Structured Interventions With Couples, Families and Groups. Washington, DC: University Press of America.

Part II

Marriage Enrichment

Three points are identified at which marriages could benefit from the impact of preventive services: before the wedding, in the critical first year, and in preparation for the middle and later years. The marriage enrichment movement is described, and an attempt is made to provide a new theoretical frame of reference for enriched marriages.

5

How Effective *Is* Marriage Preparation?

David H. Olson

Being well prepared for marriage is often seen as of little importance by both couples and society. It is still easier to get a marriage license in most states than it is to get a driver's license. To obtain a driver's license, one needs to pass a test for vision, pass a written examination on driving rules and regulations, and be able to demonstrate the ability to drive a car; and more people are hurt by divorce than by car accidents. We should not be surprised, therefore, that over 40 percent of the couples marrying this year will eventually divorce.

Because of the rising divorce rate, more interest and attention is now being paid to marriage preparation. However, most of the work with premarital couples still continues to be done by clergy, who often feel inadequately trained and have insufficient time to work effectively with these couples before the marriage ceremony. Most marriage and family therapists rarely help premarital couples prepare for marriage, but rather spend their time treating couples and families who are at the terminal stages of their relationship.

In spite of the high divorce rate, couples continue to marry—over two million did so last year. Marriage continues to be the most popular voluntary institution in our society, with over 90 percent of the people eventually marrying at least once. One out of four marriges every year involves couples in which one or both have married before, but even couples married previously often do not take time to prepare for remarriage.

Fortunately, in the last five years, there have been more systematic attempts to develop inventories and communication training programs that can be of benefit to premarital couples. If these approaches are effectively used, they can serve as a major preventive step to help couples get their marriage off to a good start. The rest of this chapter will review various ways of working with premarital couples that have been found effective.

WHY WORK WITH PREMARITAL COUPLES?

From a preventive perspective, it is essential to help couples get their relationship off to a good start. Research has consistently demonstrated that problems couples have during engagement are carried over into marriage. In addition, they develop new problems as they adjust to each other and to the experiences of married life. Therefore, unless they learn ways of effectively dealing with their current problems, they will continue to develop more problems in their marriage and eventually feel overwhelmed and unable to cope.

Another reason for working with couples at this early stage in their relationship is that they might be more able to learn positive communication and problem solving skills than they could when their problems have become more serious.

An important component of any work with premarital couples could be to help them learn that marriage is a process that takes time and energy. As in an occupation, they need to know that they should invest time, energy, and money into their marriage if they want it to be successful. It would also be important for them to start off the marriage realizing that further enrichment, and perhaps counseling, might be necessary to keep their relationship a satisfying one for both partners.

Premarital work is also important as a way of helping some couples delay or even decide against marriage. Taking prevention to its extreme, one of the ways of preventing divorce is by helping some couples see that it would be a disadvantage to marry each other at this time.

Lastly, most premarital couples are very idealistic about their relationship and have unrealistic expectations for themselves and their partners. Working with them before marriage can help them clarify their expectations for themselves and each other and become more realistic about the difficulties and challenges of their married life together.

WHY ARE PREMARITAL COUPLES SO DIFFICULT TO WORK WITH?

The saying "love is blind" is indeed applicable to most premarital couples. They are often very unrealistic about their relationship and are convinced that whatever problems they have will go away after the wedding. As a result, most couples are not interested in spending time on relationship issues.

It is safe to say that most premarital couples spend a great deal of time and energy thinking about their wedding ceremony (which last only a few hours) and by contrast have little interest in or motivation to develop their relationship. They are often afraid to challenge or discuss issues because this might threaten the partner and possibly beome serious enough to end the relationship.

Because of their denial of relationship issues, most premarital couples have not even discussed adjustments they will soon have to face such as how to deal with finances or who will handle certain household responsibilities.

So, while premarital couples are theoretically at a "teachable moment" in terms of helping them learn a great deal about themselves and each other, in practice they represent a "tough nut to crack." Any effective premarital program must, therefore, help them become more aware of their relationship issues and motivate them to begin working early before their problems become too serious.

WHAT KINDS OF PROGRAMS ARE OFFERED FOR PREMARITAL COUPLES?

If it were not for concerned clergy who often insist that couples meet with them at least once before marriage, most couples would have no premarital preparation whatsoever. Table 5.1 lists an estimate of the number of couples who receive various types of premarital services and programs. This is a ballpark estimate since there are not national statistics on the number of couples who have actually participated in these programs.

It is fair to say that about one-third of the couples currently married received no premarital service or program since they are married outside the church. About one-third of the couples have at least one or two sessions with their clergy to discuss relationship issues. Most of these clergy feel inadequately trained to work with the couples, and most of them do not use any premarital inventory to help them in this process.

Historically, many churches offered group lectures on the topic of marriage. Often, 30 to 40 couples were invited to attend several weekend sessions in which relevant topics were discussed by marriage and family professionals. The topics often included lectures on communication, conflict resolution, sexuality, finances, and values.

Recently, some churches have organized small couple workshops or retreats where premarital couples have the opportunity to discuss issues with other couples.

The most intensive and effective type of premarital counseling for couples includes structured communication and skill-building programs, but these are rarely offered or used by premarital couples. Because of the lack of trainers and inability to involve premarital couples, these programs are used by only 1 percent of couples before marriage.

In general, it is clear that most premarital couples get very little—if any—effective help in preparing for their marriage relationship. Even when programs are offered, couples do not take time or energy to become seriously involved in benefitting from these opportunities. As a result of the lack of preparation for couples, we should be surprised by the number of couples who actually manage to develop a successful relationship in spite of this major handicap.

HOW EFFECTIVE ARE THE VARIOUS PREMARITAL APPROACHES?

In the last five years, there have been a number of systematic studies investigating the effectiveness of various approaches for helping

TABLE 5.1   Services and Programs Offered to Premarital Couples

Kinds of Premarital Programs	*Estimated Percentage of Couples*
No premarital program or service	30
Dialogue with clergy (1-2 sessions) and no premarital inventory	25
Dialogue with clergy and a premarital inventory	10
Large group lectures (several sessions)	20
Small group couple dialogue	14
Premarital counseling and/or structured communication-skill-building programs (several sessions)	1

premarital couples. These studies provide helpful evidence as to what approaches seem most effective and least effective.

It is clear that large lecture courses for groups of couples are not an effective way of helping premarital couples, no matter how well the lectures are presented. A study (Norem et al., 1980) evaluated the effectiveness of five different premarital educational programs which ran from six to eight weeks. Although these programs were well conceived and the lectures well presented, no attitutde change was produced as a result. In fact, it was much like pouring water over a duck's back.

One of the negative outcomes of the lecture format was that it discouraged most couples from considering future marriage enrichment programs. It also decreased couples' willingness to go to marriage counseling if marriage problems occurred in their relationship. In other words, these lectures disappointed rather than excited them in terms of the need for and value of future marriage enrichment and counseling.

A recent study clearly demonstrated the value of using some type of premarital inventory with couples (Druckman et al., 1981). The premarital inventory used was PREPARE which is a 125-item inventory that assesses 12 content areas such as idealism, communication, conflict resolution, finances and expectations. This inventory was administered by counselors and clergy to the premarital couples. The couples' answer sheets were scored, and a 12-15 page computer printout was sent to the clergy person or counselor, who then interpreted the results and worked with the couple for one or more sessions.

The research clearly demonstrated that using PREPARE was more effective than traditional sessions with clergy or the group sessions offered to premarital couples. When PREPARE was used in combination with four intensive premarital counseling sessions by a trained marriage counselor, there was some additional benefit but not much more than was obtained from having couples simply take PREPARE and have one feedback session. This finding is somewhat surprising but demonstrates that premarital couples are not ready or willing to work on resolving conflict or to deal with serious relationship issues before marriage.

A series of systematic studies by Dr. Bernard Guerney et al. (1977) has clearly demonstrated the effectiveness of their Relationship Enhancement Program for both marital and premarital couples (Avery, 1980; Ginsberg and Vogelsong, 1977; Most and Guerney, 1981; Ridley et al., 1981). Ridley et al. (1980) clearly demonstrated that the Relationship Enhancement Program increased the premarital couple's empathy and self-disclosure skills and also increased their positive feeling about the relationship. A six-month follow-up of these couples demonstrated that most of the skills persisted even though they dropped considerably from where they were right after the program was completed. (Avery et al., 1980).

In addition to demonstrating that premarital couples can learn communication skills, Ridley et al. (1982) indicated that they can also learn problem solving and conflict resolution skills, They developed an eight-week program in which couples were trained on how to use problem-solving skills in their relationship. A six-month follow-up of these couples also demonstrated that these problem-solving skills can be learned and do persist over time (Ridley et al., 1980). Like the communication skills, couples' abilities to use the problem solving steps diminishes after they have completed the program but it is still considerably higher than before they took the program.

A significant study in the area of premarital work was done by Bader and colleagues (1980) in Canada. They developed a systematic program that encouraged couples to learn constructive conflict resolution skills and to practice them with each other in small groups. The research demonstrated that these skills are trainable and do persist over a one-year period. More importantly, the difference between the couples who had taken the program and the control group became more dramatic after one year. Specifically, couples who took the course showed an increase in their abilities to resolve conflict while the control group showed no change. Another important finding was that couples having the training more readily sought professional help for their relationship after marriage than did the control group.

A recent study by H. Norman Wright (1981) indicated that eight intensive premarital sessions with couples were of benefit. After surveying 1,000 couples after marriage, he found that those who had at least six premarital sessions felt they benefited from the experience, while those who had few sessions did not find the experience so beneficial.

These series of studies have clearly demonstrated that large lectures to groups of couples are not beneficial. Also, it is clear that using some type of permarital inventory, like PREPARE, is a very useful stimulus to involve the couple in a dialogue with each other before marriage. The studies have also clearly demonstrated that premarital couples can learn communication and conflict resolution skills and that these skills do persist after marriage.

WHAT WOULD CONSTITUTE AN EFFECTIVE PREMARITAL PROGRAM?

Ideally, it would be best if a couple could first take some type of premarital inventory and receive feedback on that instrument. Second, it would be ideal if couples could then participate in some kind of small support group where they shared their feelings and concerns with each other. Finally, it would be ideal if the couples could then receive training in communication and problem solving skills that they could use in dealing with relationship issues. This type of three-phase sequential program would take approximately six to eight weeks. The goals that could realistically be accomplished in each of these three phases are indicated in Table 5.2.

The major problem with attempting to have couples participate in such a three phase program is the fact that many couples do not come for premarital counseling until two to three months before their wedding date. As a result, it is often impossible to accomplish more than the first phase of the program. This highlights the importance of trying to involve couples in the process of marriage preparation.*at least one year before marriage.*

TABLE 5.2 Goals of a Three-Phase Premarital Program

Premarital Inventory	Couples' Discussions in Small Groups	Communication Skill Training in Couples' Groups
Increase couple's awareness of relationship strengths and potential problem areas.	Increase couple's ability and willingness to share with other couples.	Build communications skills like sympathy, empathy, and self-disclosure.
Facilitate a couple's discussion about their relationsip.	Develop other couples as friends	Build skills for resolving conflict and problem solving.
Establish relationship with clergy, counselor or married couple.	Learn how other couples relate and deal with issues.	
Prime for post-wedding enrichment or counseling.		
Referral to intensive counseling if problems too serious arise.		

When it is not possible to have couples complete the entire three phases before marriage, the process could be continued after marriage. In fact, there is some evidence (Bader et al., 1980) that couples would be more motivated and able to utilize these communication skills if they are trained within six months to a year after marriage. The important issue is that these are three valuable experiences that would help the couple get their relationship off to a good start whether they are all completed before marriage or after. The implication is that they should have these types of experiences so that they will be more prepared to face the realities and challenges of marriage.

WHO CAN DELIVER PREMARITAL SERVICES?

Based on the past, it is clear that most marriage and family therapists won't have time or interest to deliver premarital sevices. To date, clergy have been the individuals most involved with premarital couples. However, their opportunity is often limited before the wedding, and often they do not have the time or skills to work with the couples in intensive counseling after they have married.

Lay couples who are able to develop a good marriage relationship and are interested in continued marriage enrichment for themselves and others are an ideal potential resource. One group that would be ideal is ACME, an association of lay couples organized nationally and internationally by David and Vera Mace.

There are several advantages in using lay couples to work with premarital couples. First, they can use their own experience to share both the joys and frustrations of marriage with these young couples. By working with these couples before marriage, the lay couples could also serve as a useful resource and support base for the couples as they enter their first year or so of marriage. This sharing experience could also be of benefit to the marriage of the lay couple.

The kinds of services lay couples could provide would include all three previously discussed—administering and interpreting the premarital inventory, leading a couples' group, and leading a communication-skill-building group. This would naturally necessitate that the lay couples be trained in each of these areas. However, these are useful skills that would likewise enrich lay leaders' own marriages. A recent study demonstrated that lay couples can learn to train premarital couples in relationship enhancement skills (Most and Guerney, 1981).

It is clear that lay couples have been underused and would be a valuable resource for premarital preparation. Couples and clergy alike would appreciate the involvement and modeling of couples who have been able to achieve a happy and vital marriage relationship. For this to actually occur, it is important that lay couples contact their clergy or a counseling organization and offer their services in the important area of premarital preparation.

RECOMMENDATIONS REGARDING POLICIES RELATING TO PREMARITAL SERVICES

(1) Premarital preparation should be seen as a national priority to help marriages get off to a good start. The prevention of divorce begins with providing good premarital preparation.

(2) Premarital couples should be encouraged to begin the process of preparation and dealing with relationship issues at least *one year* before marriage.

(3) Premarital couples and their parents should be encouraged to spend as much money, time, and energy in preparing for the marriage relationship as they do for the wedding ceremony. This will help ensure that they see marriage as an important investment and as a process that continues for the life of the individuals.

(4) Research should be continued to find the most effective types of premarital preparation programs. It would be useful to assess the relative advantages of various types of programs to determine when each can be most appropriately and effectively offered.

(5) Lay couples should be encouraged to become actively involved with premarital couples and to work with them through their first year of married life.

REFERENCES

AVERY, A. W., C. A. RIDLEY, L. A. LESLIE, and T. MULHOLLAND (1980) "Relationship enhancement with premarital dyads: a six-month follow-up." Amer. J. of Family Therapy 8:23-30.

BADER, E., G. MICROYS, L. SINCLAIR, E. WILLETT, and B. CONWAY (1980) "Do marriage preparation programs really work? A Canadian experiment." J. of Marital and Family Therapy: 171-179.

DRUCKMAN, J. M., D. F. FOURNIER, D. H. OLSON, and B. E. ROBINSON. Effectiveness of various premarital preparation programs. Unpublished manuscript, Family Social Science, University of Minnesota, St. Paul.

GINSBERG, B. and E. VOGELSONG (1977) "Premarital relationship improvement by maximizing empathy and self-disclosure: the PRIMES program," B. G. Guerney, Jr. (ed.) Relationship enhancement, San Francisco: Jossey-Bass.

GUERNEY, B. G., Jr. [ed.] (1977) Relationship Enhancement. San Francisco: Jossey-Bass.

MOST, R. and B. G. GUERNEY, Jr. (1981) "Training leaders for premarital relationship enhancement: an empirical evaluation." Pennsylvania State University. (unpublished)

NOREM, R. H., M. SCHAEFER, J SPRINGER, and D. H. OLSON (1980) "Effectiveness of premarital education programs: outcome study and followup evaluations." Family Social Science, University of Minnesota. (unpublished)

RIDLEY, C. A., S. R. JORGENSEN, A. C. MORGAN, and A. W. AVERY (1982) "Relationship enhancement with premarital couples: an assessment of effects on relationship quality." Amer. J. of Family Therapy 10, 3: 41-48.

RIDLEY, C. A., A. W. AVERY, J. E. HARRELL, A. A. HAYES-CLEMENTS, and N. MCCUNNEY (in press) "Mutual problem solving skills training for premarital couples: a six month follow-up." J. of Applied Developmental Psychology. (in press)

RIDLEY, C. A., A. W. AVERY, JE. E. HARRELL, L. A. LESLIE, and J. DENT (1982) Conflict Management: A Premarital Training Program in Mutual Problem Solving. Tucson: Human Development Laboratory, University of Arizona.

SCHUMM, W. R. and W. DENTON (1979) "Trends in premarital counseling." J. of Marital and Family Therapy 22: 23-32.

WRIGHT, H. N. Premarital Counseling: a followup study. Christian Marriage Enrichment, 8000 East Girard, Denver, CO. (unpublished)

6

The Critical
First Year of
Marriage

Edward Bader
Carole Sinclair

Along with their congratulations and best wishes, friends and relatives often slip the bridal couple a word of warning. In doing so, are these people prophets of doom? Or are they simply being realistic advisors when they say that the first year is the hardest? Is it true that if the couple survive 365 days together the rest of their married life will be an easy ride?

It is probably impossible to overestimate the importance of the first year of marriage. So many key decisions are worked out: for example, will one play the dominant and one the submissive role, or will a kind of balance-of-power be established? How will money be managed? What frequency or pattern of lovemaking will be established? How will quarrels be resolved? Whatever patterns are established at the beginning of the marriage will likely continue for many years, and the way these patterns develop can greatly influence the future of the marriage.

David and Vera Mace (1970) describe a successful marriage as passing though three stages: These are mutual enjoyment, mutual adjustment, and mutual fulfillment. The mutual enjoyment stage is centered around the honeymoon. "Honeymoon" means "a month of honey," and even though the time the couple spend away from the everyday work world is usually less than a month, it is intended to be a time of relaxing together and enjoying each other's company and love.

The second stage of "mutual adjustment" usually comes later and lasts much longer. Although some couples start adjusting to each other long before marriage, others do not begin this task until they are living together as husband and wife. The Maces conclude that the first year of marriage is the critical year because by the end of the first year the couple has developed habits of interaction that tend to be repeated over and over in the years that follow. If these are good patterns, the marriage progressively develops. If they are bad patterns, the marriage degenerates.

> "It would be our judgment that practically all marriages that fail do so because they are unable to cope with the tasks of the adjustment period in marriage. Many of these actually break up in the early years. But even when marriages fail later in life, there is almost invariable evidence that the inadequate adaptation of the earlier years has at last caught up with them." [Mace and Mace, 1970: 67].

STAGES IN FAMILY DEVELOPMENT

From as far back as William Shakespeare's "As You Like It" we have known that every man passes through definite life changes as he progresses from birth to death. Jean Piaget (1950) and Lawrence Kohlberg (1964) have described the successive stages though which a child must go to develop into an adult, while Erik Erikson (1950), Daniel Levinson (1978), and Gail Sheehy (1974) have concentrated on the life cycle of the adult. The word "stages" is now being used in a new way to explain what is happening to families today. The emphasis is turning to exploring how the *family* as a unit passes through its various life cycles.

In an article in 1963 Michael Solomon credits the late Frances Schers with the idea of major life events affecting families. Solomon divided these events into developmental stages with specific tasks at each stage.

He defines the marriage of two people as the beginning of the development of any family. The two tasks assigned to this stage of marriage are

(1) The construction and implementation of the basic male and female roles of the marital partners that are likely to last throughout the dura-

tion of the marriage. A couple must establish ways of adequately meeting each other's needs in myriad functions. These include sexual, social, psychological, and economic satisfactions.

(2) The relinquishing by each partner of the primary relationship each has had to his or her own family. Their relationship to their families may remain important and meet many needs of the couple, but it must become secondary to the new relationship to each other.

The work of Elizabeth Carter and Monica McGoldrick (1980) parallels Solomon's. They assign similar tasks to the beginning of marriage which they describe as "the joining of families." The emotional process requires a commitment to the new system and these two tasks:

(1) formation of the marital system, and
(2) realignment of relationships with extended family and friends to include spouse.

These writers have referred to what have been found to be two especially "touchy" areas in the first year of marriage which have been further described in the research project to be described in this chapter (Bader et al., 1980).

In preparing for our research study we contacted engaged couples though the churches in which they were to be married. They were then randomly assigned to either an "experimental" group which took part in group discussions, both before the marriage and during the first year of marriage, or a "control" group which received no marriage program. A preliminary interview was done with members of both groups approximately three months before the wedding. A second interview was done approximately three months after the wedding. The third interview took place one year after the wedding. A fourth and final interview was done five years after the wedding. Of the 63 couples who took part in the original research, 57 were located and participated in all four interviews.

Establishing New Roles

Household chores may seem a surprisingly trivial area of disagreement, but our research study showed that 87 percent of the couples interviewed six months after the wedding marked this as an area of disagreement. After one year of marriage, this figure rose to 91 percent! In both interviews it was ranked as the most frequent area of disagreement.

A closer examination of the life style of most young married couples today gives some clues to the high level of irritation that often surrounds household tasks. Usually both husband and wife are working full-time, sometimes with the added complications of shift work. Neither feels particularly energetic when arriving home to face the prospect of cooking supper, doing the dishes, washing clothes, cleaning the apartment or house, and so on. And if one partner feels the other is not doing his or her fair share an argument can easily erupt.

Often the family backgrounds of both partners are important factors in determining which partner assumes which task—for instance, if both partners come from families in which the upkeep of the bathroom was the responsibility of the mother, they will probably easily agree that the woman will be in charge of that area. However, if either father shared in or took charge of cleaning the bathroom, then the couple has two models from which to choose. After all, no one really enjoys cleaning toilet bowls, and most people would definitely prefer having the partner take on this sometimes unpleasant chore.

The list goes on. Taking out the garbage; making the bed; cleaning the apartment or house; taking the laundry to the laundromat; ironing; cooking; shopping—these are the nitty-gritty parts of a shared life. The traditional male/female roles don't necessarily apply when deciding who should do which task.

Most couples must make this division with no acceptable models to guide them. They often know they do not want to follow their parents' roles but they aren't sure what they want for themselves.

Leaving Home

The second area of frequent disagreement is family ties. Those who have written about the normal development of the family insist that they do not recommend giving up family ties and family loyalties, but they do emphasize the importance of keeping the needs of the marriage partner ahead of those of one's family of origin. If the young wife feels that her husband puts his family ahead of her when decisions are being made, she will be disappointed and hurt. And the husband who believes that his wife puts her parents' needs or wishes ahead of him will resent their influence and do his best to eliminate or decrease it.

The first year of marriage becomes the time during which many families exert subtle, or even obvious, pressures on their children, pushing them to spend time at the parental home and sometimes demanding that they give them even more attention than they did before they were married. If their invitations to Sunday dinners and family celebrations are turned down, parents can become angry or so disappointed that their child feels guilty. Mother's Day, Thanksgiving, and Christmas become days of tension as the newly married couple try to achieve a shaky balance of their own wishes and needs while keeping both sets of parents at least partly satisfied.

Robert Stahmann and William Hiebert (1980) further develop the importance of "leaving home." "To put it in other terms, the child has become an adult. The person no longer asks his or her parents to mother and father him" (p. 69).

Stahmann and Hiebert list four negative results on the new marriage if either spouse fails to "leave home":

(1) They keep getting tangled up in family problems. Their own marriage relationship is continually in crisis because of crises going on in the larger family.

(2) Because families that hang on to their children prevent them from growing up emotionally and psychologically, their children tend to look for another parent to take care of them—not for a peer, a fellow adult with whom they can establish an intimate relationship.

(3) Research on psychosomatic illnesses indicates that people who are still emotionally entangled with their families are ill more frequently than those who have established their independence.

(4) Because their parents did not want them to grow up and leave home, they find it easier to function as dependent children rather than self-reliant adults.

Newly married couples deal with their families in various ways. Some remain entangled and face the consequences outlined by Stahmann and Hiebert. Others cut off their families emotionally or in frequency of contact, either before or early in the marriage. They attempt to gain their independence by ignoring their families or simply avoiding seeing them. Monica McGoldrick (1980) believes the usual pattern is a combination of some contact, some closeness, and some generally avoided issues. "Whatever the patterns of difficulty with extended family—conflict, enmeshment, distance or cutoff—the lack of resolution of these relationships is the major problem in negotiating this phase of the family life cycle" (p. 104).

One reason why separating from families is so difficult is that there are various combinations or triangles that can become intertwined. A man may marry a stronger willed woman, secretly hoping she will fight his battles with his domineering parents. A father may blame his son-in-law for his daughter's infrequent visits, fantasizing that she would prefer to spend most of her free time at the family home. Brothers and sisters often resent the addition of an outsider to the family circle, especially if the new member has qualities or attitudes that they see as different, as superior or inferior, to their own.

The normal difficulties of "fitting in" to another family are compounded when the members of the couple come from widely different cultural, ethnic, or religious backgrounds. Although these very differences can become a source of strength for the couple, the first year usually contains many shocks and surprises, demanding that both adapt to each other's attitudes and needs. Special problems can emerge if the newly married couple are either quite young, pregnant, or financially dependent on their families. When two or three of these conditions are present, the difficulties facing the couple will be extreme and outside help may be essential. Premarital counseling with underage couples has proved to be helpful (Shonick, 1975; Meyer 1977; Rolfe, 1980) but some postwedding assistance may also be needed.

WHAT CAN BE DONE TO HELP?

What can be done to make the first-year transition smoother? Dr. Russell Dicks (1963) concluded his book *Premarital Guidance* with a short chapter on postwedding counseling. Speaking of the disappointments and irritations that appear shortly after the wedding he says bluntly

Sometimes it is simply homesickness that is taking its toll, sometimes the personal habits of the mate are irritating factors. These habits may have been well concealed during courtship, but quickly rear their ugly heads after the wedding. The courtship is a time of deceit. After the wedding the deceit is usually detected [p. 135].

He suggests that the pastor-counselor can do much to help at this stage of the marriage. Besides any counseling which may be given to the couple by the clergy, marriage counselors, or physicians, it should be added that there are an increasing number of preventive or educational programs available to the newly married.

Claude Guldner (1971) was probably the first to establish a postwedding program during the early months of marriage. Dissatisfied with the existing premarriage counseling format, he asked 30 couples to return after the wedding for a series of small group discussions. The couples were subdivided into three groups: One met approximately one month after the wedding; the second group met three months after the wedding; and the final group met six months after the wedding. The final group was the most receptive and gained the most benefits.

Other more recent programs have been quite successful in aiding newly married couples to adjust during the first year of marriage (e.g., the study by H. Norman Wright, 1981, described in Chapter 5 of this volume and the Growth in Marriage for Newlyweds program set up by Doris and Jerry Thompson in Kansas City, Missouri).

In the Bader et al. research study the preventive program was divided into two segments, with five sessions prior to the wedding and three sessions approximately six months after the wedding. Video tapes were used to stimulate discussion, and each group was limited to five to seven couples.

The two key areas of adjustment, establishing new roles and leaving home, were discussed in both the pre- and postwedding segments. The Teleketic film "You Haven't Changed a Bit", which dramatizes both areas was used before the wedding; "They Appreciate You More" by the National Film Board of Canada and "Johnny Lingo" by Brigham Young University illustrated the two areas in the postwedding segment. A humorous but useful list entitled "Who Does What?" (see Appendix) is now being used for both couple and group discussion before the wedding; the same list is filled out during the postwedding sessions to see in what ways the list has changed.

The research results showed that some interesting changes took place during the first year. One of the hypotheses being tested was that couples who took part in pre- and postwedding programs would be less likely to engage in destructive conflict with each other than those who had not. As a test of the couples' ability to resolve conflict constructively, couples were asked to assess and solve a series of hypothetical marriage problems. Transcripts of the taped discussions were rated on a three-point rating scale. Generally, a score of 1 was given to couples who had much difficulty listening to one another, displayed hostility to each other either directly or indirectly, seemed caught in a power struggle, and/or played somewhat destructive psychological games with each other. A score of 2 was given to couples who had some difficulty listening to each other, who tended to agree at the moment but displayed no apparent hostility or power struggle. A score of 3 was given to couples who readily listened, could adapt their points of view or respond to what they heard, were supportive of each other and receptive to the other's ideas, and readily admitted and dealt with differences of opinion. The results indicated that couples who took no program showed almost no change over the four interviews, while the couples who had taken the program showed a steady increase in their ability to resolve conflict constructively.

One important aspect of the improvement of couples who took the program was that their greatest increase in ability to resolve conflict occurred after the postwedding sessions. Even though they took part in fewer sessions (three), their improvement was greater than after the five prewedding sessions. This may indicate that they are more receptive and more capable of change after the wedding and honeymoon are behind them. A second important (and encouraging) result is the continuing ability of these couples to resolve conflict constructively even after five years. It appears that a skill learned at such a teachable moment is retained and reapplied to new problems if and when they arise.

The second major hypothesis of the research study was that couples taking part in the program would seek help in solving either individual or marriage problems more readily than those who did not take part. Here again the couples who took the program named more helpers than the couples who did not at both the six-month and one-year interviews. The second difference in seeking help was found in the use of professional counselors. The couples that were not involved in the program showed a marked decrease while the program couples showed a small, but steady, increase.

At the five-year interview a different question was asked: All of the couples were asked if one or both had received any professional counseling or had taken part in either consciousness raising, Marriage Encounter, or Marriage Enrichment groups. Of the experimental couples, 38 percent had at least one partner who answered "Yes," while only one woman (5 percent) of the control couples had received help (and this occured only when the marriage had begun to fall apart).

These final findings are particularly important (and again encouraging) because they indicate that a good experience with a preventive and educational program at one juncture predisposes the participants to similar programs later on. Thus a link is possible between the first premarriage program before the new family is formed extending through the critical first year, bracketing a major change in family structure when the first child is born if both pre- and postnatal programs are available, assisting parents through all the varied stages of raising their own children until it is time for the parents to release them so that they can leave home and begin the family cycle once again (e.g., Claude Guldner's Warranty System, and pre- and postretirement programs like Katie Denyer's in Ottawa, Ontario).

The key is a good beginning. That is why effective premarriage programs like those described by David Olson, and postwedding programs during the critical first year such as those described above can be so beneficial in helping families to progress though the various stages of the life cycle.

Appendix:
Who Does What? A Questionnaire
for Pre- and Postwedding Couples

(1) Who puts out the garbage?
(2) Who cooks most of the meals?
(3) Who washes the dishes?
(4) Who does the cleaning?
(5) Who decides the budget?
(6) Who makes the bed?
(7) Who does the laundry?
(8) Who shops for groceries?
(9) Who puts gas in the car?
(10) Who fixes small things in the house? car?
(11) Who invites the company over?
(12) Who waters the plants?
(13) Who initiates sexual intercourse?
(14) Who pays the bills?
(15) Who changes the light bulbs?

(16) Who cleans the toilet bowl?
(17) Who makes up after a fight?
(18) Who is responsible for contraception?
(19) Who starts the fight?
(20) Who decided where you went for Christmas Dinner?

REFERENCES

BADER, E., G. MICROYS, C. SINCLAIR, E. WILLETT, and B. CONWAY (1980) "Do marriage preparation programs really work? A Canadian experiment." J. of Maritial and Family Therapy 6: 171-179.

CARTER, E. A. and M. MCGOLDRICK (1980) "The family life cycle and family therapy," in E. A. Carter and M. McGoldrick (eds.) The Family Life Cycle: A Framework for Family Therapy. New York: Gardner.

DICKS, R. L. (1963) Premarital Guidance. Englewood Cliffs, N.J.: Prentice-Hall.

ELKIN, M. (1977) "Premarital counseling for minors: The Los Angeles experience." The Family Coordinator 26: 429-443.

ERIKSON, E. H. (1950) Childhood and Society. New York: Norton.

GULDNER, C. (1971) "The post-marital: an alternative fo pre-marital counseling." The Family Coordinator 20: 115-119.

KOHLBERG, L. (1964) "Development of moral character and moral ideology," In M. L. Hoffman and L. W. Hoffman (eds.) Child Development Research, volume 1. New York: Russell Sage.

LEVINSON, D. (1978) The Seasons of a Man's Life. New York: Knopf.

MACE, D. and V. MACE (1970) "What you build into your marriage," in R. Raban et al. Marriage: An Interfaith Guide for All Couples. New York: Association Press.

MCGOLDRICK, M. (1980) "The joining of families through marriage: the new couple," in E. A. Carter and M. McGoldrick (eds.) The Family Life Cycle: A Framework for Family Therapy. New York: Gardner.

PIAGET, J. (1950) Psychology of Intelligence. New York: Harcourt Brace Jovanovich.

ROLFE, D. J. and M. W. ROOSA (1980) "Mandatory premarriage counseling for minors: procedure, follow-up, and findings." (unpublished)

SHEEHY, G. (1974) Passages. New York: E.P. Dutton.

SHONICK, H. (1975) "Pre-marital counseling: three years' experience of a unique service." The Family Coordinator 24: 321-324.

SOLOMON, M. (1973) "A developmental conceptual premise for family therapy." Family Process 12: 179-188.

STAHMANN, R. R. and W. J. HIEBERT (1980) Premarital Counseling. Lexington, MA: D.C. Heath.

WRIGHT, H. N. Premarital counseling: a followup study. Christian Marriage Enrichment, 8000 East Girard, Denver, Colorado. (unpublished)

7

Preparing Couples for Mid-Life and the Later Years

Robert P. Travis
Patricia Y. Travis

We have made America older by our reluctance to have as many children as we used to and by our great advances in medical health technology. Considering just their sheer numbers, older people must be reckoned with today.

Perhaps we who are growing old are the only ones who truly know how wise we are. The advertising media direct us to hide our wrinkles, our varicose veins, our graying hair. The message is "Try to stay as young as you can; and then, when you can't keep it up any longer, tell yourself you don't care and go ahead and and submit to your age."

But maybe there is a better way: to build in the earlier years the kinds of foundations upon which life in the later years can rest securely and, particularly, to develop the kinds of marriages that will blossom into warm companionship and loving intimacy when our failing powers most need supports of that kind. With the continuing extension of the lifespan, today's marriages could last a long time and be a powerful source of emotional security when other resources begin to fail. Any preventive service to families must therefore include a clear understanding of what we now know about marriage in the later years, and how to plan ahead for the rewards it offers to the couple who go hand in hand to the end of the road.

For couples, the key to preparing for middle age and beyond is realizing that marriage itself is a process. If more of us could keep up with this process though open communication, there probably would be little need to experience the "crisis" of middle age and the "empty nest" syndrome.

We recently counseled with a couple who had been married 30 years. He was 51 and successful in business; she was 49 and successful in civic work. They had also been successful in raising three children who were in the process of establishing their own lives. To all outside appearances, this couple was ready to embark on the "harvest years" of their lives.

Then, they took their first long look at each other in years and discovered that they were strangers in an empty house. Their relationship had slipped away almost unnoticed. Even their long established familiarity with each other became strained. They talked about divorce. It seemed to be the only common thing they could discuss.

Their scenario may seem a little extreme; but in one form or another, it is a recurring theme. A significant portion of American divorcees occur when the children are well into their teen years. The saddest part of this story is that it could have had a happier ending.

Emotional poverty can occur in marriages of any duration, but in the middle years it can become particularly acute. The investment of all those years together, building the fringe benefits of the good life and creating a good family, can add substance to the unique partnership of marriage only if it is woven together by the thread of affection. Affection is the single most important ingredient that is blended thoughout the many changes produced by time and circumstance. It is the common bond that gives heart and strength to the shared life.

The "middle marriage" is the time to cultivate the strengths of the marital dyad. If the intervening years have taken too much of a toll, this new experience may not provide the potential to which so many couples look forward. Obviously the marriage crisis of the middle years has some of its roots in the early years of marriage.

There are at least three "adjustment" periods in marriage that can influence the affectional needs which a couple shares. It's helpful to see these as balance points in which the scale can be turned either in one direction or another. Keeping the balance between being a partner, being a parent, and being a person can be crucial to the mid-years and beyond.

THE RELATIONSHIP AND THE MARRIAGE

First, there is the balance between the interpersonal relationship and the marriage itself. Most couples readily admit to the often dramatic difference between their relationship before they decided to get married and the early years of married life. This was described by Bader and Sinclair in this volume. Before marriage both partners were "putting their best foot forward" and trying to be creative in relating with each other. Treating each other as very special people was exciting. The surprise gifts, flowers, poems, long gazes, lingering touches; the greetings, the good-byes, the long talks in which you discovered so much, the long walks when silence was golden all created that unique intimacy that led to the decision to marry.

Then, for many couples, those behaviors stop. They begin to take each other for granted. The reason seems to be that they view marriage as *the goal* they've finally reached rather than as a process though which their relationship can grow and evolve (Travis and Travis, 1979). Consequently, quite a few changes can occur soon after the wedding day. Marriage becomes the ritual that allows those involved to establish a new way of relating to one another (Haley, 1973). Now, as husband and wife, new expectations and roles begin to emerge. Day-to-day activities may become a routine centered around the "maintenance needs" of the marriage. Often negotiating these needs becomes a primary source of communication, lecturing, or pleading. It is no wonder that so often the "romance" and good feelings of the relationship become overwhelmed by the daily routines of life.

Frequently, we see the relationship thrown out of balance with the marriage by such issues as who pays the bills, vacuums the floor, cooks the meals, cleans up after dinner, mows the lawn, takes out the garbage, and so on. These concerns all but overwhelm the intimacy of the relationship. These negotiations become the focal point of the marriage, leaving little time for creativity. It is often helpful to remember that with the exception of child rearing and scheduling visits with in-laws, everything that maintains marriage as a socio-economic unit would also have to be accomplished in some way by the individual partners *even if they were not married.* In other words, doing the "maintenance needs" does not a marriage make. A marriage is made up of three units: each of the individual partners and their relationship. This relationship, which preceded the marriage, should never lose out *because of the marriage.* Indeed, marriage is the celebration of the relationship. Therefore the relationship, that vital third entity of the marriage, should be considered a developing and evolving process of the highest priority.

There are several other changes that can occur after marriage that tend to keep the relationship off balance. One is an attitude that can be described as "since we're married now, you know I love you and this is the way it will be until I tell you differently." This attitude means again that marriage was a goal to be reached and the relationship should just take care of itself. Consequently, partners begin to take each other for granted, and their relationship (which they once carefully and joyfully created) is also taken for granted. Taking each other for granted can result in a devastating loss of the intimate potential of marriage. And intimacy, in this respect, is much more than sex.

For some married couples, the intimacy that they once experienced in their relationship is gradually replaced by foreplay and sexual intercourse. In other words, the couples' sex life replaces the intimacy of the "non-sex-life." This can reach such proportion that any touch or caress is interpreted as a signal that the partner wants or expects a sexual experience.

We have heard both husbands and wives say how much they really wanted to be more affectionate but didn't because they were afraid their partner would misinterpret their need. We recently heard a wife say, "If only he would hold me without my thinking he has something else on his mind." It seems strange that something as nice as a touch, a caress, or an arm around the shoulder can produce such negative feelings.

Sex remains a valuable source of pleasure and intimacy during mid-life and beyond, but partners must learn to touch, caress and hold *for the pleasure of the moment* without the automatic implied commitment to sexual activity. Sex (foreplay and intercourse) can rarely fill the void of emotional poverty. When a husband or wife can freely ask to be hugged or stroked, secure in the belief that there is no other goal, then a mutually fulfilling marriage is almost assured for the middle years.

BEING A PARENT VERSUS
BEING A PARTNER

We have seen how the change in the balance point between the relationship and the marriage can produce a loss of feeling special with each other. Often this loss is further accentuated by the second major life-cycle change in the marriage, childbirth and care of the young. This can be described as the balancing point between being a parent and a partner in the marriage. Parenting often dramatically changes the structure and the dynamics of the marital pair. Many couples discover that this time of excitement and joy is also a period of stress because the social context, the intimacy, and the role structure that they had developed are now altered—often drastically. The new arrival may also intensify any resentment that was present in the marriage as well as demand extensive attention from both partners.

This brings a new era of negotiating the organization of daily living. Frequently, achieving the all-consuming goal of nurturing, training, and educating children now becomes the main task of married life. It becomes a common goal—frequently the only goal—shared by both husband and wife. Once again, the maintenance and enjoyment of their interpersonal relationship is out of balance with parenting. The quality of the relationship can become so impaired that each partner feels emotionally deprived.

Husbands and wives would do well to remember that the quality of their shared life is related to their interpersonal creativity and intimacy just as much as to their involvement in the reproductive cycle, and that these are not mutually exclusive. It is essential for partners to maintain a separate strength in their interpersonal relationship throughout their marriage, and perhaps particularly during the life-cycle change of parenting.

The advent of chldren can help foster this strength, but they cannot be its only source. If this is allowed to happen, the mid-years can be frighteningly hollow.

Married couples should keep their own relationship in high priority by making leisure time for just the two of them. To repeatedly sacrifice their creative-private time for the children is to cheat the total family of a primary source of strength. It would be well for partners to remember that the mother/father relationship to the children is separate and distinct from their wife/husband relationship to each other.

The center of the family is the marital dyad. It is imperative that couples realize that *the quality of the husband-wife relationship reflects the total quality of family life.* If this emphasis is maintained through the childbearing and child rearing years, the relationship will not only survive when the children leave home but will continue to be a primary source of strength and satisfaction.

BEING A PERSON VERSUS BEING A PARTNER

The third major balance point occurs between being a person and being a partner. This balance point is not associated with a specific event such as getting married or becoming parents. It can become critical at any time when the individual's goals and ambitions become more important and meaningful than those of the relationship. This is when "getting ahead" and "winning the race" can mean losing the marriage.

People pursue their professions for different reasons. For some it's just a means to an end, while for others it's the most important concern in their life. For the latter, their success and happiness in life is defined by their work. Retirement hits them very hard.

There are more dual-career couples now than ever before. This can severely change the traditional household and childcare roles in the family (Berger, 1979). Sometimes, when couples follow an egalitarian strategy in handling these problems, they can move closer together in their relationship. All too often, however, we have seen both husbands and wives direct their creative energies toward their careers, community service, church activities, or hobbies to the point that their relationship is lost in the shuffle to get things done—separately.

There can be a healthy balance between individual development in terms of work, hobbies, leisure time, and so forth, and relationship time. They do not have to be mutually exclusive. Just as with the other guidelines mentioned above, if the relationship is kept in central focus as a productive and pleasurable part of a couple's life, then time-out to be creative in individually meaningful and satisfying pursuits can be a positive experience for all concerned. The opposite is true where the relationship constantly competes for its share in that most scarce commodity of all—time.

MAINTAINING THE BALANCE

Couples whose marriage relationship has been off-balance during the earlier years may find the new pressures of the middle years particularly difficult. For most couples, there are at least 15 years of marriage after their last child leaves home (Mead and Kaplan, 1965). Almost certainly, this will be much more time than they had together before the arrival of the first child.

This time, alone together again, is also a different time psychologically and physiologically. We've all heard about female menopause and, more recently, the male climacteric. A host of people breeze through these periods with minimal discomfort, but we rarely hear of them. We tend to label these physiological changes as "crisis periods" and perpetuate an expectation of dreaded symptoms to which many people succumb. This is not to deny that there are some very real changes at this time in one's life; but we do suggest that individuals do not have to follow the classic descriptions because of an attitude of "after all, what else can you expect?" Regardless of biological changes, there can be little question that psychological and social factors have a profound impact on how husbands and wives react to this period of mid-life.

Thus far we have stressed the quality of the intimacy-based marriage as the mainstay of effective functioning in the middle years. It is in this climate that couples can best find a mutually enhancing marital relationship that meets the need of genuinely relating to another person—the need to express feelings and to hold, to touch, and to be held. We have stressed these attributes of intimacy because couples shoud be aware that such needs do not, as is often supposed, atrophy or end with the aging process.

The need for intimacy is, indeed, the most notable exception to other kinds of needs and changes associated with aging. If we were to take seriously everything that has been written about the aging process, we would be convinced that nothing—physiologically or psychologically—is as good or as strong as it used to be when we were young. But surely, the need for intimate attachment and feelings of personal identity does not decline with time, greying hair, or wrinkled brows.

In fact, the middle years actually offer couples an opportunity to explore new dimensions of their relationship. It is a time when both partners need each other's support and understanding. Often, it is a time that offers more financial security than the child-rearing years could. It is also a time of increased freedom and spontaneity. The phrase "starting over again" seems appropriate here for, as with all the family-life stages, the best approach is to use whatever resources you have at any given time as effectively as you can. There are so many opportunities for enriching one's life, and every lifestage offers its own resources for fulfillment. The middle years can be a time for recommitment—a time to discover that familiar partner in new and different ways.

TOUCH: THE BRIDGE TO COMMUNICATION

One of the most important factors in achieving an effective marriage is the ability to communicate openly. Open communication means a representation of self that is conveyed in a manner that shows genuine care and regard for the partner. Particularly, it includes the ability to listen.

Couples can foster this type of communication through touch. Married partners who really experience and appreciate their ability to talk freely with each other also seem to have a confident and trusting nonverbal physical communication. The basis for productively communicating in either of these styles is the same (i.e., "I can talk to you with no strings attached; I can touch you with no strings attached").

The ability to communicate (verbally or nonverbally) with no strings attached is not always easily achieved. It is particularly difficult for couples who have reached the middle years of marriage without having developed this skill. Difficult, yes, but not impossible provided that both partners are willing to risk and be vulnerable. The intrinsic rewards in this type of communication are to enhance one's self-esteem and to heighten one's appreciation of the partner. This is a healthy and pleasurable alternative to emotional poverty.

With the reemphasis on the marriage relationship in the middle years, partners can find a beautiful source of mutual joy, comfort and emotional sustenance. During these years, couples need a place that is uniquely theirs—a respite, a nourishment, a place simply *to be.* Marriage can provide this vital security provided that both husband and wife can cultivate a rich climate of emotional and sensual pleasure and fulfillment.

With this background, the marital dyad can establish a common ground and strength and purpose that can help them negotiate their differences and face their personal assortment of life stresses. With this type of commitment to interpersonal development, couples can take advantage of the middle years and expand their adaptive and creative moods in terms ot interests, sexuality, new involvements, pleasurable activities, and simply take time to experience and belong.

This is the time to expand a kind of self-awareness with the utmost confidence that each partner wants only the best for the other. "Growing individually together" can have special meaning during this phase of the life cycle.

There is some evidence to show that couples in later life actually experience a new high in marital happiness. For example, Deutscher (1967) noted that the majority of middle-aged couples found this stage of marriage as a time of new freedoms: from being economically responsible for children, from housework and chores, and freedom to be oneself for the first time since the children came along. In a more recent study (Rollins and Feldman, 1970) and in a national survey (Campbell, 1975), it was found that marital happiness was highest in newlyweds, declined with the coming of children, and turned up again when the children left home. There seems to be little doubt that the new freedom of the mid-years offers, at least potentially, a different opportunity for couples to develop personal and interpersonal skills.

It seems adults have new stages of development just as growing children do. This awareness of new options in the middle years may create an intimate environment in which the individual thrives and the quality of life is enhanced for both partners.

BEYOND MIDLIFE

Persons of age 65 and older are increasing both in number, and in proportion to the total population (Shanas, 1980). In 1950 there were about 12.3 million people 65 and over—11 percent of the population, or one out of every nine Americans. Of those 65 and over, four of every five have living children (Shanas, 1978). For those with children, approximately one-half live close to at least one child and see at least one child often. Other relatives often provide some helping functions for those couples who do not have children.

In a sense, age 65 and beyond is a time of reentering the family unit. It is largely from the strength of the family, including spouse, sibling, children, and other kin, that the older person maintains a functional integration in society. The emotional support and helping services that the extended family can provide offer the elderly a "safe harbor" in which to securely and effectively function (Shanas, 1980).

This type of social support, together with that provided by friends and neighbors, can be a substantial aid in helping the person live a productive life. This does not mean to imply that 65 and older is the "helpless" period of the life in which parents become "dependent" on their children, relatives, or friends. We all age psychologically, physiologically, and emotionally at different rates. At some point, however, everyone appreciates a little help, understanding, and encouragement. We need this when we are young, aged, and in all the years in between. This is a part of living fully through each life cycle.

We repeatedly remind our patients—of all ages—to use their assets to the best of their ability. Capitalize on your strengths! This means taking full advantage of what each life cycle change offers. This includes the relationship, the marriage, and the family, the middle years as well as the later years. Creating the most out of each of the "phases"—indeed, of life itself—is to take advantage of your strengths, your abilities, and your assets. Learn to explore *possibilities*.

There are changes with the middle years, with retirement, and with aging. Taking advantage of these changes with the unrestricted expression of your capabilities is to appreciate the process of living. This is a different philosophy for the more common "liability" model. Looking at what we don't have is often an American pasttime. Finding the disadvantages is often easier than accentuating the positive or looking for growth through change. How many fall victim to depression and lowered self-esteem because the middle years are *without* children, retirement is *without* fulfilling work, and old age is *without* strength and agility. In fact, the "prime of life" is doing the best you can with what you have, and this can occur at *any* age.

Walking slowly with caution is an *advantage* of old age as running fast in youth is an *advantage* of being young. Both are complete, both can be fulfilling, and both can be an exercise in not taking your assets for granted but rather in using them fully.

It's time to stop and smell the flowers. On second thought, let's plant some.

REFERENCES

BERGER, M. (1979) "Men's new family roles: some implications for therapists." The Family Coordinator: 638-646.

CAMPBELL, A. (1975) "The American way of mating: marriage, si; chidren, maybe." Psychology Today (May).

DEUTSCHER, I. (1967) "The quality of post-parental life, pp. 263-268. In B. L. Neugarten (ed.) Middle Age and Aging. Chicago: Univ. of Chicago Press.

HALEY, J. (1973) Uncommon Therapy. New York: Norton.

MEAD, M. and F. B. KAPLAN [eds.] (1965) American Woman: The Report of the President's Commission. New York: Scribner.

ROLLINGS, B. C., and N. FELDMAN (1970) "Marital satisfaction over the family life cycle." J. of Marriage and the Family. 32: 20-28.

SHANAS, E. (1980) "Older people and their families: the new pioneers." J. of Marriage and the Family. 42: 9-15.

SHANAS, E. (1978) A National Survey of the Aged. Final Report to the Administration on Aging. Washington, DC: U.S. Department of Health, Education, and Welfare.

TRAVIS, R. P. and P. Y. TRAVIS (1979) Vitalizing Intimacy in Marriage. Chicago: Nelson-Hall.

8

The Marriage Enrichment Movement

David R. Mace

It was 1943, and World War II was being fought around the globe. In the early months of that year, a small group of us opened the first marriage counseling agency in Europe, in the West End of London, which has continued to offer service ever since. It was sorely needed—the war had been very hard on Britain's families.

Our counseling sessions were often punctuated by shattering explosions, but we believed strongly in what we were doing. When the war was over, marriage counseling would still be needed for the immense task of reconstruction. The Queen had spoken in a broadcast message of the "great rebuilding of family life" that the nation would have to undertake.

A decade earlier three marriage counseling services had already been established in the United States—in Los Angeles, in Philadelphia, and in New York City. Since then marriage and family therapy has developed extensively, and the need has continued to increase.

In those early days, however, we took a very simplistic view of the matter. We believed that most marriages were on the whole successful, but that just a few here and there got into trouble and needed outside help. Marriage counseling was therefore seen as an emerging new service that would be available to the relatively few people who might need it. What we didn't full grasp was that profound cultural changes were taking place that would compel us to reexamine all our traditional concepts of marriage and family life.

We should have listened more carefully to Ernest W. Burgess, who has been called the "father" of American family sociology, when he said (Burgess and Locke, 1945) that marriage and the family were in transition "from institution to companionship." Marriage, he said, had come to be viewed as a source of personal fulfillment rather than as a social duty. The implication was that couples could no longer be kept together by external coercion—their relationships must be sustained by internal cohesion.

We now know, only too well, that this change in our expectations of marriage has made the task very much more difficult. Indeed, Nelson Foote, a disciple of Ernest Burgess, put it starkly when he said that if modern couples were to realize their wishes for a close, intimate, and loving relationship, most of them would need to be *trained* in what he called "interpersonal competence" (Foote and Cottrell, 1955). Or, as Clark Vincent expressed it later, the "myth of naturalism"—that we are all endowed with the skills necessary to make marriage work— must be abandoned (Vincent, 1973). This concept was further supported by the opinion of psychiatrist Don Jackson, one of the founders of family therapy, who said that the proportion of American married couples who were achieving the highest levels of marital satisfaction did not in his opinion exceed 5-10 percent (Lederer and Jackson, 1968).

These were the views being expressed in 1949 when after seven intensive years of helping to build up the marriage guidance services in Britain, I moved to the United States. In 1960, with my wife Vera, I then put in another seven years developing the American Association of Marriage Counselors (now renamed the American Association for Marital and Family Therapy, AAMFT). Although the rates for marriage break-ups were (and still are) decidedly higher in the New World, I was however still of the opinion that if only we had enough competent counseling services, much could be done to arrest the rising divorce rate.

Since that time, accredited membership of the AAMFT has grown to more than 10,000—a large proportion of them working as full-time professionals. The standards of competence have steadily improved. Yet in the opinion of careful observers, these and other services to marriage constitute no more than a drop in the bucket. Well over a million marriages each year in the United States now end in divorce, and if the present rate were to continue, at least two out of every five marriages would eventually break up.

In addition to this, the searching light of inquiry is now being directed toward the so-called "stable" marriages that *don't* break up. Initiated by Murray Straus, extensive studies of "family violence" are showing that stress in these marriages has been producing the misery of "battered wives," "battered children," and even "battered husbands" on a tragic scale.

So the smug idea that all is well in the marriages that *don't* break up is being rudely shaken. It is consequently little wonder that many are arriving at the conclusion that, whatever was true in the past, the marriage relationship is becoming increasingly unworkable in our contemporary culture.

IS THERE A BETTER WAY?

Confronted by these facts, I found myself looking for better answers. I could not abandon my conviction that family life was necessary for the maintenance of personal growth and of social order. I still believed that the quality of relationships in any community is ultimately a product of the quality of relationships in the families that make up the community, and that the quality of family relationships, at least in a two-parent family, is determined by the quality of the marriage that initiates the family.

Moreover, I knew very well that marriage is a rich and satisfying experience for some couples, even though we must now acknowledge that they are very much in the minority. And I could observe that the children of those truly loving marriages were, for the most part, the kind of people who contribute very positively to the common weal. The dilemma, therefore, was "If really creative marriages are possible, and if the general well-being depends on having enough of them, what can we do to bring about a great increase in their number?"

I was compelled to admit, as I viewed the marriage counseling services we have so successfully built up, that this is only a partial answer. Without doubt, these services have "saved" many marriages from breakdown; or, where this has not been possible or desirable, they have enabled the persons concerned to take stock of their life situations and to do better the "second time around." Marriage counseling has certainly justified itself as a remedial service, and in our present society I cannot imagine how we could manage without it.

Nevertheless, in the light of today's situation, it is simply not, by itself, the complete answer. Therefore, I now strongly believe that we must supplement our existing *remedial* services to marriages with complementary *preventive* services.

In 1962, while Vera and I were thinking along those lines, we were invited to lead a weekend program for a group of married couples at Kirkridge, a retreat center in Western Pennsylvania. We felt poorly equipped for this task but we went. And what happened on that weekend gave us a great deal of encouragement and hope. We now see it as a significant part of the beginning of the marriage enrichment movement in North America.

During the same year (but unknown to us) a Catholic priest in Spain, Father Gabrael Calvo, gathered together a group of couples in Barcelona for a weekend retreat. This turned out to be the beginning of the Marriage Encounter movement which has now spread extensively throughout the Christian world. Our first 1962 weekend was followed by other similar opportunities. In 1964, Leon Smith, a former graduate student of mine, with his wife Antoinette began to develop marriage enrichment weekends, organized nationally by the United Methodist Church. As the demand for these experiences increased, we began together to design training programs for leader couples. Our first programs were organized through the Society of Friends (Quakers) to which Vera and I belong.

These three main streams have continued, and many other people began to get involved. Vera and I now worked on four continents with thousands of couples in intensive small groups. It has been a slow, groping process of learning what is effective and what is not; we know that we and others are still only at the beginning of something really new and exciting. However, we now feel that we are coming within reach of really effective answers to the questions we had been asking.

The marriage enrichment movement is still spreading and growing. Marriage Encounter has divided into three separate groups—National, International, and Worldwide. It has also extended its scope from the original Catholic base to include "expressions" in a number of Protestant churches. Our own model and that of the Smiths have now been largely combined, and a number of new patterns have developed and are still emerging (such as the program described in the excellent book by Hof and Miller, 1981).

In 1973, Vera and I made an important decision. In that year, on our wedding anniversary in July, we launched the Association of Couples for Marriage Enrichment (ACME) which is now an international organization. Its purpose was, and is, to attempt to give shape and directions to the developing marriage enrichment movement, and especially to establish standards for the selection, training, and certification of leader couples. Later, in 1975, we brought together a wide selection of organizations in the United States that were offering marriage enrichment programs on a national scale and established the Council of Affiliated Marriage Enrichment Organizations (CAMEO) for which ACME serves as coordinator and whose constituent bodies meet every year for consultation and mutual support.

At first the family specialists showed little interest in marriage enrichment. In part this was because they didn't really understand what we were doing. But it was also true that they felt threatened by something that seemed to be competing with them. These attitudes are now largely disappearing. For example, at its annual meeting in 1980, the prestigious National Council on Family Relations (NCFR) established a "focus group" on marriage and family enrichment, and in 1981 it renamed its section on education the Education and Enrichment Section. A considerable number of graduate students in the family field have also shown eager interest in enrichment, and many doctoral dissertations have been reports on research projects based on marriage enrichment groups.

THEORETICAL FOUNDATIONS

Marriage counseling was once called, derisively, "a practice in search of a theory," but now with the development of family therapy, that is far from the truth. From the outside, marriage enrichment has looked very much as if it might follow the same path, but some of us want to affirm very positively that this is not the case. At first the tendency was to view the marriage enrichment weekend as a new gimmick—a craze that would last for a time and then be forgotten. Part of the hesitation of the specialists to recognize marriage enrichment was probably based on this view. As someone once expressed it: "Here's a new idea—let's go out and meet it with a gun!"

One of our difficulties in developing theory has been that marriage enrichment represents a rather drastic departure from generally accepted patterns of serving families. Two examples will suffice:

First, marriage enrichment leaders work not as individuals but as *couples,* and their role is not primarily to be authority figures who have the answers; rather they function as "participating facilitators," and experience shows convincingly that it is their *modeling* rather than teaching or therapeutic intervention that provides their major dynamic. One inevitable implication of this is that *selection* of the persons who provide leadership, and the *quality of their interaction with each other* (factors which are virtually ignored in professional accreditation) are at least as important as the training process.

Second, since most of the action in marriage enrichment is in fact group interaction, we might presume that knowledge of group dynamics would be of central importance. However, the married couples in our groups are established social units. It is now quite clear that the dynamics of a group of such couples, led by a similar modeling leader couple, are radically different from those of a group of individuals with no shared past or future, led by a separate individual. We have known instances where specialists in group dynamics have come near to wrecking married couple groups that they tried to lead. These and other important differences must be taken into account in developing marriage enrichment theory. All that is possible here is to outline briefly a hypothetical frame of reference that is now beginning to emerge. It will be best, I believe, if I speak of this personally.

After long years of marriage counseling in which I was seeing the inside picture of married couples in serious trouble, in our marriage enrichment groups I then found myself looking at the inside of marriages that were ostensibly *not* in serious trouble. It occurred to me that this provided a valuable opportunity to make a comparison between the two.

I soon found, however, that this was an impossible task, for the simple reason that there were no clear or definite differences! I have now come to accept the fact that, with the exception of a small number (say, 10 percent) at both ends of the continuum, all married couples are very much alike, so far as the tasks of adjustment that confront them are concerned. I did not expect to find this, but I am now convinced of it.

I would put it in this way. Given the expectation of a loving companionship which is widespread today, marriage has become a complex and difficult task for almost all couples and an impossible task for some. The concept of the suitability of the couple for each other—of their compatibility as we like to call it—seems not to be nearly so important as the early researchers assumed. There are in fact many areas of apparent incompatibility in *all marriages* and the important key to success is what kind of *coping system* is available for the adjustment process.

From this basic assumption, I began to look at the ways in which couples attempt to cope. Over time I came to the conclusion that there are what I call three "essentials" for success in a close relationship. Given these, most marriages can be gradually adjusted to become mutually fulfilling or at least mutually acceptable. In the absence of the essentials, however, I believe that the chances of success are very poor indeed. What, then, are the essentials?

(1) First and foremost, a commitment on the part of both partners to ongoing relational growth. I find that the growth processes in a marriage coincide neatly with the biological laws of growth. There are three of these: the developmental process of unfolding of inherent potential; the capacity to reach out for resources needed and to make use of support systems; and the power to adapt to crisis situations when they arise. So my first objective is to secure from a couple seeking enrichment a joint commitment to ongoing growth.

I find that the dynamic for this commitment is hope. Every married couple begin their shared life with a dream. But their dream is usually unfulfilled, and hope diminishes or dies. It can, however, be re-awakened. This happens most powerfully when they actually witness the interaction of other couples who are successfully growing. A change then occurs. It is not, however, at this stage a *behavioral* change, it is only an *attitudinal* change. But with the provision of a suitable *support system*—a group of couples mutually committed to growth and change—new behavior becomes possible over time. Roughly, I estimate that reorientation can happen in the course of about a year.

(2) The second essential is *an effectively functioning communication system*. The levels of communication in most marriages are deplorably low. But that can be rapidly changed in a supportive atmosphere. Once the channels of in-depth communication are opened up, a tangled web of misconception can be cleared away. Until this is done, no real growth is possible. Until the couple perceive and accept each other as they really are, the thrust of most of their efforts to improve the relationship is misdirected and the energy exerted is wasted, leading to a state of disillusionment and despair.

(3) The third essential is *to learn to use conflict and anger as raw materials for growth.* This I find to be the most critical factor in American marriages today. I am more and more convinced that the management of anger is the key issue; but it is a subject which as yet has been given too little attention.

I now believe that the state of being married generates anger on a pretty large scale in most couples; and almost inevitably so in the modern equalitarian marriage. Far from being a negative, destructive force, however, anger as I now perceive it is the defense system of the ego, and an essential, positive, and healthy element in marriage. I see love and anger as two cooperating emotions which together establish and maintain the necessary balance in a close relationship—allowing it to be close enough for warmth and intimacy, yet not close enough to violate the necessary separateness of the two persons involved. This will be further elaborated in Chapter 9.

I have described the primary coping system very briefly. In conclusion, it must be stressed that the three essentials are interdependent. A successful marriage must have *all of them.* One without the other two, or even two without the third, will not be enough.

Once we have grasped the importance of the primary coping system, we can put in proper perspective what I call the secondary adjustment areas in marriage—issues such as sex, in-laws, time and money management, parenting, and the like. These all represent where the inner success or failure of the marriage is acted out and demonstrated. In my judgment, all marital failure start from within and inevitably produce external manifestations in the form of symptoms. To focus on the symptoms, and not go back to the root cause, it as ineffective here as it would be in the practice of medicine.

MARRIAGE ENRICHMENT IN PRACTICE

Marriage enrichment differs from marital therapy in at least two important respects. First, its focus is *not* on "problems." It does not deny the fact that some couples suffer from pathological conditions, and cannot function normally till these have been cleared up. We do not, however, recommend that such couples should look to marriage enrichment to overcome their difficulties. They require *treatment,* personally or relationally, by highly trained and qualified therapists.

The emphasis in marriage therapy, therefore, has to be on diag-
nosing and treating the pathology. In marriage enrichment, by
contrast, the emphasis is on promoting relational growth by encouraging the couple to discover and claim their unappropriated relational
potential. The assumption is that couples coming to marriage enrichment are free from complicated conditions that can only be cleared up
by therapy. If it should turn out to be otherwise, all trained marriage
enrichment leader couples should know how to refer couples with
serious difficulties to qualified marriage counselors. We also consider
that couples who have successfully completed marital therapy should
then be ready for a new phase of relational growth and could profitably
proceed to a marriage enrichment experience. Some therapists do
make such referrals. There are also, in these days, more and more
therapists who, with their spouses, have taken training in marriage
enrichment and are qualified to work in both fields. The chapter in
this book by Claude Guldner discusses this issue.

The second difference between therapy and enrichment lies in the
methods employed. Although group process is used by some marital
therapists, the usual procedure is to schedule a series of interviews
with the couple (with or without other family members). The focus is
strongly on the interaction patterns of husband and wife, and the
interviews are flexibly structured to deal with whatever calls for
attention.

In marriage enrichment, so far at least, the major focus is on
couples interacting with each other. The interactions are of three
kinds: between the leader couple and the total group; between couples
and other couples in the total group; and between husband and wife,
either in the group or in a separate place.

The objectives in this process are also three. First, the leader
couple excercise a modified *teaching* role. They present the marriage
enrichment concepts, usually in short talks or in dialogue with each
other, often using diagrams to illustrate the material. This teaching is
needed because the couples generally are not familiar with the theoretical concepts and need to change their thinking before they can be
ready to change their behavior.

Teaching in marriage enrichment, however, is never confined to
cognitive material. The procedure is always "tell and show." So the
leader couple will model what they teach, usually by turning directly
to each other and illustrating the point through their relational
experience. The second objective is therefore that of *modeling.*

The third step is to provide the couples in the group with an opportunity to *apply* what has been explained and modeled to their own interpersonal situation. This is done by direct dialogue with each other. A useful intermediate step, first developed by Marriage Encounter, is for the members of the group to reflect on what they have learned, write down their reactions, and then share these with their partners either in private dialogue or openly in the group.

Exercises have been extensively devised to promote these processes. But in essence, these three basic steps represent marriage enrichment methodology: the presentation of a relational concept, the modeling of the concept by the leader couple, and the application of the concept to their own relationship by the couples within the group. As already explained, the objective is to bring about attitudinal change, including a commitment if possible to adopt new and more satisfying behaviors, and to generate the dynamic of hope that the desired behavioral change can be brought about over time.

As already indicated, a great deal of experimentation is currently going on, and new ideas and methods are being constantly tested. All couples do not come to marriage enrichment events in a receptive frame of mind, and these may gain little from the experience. But for many others, the experience turns out to be truly life changing.

The marriage enrichment experience can be planned in a number of ways. The most popular pattern has always been the weekend residential retreat. However, for couples unable to get away or to afford the cost, a "growth group" with sequential meetings spaced over six to eight weeks, can be substituted. Experience strongly suggests that a minimum of 15 to 18 hours in the group is highly desirable for an effective experience, although the mini-retreat (covering 9 to 12 hours and going home overnight) has been developed as an "introduction to marriage enrichment"—a chance to become oriented to the basic concepts.

Effective as these relatively brief experiences are, it is becoming more and more clear that the first experience needs to be followed up by what we call "support systems." ACME now has a number of local chapters in which couples who so desire are placed in "support groups." The couples contract to meet in each other's homes at regular intervals (usually every three or four weeks) for about a year. They thus make themselves accountable to each other to carry out the growth processes they feel they need to make their marriages more satisfying with the help of the group. Such couples almost invariably develop deep and lasting friendships, and sometimes extend their association to form family clusters, involving their children and other relatives. It ie surprising how many lonely couples there are in typical American communities.

SUGGESTIONS FOR FUTURE POLICY

I see marriage enrichment at present as just beginning, and functioning at this stage at a very elementary level. Yet I think we now know enough to catch glimpses of its enormous possibilities. Consider what could happen if increasing numbers of marriages could be made to function at much higher levels of loving intimacy. Consider what this could contribute to the mental health of the individuals concerned. Consider what that kind of emotional climate could make possible for children growing up in such homes. Consider how our society could be changed as we produced more and more deeply happy and creative people and what this could do to cut back our rates for crime, delinquency, mental illness, social maladjustment, and the like.

These, I believe, are now practical possibilities. We are already beginning, in our ACME chapters and in some churches, to see couples getting together in the joint pursuit of ongoing personal and relational growth. These people are readily available for investigation and longitudinal research, but so far no very precise research methodology has been evolved to measure their growth.

We still have a great deal to learn about marriage enrichment. So far we have only touched its outer fringes. We have applied it only to limited numbers of people for very short periods of time. Far greater possibilities await our exploration.

Probably the most exciting possibility for the future lies in the intensive use of marriage enrichment with newlyweds. I look to the day when we shall be able to guide couples continuously from the premarital period, through their critical first year together, and into their parental tasks, beginning before the birth of their first child and continuing right on through the life cycle. Such a program could furnish them, at each appropriate point in their growth together, with whatever they need to make the best possible use of their resources. Once this kind of service is provided and accepted by the couples, a vast amount of human misery can be prevented and the precious resources of personal and relational potential can be released in the service of mankind.

Is this a pipe dream? The future alone can tell. What we can say, however, with reasonable certainty, is that the enrichment of marriages and families seems now to be a practical possibility, as it has never been before. And that, surely, is something to get excited about!

In the limited space available here, I have been able to do little more than provide a rough sketch of the marriage enrichment movement. For more detail, see the reference list. Listed there are three books that I have either authored or coauthored and which I recommend for further information concerning these programs. The address of the Association for Couples for Marriage Enrichment (ACME) is 459 S. Church Street, P.O. Box 10596, Winston-Salem, N.C. 27108. Phone (919) 724-1526.

REFERENCES

BURGESS, E. W. and H. J. LOCKE (1945) The Family: From Institution to Companionship. New York: American Book Co.

FOOTE, N. N. and L. S. COTTRELL (1955) Identity and Interpersonal Competence. Chicago: Univ. of Chicago Press.

HOF. L. and W. R. MILLER (1981) Marriage Enrichment: Philosophy, Process, and Program. Bowie, MD: Brady.

LEDERER, W. J. and D. D. JACKSON (1968) The Mirages of Marriage. New York: Norton.

MACE, D. (1983) Close Companions: The Marriage Enhancement Handbook. New York: Continuum.

——— (1982) Love and Anger in Marriage. Grand Rapids, Mich.: Zondervan.

——— and V. MACE (1974) We Can Have Better Marriages. Nashville: Abingdon.

STRAUS, M., R. GELLES, and S. STEINMETZ (1980) Behind Closed Doors: Violence in the American Family. New York: Anchor.

VINCENT, C. (1973) Sexual and Marital Health. New York: McGraw-Hill.

9

Enriched Marriage as a Reciprocally Resonant Relationship

Barbara Fishman
Robert Fishman

The development of marriage enrichment in recent years raises the question of how a mutually satisfying couple relationship really functions. Increasingly, the widely accepted theories of marital interaction seem not to be adequate. In this chapter, we offer a rather different way of understanding married love as a special form of bonding between the partners. We see this as a "reciprocally resonant" relationship, characterized by an ongoing pulsation between the shared experience of an "Us" and the individual experiences of participating selves. The Us should not be viewed as an entity but as a process which slowly evolves as the couple move through family life. Shifts in the phases of famiy development allow for more intense experiences of that Us at certain times of life and more intense experiences of the I at other times.

The reciprocally resonant relationship is only one form of coupling; it is by no means achieved or desired by everyone. Given the emphasis placed on individuality and personal autonomy in our culture, many people find it difficult to create or even to value the Us. When these "I"-centered people bond, they form what has been called exchange relationships which are characterized by the existence of a "you" and "me" that remain inviolable and an Us that barely exists. Neither partner assumes that the other can be fully trusted, personal goals are primary, and self-interest is rarely forgotten. Contracts are developed with rights and privileges spelled out, and the connection lasts only as long as personal needs are fulfilled. In contrast, the creation of an Us in a reciprocally resonant relationship is a powerful experience that has great impact on the participating selves. When such people bond, neither individual remains untouched.

The enmeshed relationship is still another form of coupling, at the other end of the spectrum from the exchange relationship. People who develop enmeshed relationships create an all-pervasive Us, allowing barely any existence for the individual selves. The enmeshed experience is static and does not allow for the rhythmic pulsing between selves and Us which is characteristic if a reciprocal resonant relationship. People who are enmeshed are tremendously fearful of the loss of the *other* so they pattern as much of their behavior as is possible on an Us design. This is the obverse of people in an exchange relationship who fear the loss of *self* in every interaction. Both patterns rigidify the natural processes that take place as families evolve over the life cycle (Carter and McGoldrick, 1980; Minuchin, 1974). In enmeshed relationships, personal goals and individual rights or privileges almost always give way to the needs of the Us, and the connection holds even more rigidly when the going gets rough.

Having identified both exchange and enmeshed forms of coupling as distinct from the reciprocally resonant experience, we may now proceed with a map that outlines the paths taken in these three forms of coupling. Hopefully, it can serve as a guide to those working with people who prefer one or another form. We pay special attention to the reciprocally resonant relationship because it permits individual identity as well as the joining of identities, and because its paths have not hitherto been clearly charted.

RECIPROCALLY RESONANT
RELATIONSHIPS

Couples who reciprocally resonate experience a rhythmical pulsing (Roberts, 1980) between the participating selves and the Us (see

Diagram 9.1). There are endless gradations in the distance between the individual selves who make up a couple, although we have chosen to abstract only three phases of this process. In just a few moments, the Us may move in and out of awareness as each person experiences either an individual or a shared perception of the world. In this process, a self is never lost although at one moment it may be background and at the next foreground.

During phase A when individual selves are most distinct and the Us is minimal, people are involved in separate activities, barely thinking about the other or about shared perceptions of the world. She may be working at a computer, fully involved with the task at hand, while he may be teaching a class, again totally involved. Each person feels comfortable functioning independently in the world.

During phase B, there is a clear but limited sense of the Us. Talking about some news of the day, jointly doing everyday chores, making occasional eye contact while socializing with friends, all continue to verify the couple's special relationship. While each person is primarily concerned with personal thoughts, the presence of the other is only peripheral. Deciding about the choice of a tie, he will be affected by their common taste in clothes which has been created over many conversations and many purchases, but the actual decision is his.

The most intense experience of the Us is in phase C during which the couple have a fully shared experience of the world. Berger and Kellner (1970) described such coupling as reality building, during which each person's tastes, opinions, and basic assumptions about the world change as they are exposed to the scrutiny of the significant other. A new reality emerges, different to some degree from the reality of each individual partner and certainly different from other couples. For example, a couple may see a movie together and share their preceptions, creating a mutual vision, different from either one's individual experience. At different times one or the other may have more impact on that vision, but since each voice is valued, tallies are not kept. Still another example of phase C might occur in a sexual interaction during which bodies resonate; one may lead while the other follows, but again, mutual respect prevails. In these shared experiences of the world, selves are momentarily forgotten. Communication is free-flowing; no rigid boundaries exist between what is thought, felt, and said. He may finish her sentence without interrupting her thought. There is no clear separation between what she perceives in relation to him and what he perceives in relation to her. They are creating a self-transcendent reality which allows their thoughts and

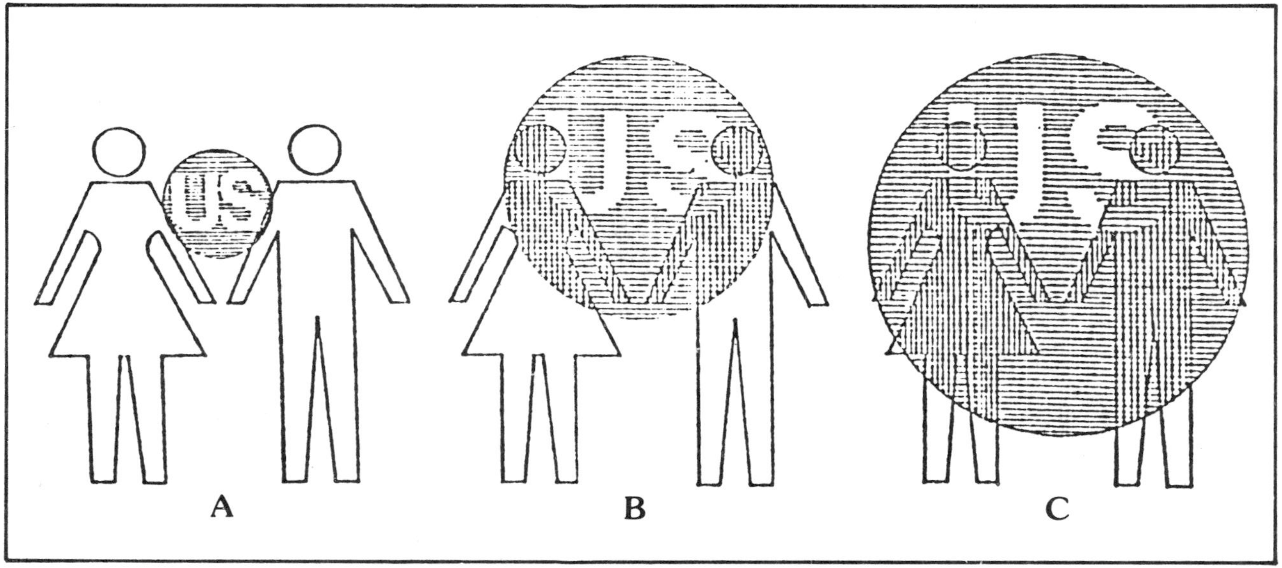

Diagram 9.1   The Reciprocally Resonant Relationship

feelings to take them where they will. They are close and in the present; having been here before, they want to be here again. Unfortunately, phase C can also conjure up fears of too much dependency, possible hurt, and loss. She may fear not being sufficiently valued and in that sense, loses her individual self. Thinking linearly, people often want to feel "whole" first, with enough self-esteem to protect themselves from the other, but a respectful diadic dance can be learned only in interaction. In a circular process, reciprocally resonant coupling affects and is affected by each person's sense of self. Trust that he does not want to negate her worth implies that anger is not expressed through violence or judgemental name calling. When anger is felt, it does not negate the worth of the other, nor does it lead to threats of separation. Basically, each maintains a trust that whatever the conflict is, each person is committed to the Us.

In summary:

- The reciprocally resonant relationship pulsates between perceptions of the selves and perceptions of the Us. It involves a recognition that changes from phase to phase are essential and cannot be avoided.
- It is based on the mutual respect that self-respecting people insist upon, and trust that one is not trying to undermine the other's worth.
- Finally, it involves commitment to a long-term relationship in spite of short-term anger.

People in reciprocally resonant relationships have their own particular set of problems. One person may find it difficult to let go of a relationship phase. Enjoying the ecstasy of phase C, they can feel that it is intolerable to let go and move on to phase A or B. Anger or irritability can develop in the wake of one person holding on too tightly to any phase, He may feel that her clinging to sexuality is inhibiting the rightful concerns of his individual self, just as if they were in an enmeshed relationship. On the other hand, when someone has been in phase A for too long, he or she can feel too disconnected, as if they were in an exchange relationship. She may feel that his involvement with work negates her need for Us experiences. Phase A or C can respectively resemble either the exchange or the enmeshed relationship, and the resemblance can awaken troubled feelings.

People in our culture have difficulty creating a reciprocally resonant relationship because cultural norms identify individuality and self-sufficiency as an ideal while mutual dependency is labeled as sick or at least regressive. However, the very organization of an Us is composed of individuals who need the other to create their whole. When functioning as a couple, each person is incomplete without a mate, Because of these cultural norms, those who live in a reciprocally resonant relationship could think of themselves as deviant, too independent, poorly mated. Without a clearly charted and well-accepted course, the struggle to create and maintain a reciprocally resonant relationship is often difficult.

EXCHANGE RELATIONSHIPS

By definition, the exchange relationship has a barely existent Us. Shared perceptions are rare, and they are suspect when they occur. Fear of a loss of self leads participants to limit their conversation and their time together. Perhaps a child with whom both interact or a living space both share creates some experience of common goals, but the fullness of a shared reality that characterizes a reciprocally resonant relationship does not exit. Each person may create a pulsing with others—colleagues at work, friends who shop together or play ball together—but that close relationship does not exist between the couple. Men and women who fear losing their newly won independence from traditional roles will often develop exchange relationships, not perceiving that they can have both connection and individuation in a reciprocally resonant relationship.

An exchange relationship does not follow the ebbs and flows of closeness in an organic pattern; instead, it is legalistic. Contracts are used to determine behavior, and when they do not work, separation follows. Even the words of Paul Simon—"You like to sleep with the window open, I like to sleep with the window closed, so good-bye, goodbye, goodbye"—are a contemporary comment on loss due to the prevalence of the exchange relationship.

People in exchanging relationships tend to think strategically, intently figuring out what the other is doing and what the other's motives are. They continually scan the environment for present or future advantages. This kind of information is essential in order to maximize self-interest since with it the person can readjust behavior to increase advantages or decrease liabilities. Ideally, these people create fair connections in which both equally share in the burdens as well as the joys of family life. He may exchange his hard earned money for the comforts of a home, while she may provide those comforts in exchange for what the money can buy for her in luxuries. He may exchange his commitment to her for her sexual companionship, while she may provide that sexual companionship for the opportunity to bear children. The exchange relationship is certainly a cultural pattern which has existed though time and has provided people with many of the satisfactions that family life has to offer. It can be successful in its own terms while not approaching the trust and closeness that characterize a reciprocally resonant relationship.

THE ENMESHED RELATIONSHIP

Because therapists encounter enmeshed relationships in a large number of the families who visit their offices, there may be an illusion that enmeshment is the only form of intense diadic connection. Inadvertently, family therapists who believe in this illusion contribute to the pervasiveness of the contemporary cultural norm which stresses individuation and negates the self-transcendent Us.

The enmeshed pattern consists of an all-important but static Us, making this relationship significantly different from the reciprocally resonant experience. Rather than flowing in and out of the Us, enmeshed people get stuck with it, desperately fearing loss of the other. With little space for individual experiences of the world, the couple's shared experiences become their only reality. Only the present and past are comfortable as the enmeshed couple fear any change that the future may bring. We can say that the enmeshed pattern is morphostatic or unchanging while the reciprocally resonant pattern is morphogenetic or ever-changing (Hoffman, 1981).

Couples who are in enmeshed relationships rigidly apportion the distribution of power. He may be in need of being right while she may accommodate by allowing him to determine the shape of their interactions. Their shared reality is, in this case, consistently and unfailingly more his than hers. Ann Sexton, the poet, describes the experience well:

We are stripped to the bone and we swim in tandem and go up and up the river, the identical river called Mine and we enter together. No one's alone.

Clearly, this is not a relationship built on mutual respect. One person prevails while the other, often resentful, searches for indirect patterns of influence. Physical illness, addiction, or frequently a child becomes the conduit through which such indirect influence is asserted. What looks like closeness is instead fear, resentment, and indirect, stilted communication.

Given this analysis, we suggest that marital discord may occur for the following reasons: First, each member of the couple may use a different relationship map. He may expect an enmeshed relationship while she may expect an exchange relationship. Clinical experience indicates that this may be a phenomenon of some prevalence, and therefore worthy of research. Are males in our culture socialized to want the traditional caring that is part of an enmeshed relationship while females are socialized to want the personal freedom associated with an exchange relationship? Second, marital discord may be a product of a couple's inability to create an ideal version of their jointly held relationship map. Perhaps they want the independence of an exchange relationship but never quite agree on what is the nature of an ideal fair trade. Third, clinical experience indicates that people often talk about wanting relationships that can be described as exchange or enmeshed but they have secret dreams of something different—a relationship that offers a deeper experience of loving as well as individuation.

BONDING THROUGHOUT THE LIFE CYCLE

All couples have to deal with the changes inherent in the life cycle experience. Being young and in love is qualitatively different from being married and parenting several school age children, and different also from the companionship that characterizes relationships after children have been launched. The quality of the relationship itself changes to accommodate the tasks of each developmental stage. While people in exchange or enmeshed relationships have great difficulty accommodating to developmental changes, those in recip-rocally resonant relationships more easily manage these demands.

A look at the diagram 9.2 illustrates the changes that occur in recip-rocally resonant relationships over the life cycle. While such changes may occur in any type of marriage, it is more likely that people in static relationships will have more trouble with life cycle transitions.

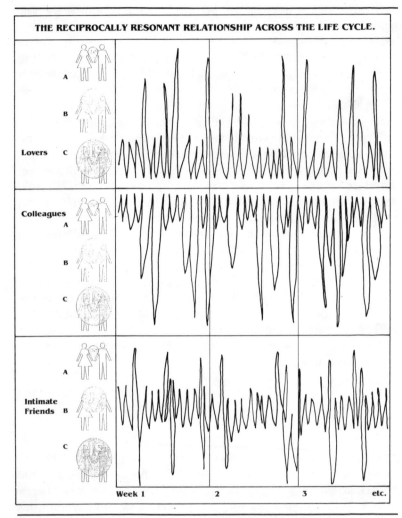

THE RECIPROCALLY RESONANT RELATIONSHIP ACROSS THE LIFE CYCLE.

Diagram 9.2   The Reciprocally Resonant Relationship Across the Life Cycle

We therefore focus on the reciprocally resonant experience. During the first stage, the couple have many phase C experiences. Deeply involved with each other and with the business of creating shared perceptions of the world, their experiences of the Us are often ecstatic. We call them lovers.

Soon, all too soon, this stage is over to be replaced by the colleague-ship that occurs as the couple create a home, have children, and develop work lives. While the dyad continues to have experiences of all three phases of reciprocal resonance, phase A occurs with greater frequency. In our culture, this is a time of hard work. Most people spend a good thirty years nurturing children and building careers. It is a stage when people invest in their relationships with children or their associates at work rather than with a lover. Many people feel deprived because they have so little time to experience phase C; some say that they are no longer "in love", not understanding that the infrequency of phase C is a developmental shift in the quality of their relationship. We may call these people colleagues.

Finally, as the pressures of child rearing and career development diminish, people experience phase B with greater frequency. Two people who were lovers and became colleagues now know the pleasure of being lifelong companions. While all three phases of the reciprocally resonant pattern still occur, now phase C is somewhat more frequent and phase A is less frequent as the hard work of youth is over. The later years are a time to enjoy both the well-developed self that each person has worked to achieve, and the established Us which the couple can easily enter into and leave at will. These couples are intimate friends.

Some couples experience a reciprocally resonant relationship at one stage of the life cycle but cannot maintain it during the next stage; lovers cannot always do well as colleagues and conversely, colleagues do not always make good lovers. People bring different interpersonal talents as well as developmental gaps to a relationship and they need the other to match them in a complementary fashion. That match may work well at one time and fail at another. The struggle to live well in a relationship requires that each person monitor this match, attending to their personal gaps in development as well as their joint capacity to complement each other.

CONCLUSION

The reciprocally resonant relationship is characterized by the ebb and flow between a subsystem called the self and the system called an Us. Each has different rules that govern behavior, and the reciprocally resonant couple pulsates between those two levels of being. We hypothesize that this pulsation is a physiological phenomenon, tying us as human beings to other living beings, all of whom experience that rhythmical relationship inherent in the rotation of the sun and the moon, the experience of day and night, and the ebb and flow of the tides. Isomorphically, living beings have the rhythmical experience of breathing and of a heartbeat, to name but two examples of our physiological responses.

The reciprocally resonant relationship is also a cultural experience, as it is enacted in a particular society with its particular rendition of coupling during the life course. We offer this analysis as an alternative to both the enmeshed and the exchange forms of relationships, hoping that those who work with married couples may find it useful. It seems to have particular relevance to the new and rapidly developing field of marriage enrichment.

REFERENCES

BERGER, P. and H. KELLNER (1970) "Marriage and the construction of reality," in H. P. Dreitzel (ed.) Recent Sociology 2. New York: Macmillan.

CARTER, E. and McGOLDRICK [eds.] (1980) The Family Life Cycle: A Framework for Family Therapy. New York: Gardner.

HOFFMAN, L. (1981) Foundation of Family Therapy. New York: Basic Books.

MINUCHIN, S. (1974) Families and Family Therapy. Cambridge: Harvard Univ. Press.

ROBERTS, A. (1980) "Rhythmical patterning in human behavior." Resources for Human Development, Ardmore, PA. (unpublished)

Part III

Parenthood and Whole Family Enrichment

The concept of wellness is now expanded from the marriage relationship to the wider family unit. This process begins with the birth of the first child, expands with the infant's early development, continues through the period between infancy and adolescence, and then finally to the movement of all the children toward independence. At each and every stage, the wider family group can be enriched through creative interaction with other families.

10

Preparing for Parenthood During Pregnancy and Early Infancy

Ann Ellwood

Gene and Sue Milton looked forward to the birth of their first child. However, they were having difficulty deciding whether or not Sue would return to her job as a librarian once the baby arrived. Sue enjoyed her owk and the financial assistance it provided, but she and Gene were both very concerned about giving their child the best parenting possible. Sue's parents felt strongly that a woman should be more than a housewife. The Miltons found it hard to pinpoint their own needs and preferences in the midst of such pressure from others.

Gene and Sue began attending a MELD parent education group three months before the birth of their son. They found that other members were struggling with the work issue. The group's facilitators organized a panel presentation featuring fathers and mothers who worked full time, part time, and not at all. After the panel, group members discussed their individual feelings and needs. Gene and Sue were able to make a decision that seemed right for them shortly after this particular session. At future group meetings, continued support from others helped maintain the Miltons' confidence in their choice.

Participation in the MELD group prepared the Miltons for each new phase of parenthood. It helped them deal constructively with the questions and difficulties first-time parents inevitably encounter. During one meeting, their MELD group covered the most recent information about effects of maternal nutrition on the fetus. Gene and Sue read some interesting material and heard a brief presentation by a facilitator. Then they analyzed their own nutritional intake, asked questions, shared knowledge, and discussed some techniques for improving nutrition.

Each session of the MELD group covered a new topic, and members chose the particular subjects they wished to explore. Thus they learned about child development, health care, safety, postpartum blues, and more as these issues arose. In addition to receiving the latest facts, they listened to personal experiences of people with whom they could identify closely. Gene and Sue greatly appreciated being able to share experiences and solve problems with people who were at similar points in their lives and were encountering some of the same joys and difficulties.

THE MELD PROGRAM

What Is MELD?

MELD (formerly Minnesota Early Learning Design) is a program providing information and support for first-time parents. The program involves peers in self-help group format—it involves parents in helping other parents. MELD's primary goal is to present the most useful information available in the most supportive environment that can be created.

Experienced parents volunteer to facilitate MELD groups. They receive extensive training and assistance during their two years of service. The men and women who participate in MELD groups join when they are expecting their first child. The groups meet twice a month until the children are two years old. Meetings follow a carefully designed curriculum that focuses upon health, child development and guidance, family management, and parent development. The caring network that grows among participants, facilitators, MELD staff members, and community resource people becomes a rich source of support for the members and facilitators.

Who Participates in the MELD Program?

A wide variety of parents attend MELD groups. They are recruited though the health care system, childbirth classes, newspaper articles, and (most effectively) by word of mouth. Men, women, single parents, couples, those living traditional or nontraditional lives, individuals from many different socioeconomic, religious, and racial backgrounds—all who are becoming parents for the first time can participate in and benefit from the MELD program.

MELD participants are usually committed to the task or parenting. They may be seeking to provide a different kind of parenting than they received. Some of the men are eager to share child rearing responsibilities with their wives. A few fathers even make career adjustments in order to care for their babies while their wives continue to work.

Both male and female single parents receive useful information and support from their MELD group. They also help the more traditional couples learn about the realities of raising a child in a one-parent family.

Men and women often feel a lack of preparation for parenting that makes them eager to learn. MELD participants seem especially aware of the changes child rearing brings to their lives. They want to enhance their ability to carry out their new roles and responsibilities effectively. Before joining a MELD group, prospective parents may have been frustrated by the enormous amount of information, both printed and oral, that is available and is so difficult to sort though. Additionally, they may be acutely aware of a need for more assistance from others. Modern day mobility, which often leads to separation from family and friends, leaves many without the network of helpful others that once provided guidance and support during the first encounter with parenthood. Thus, men and women come to MELD at a particularly "teachable" moment in their lives.

Who Are the Facilitators and What Do They Do?

MELD groups are led by three or four facilitators who share their responsibilities. The facilitators are experienced parents whose children are generally five years old or younger. They volunteer their services for a two-year period. Facilitators usually join as couples, and every group has at least one male and one female to provide role models for parents of both sexes.

MELD's volunteers are chosen because of their concern for parenting and because they can serve as healthy role models. Their primary functions include planning activities for each session, presenting information at the meetings, and facilitating the group process. Facilitators help parents share thoughts and feelings and develop solutions to problems. They do not function as therapists. They serve as models for constructive parenting, and help members who have serious difficulties to find appropriate professional assistance when necessary.

Each volunteer participates in at least 40 hours of training prior to and during the course of his or her involvement with MELD. This training is provided free of charge. In addition, reimbursement for childcare and transportation expenses is available for those who need it.

What Are MELD Groups Like?

MELD parents join a group during the last trimester of pregnancy. Groups meet every other week, usually for three hours in the evening. A portion of each session is used to present material from the curriculum that is relevant to the current experiences of the members. In addition, concerns are shared, common problems are discussed, and individual solutions are developed.

Sometimes guest speakers are invited to MELD groups. A lawyer might describe laws concerning estates, wills, and guardians in the event that natural parents die. Several guests who have chosen a variety of childcare arrangements might make a panel presentation.

MELD participants also use group time to exchange resources for bargains, jobs, housing, and other concerns that are not specifically oriented toward parenting. At each meeting, parents can borrow from a book box filled with resources MELD parents has found useful. Finally, besides attending the regular meetings, MELD parents often socialize with each other, hold picnics or parties, take baby swimming classes together, organize baby-sitting co-ops, and more.

What Benefits Result from the MELD Program?

The first-time parents who participate in MELD groups, their children, the experienced parents who serve as volunteer facilitators, and the community at large can all benefit from MELD's program.

MELD helps participants gain the competence and confidence they need to function effectively as parents, as partners, and as individuals. While MELD's primary function is to promote constructive parenting, MELD groups also promote mental health. Confident, relaxed parents who have the backing of a reliable support network and know how to use their community's resources can act more effectively as parents and people. Many MELD parents gain knowledge and abilities that they can apply at work and in other settings as well as at home. For example, participants often improve their communication skills and can apply these skills to enhance their interactions with others.

MELD's volunteer facilitators gain as much as participants. The training facilitators receive and their group experiences stimulate personal growth and the development of leadership skills. Additionally, facilitators receive pertinent child rearing information and also the support and friendship of group members, other facilitators, and MELD staff members. Partners especially appreciate the opportunity to work together outside the home; this enhances their commitment to parenting. According to one facilitator, "I'm a better wife, I'm a better mother, I'm a better friend."

Children of MELD participants and facilitators benefit in many ways. MELD helps parents learn how to meet their children's physical, psychological/emotional, and cognitive needs more adequately. Parents learn to respect and appreciate the uniqueness of each child—to be sensitive to each child's special needs and interests.

Additionally, MELD helps communities and individuals realize that good parenting is a learned skill. Through participation in a MELD group, members learn about mental and physical health care resources that can provide assistance, and they become more confident and skillful in using these resources. They learn how to communicate their needs more clearly, and how to fill their needs as parents and as people more adequately. A powerful support system develops in their MELD group; this natural network serves many of the functions that used to be handled by extended families.

THE MELD ORGANIZATION

What Is MELD's Philosophy?

MELD believes that there is no one right way to parent. Rather, we encourage respect and appreciation for the uniqueness of each individual. We believe each person can make his or her own best choices. Additionally, we believe that parents can learn from and support each other. This peer, self-help process enhances the wellness of the entire family.

How Has MELD Evolved?

In 1973, The Lilly Endowment, Inc. responded to then-Senator Walter Mondale's interest in families by offering a research and development grant to explore new ways to strengthen families. MELD was established as a result of that grant. During the first year, the MELD staff reviewed literature, surveyed community needs, and assessed resources related to young children, parenting, and early learning. Staff members attended conferences and seminars throughout the United States. They also met regularly with a parent advisory committee to discuss their progress and explore possibilities for MELD's future directions. The original purpose for a MELD program, written in 1974, grew from this year of research.

Five parent groups were started in Minneapolis during the MELD program's pilot period, 1975-1978. The program served 89 parents, and 19 volunteer facilitators were trained during this time. Evaluation of these original groups indicated that the MELD model is a very cost-effective way to support family life. At the same time, with little dissemination, MELD began to receive requests for information from across the country. Many included inquiries about duplicating the program.

MELD began a three-year replication stage in 1978. From the beginning, it has been committed to developing a program that could be duplicated in other locations. To that end, the MELD process, curriculum, manuals, and training procedures have all been designed for easy use in distant locations. During the replication stage, new groups were begun in nonurban and out-of-state sites in New Mexico, Wisconsin, and Minnesota. The curriculum was refined and expanded, and manuals detailing procedures for recruitment, training, support, and coordination were completed. At the same time, the MYM (MELD's Young Moms) program was developed to more fully meet the needs of adolescent mothers. MELD's standard curriculum and procedures have been adapted for use in MYM groups.

What Is MELD's Current Status?

- MELD has grown from 5 experimental groups in 1978 to 50 groups as of June, 1981.
- Over 1000 parents and volunteer facilitators have been used.
- Groups are currently operating in Minneapolis, St. Paul, Blue Earth, and LeSueur, Minnesota; Albuquerque, New Mexico; and Milwaukee, Wisconsin. Programs are planned for Duluth and Rochester, Minnesota; Corpus Christi, Texas; and Rockford and East St. Louis, Illinois.
- MYM groups are underway in two Twin Cities locations. Replications have begun in Milwaukee, Wisconsin, and Sioux Falls, South Dakota.
- MELD is also developing a variation to serve Hispanic parents. A bicultural, bilingual program will be offered in Minneapolis in cooperation with Centro Cultural Chicano.
- Graduates of the two-year program are declaring their wish to stay in MELD groups and "raise our children together." Some have become facilitators of new groups.

How Does MELD Use the Peer, Self-Help Model?

MELD's peer, self-help model uses people who have already experienced and successfully negotiated particular concerns in life to teach, guide, and encourage others who are currently experiencing these concerns. Thus, a woman who has nursed an infant is pleased to help a new mother interested in learning how to nurse. A group member who already knows a great deal about nutrition can share this knowledge with others who want such information. New parents need and appreciate support from their peers and from someone who has "been there." The MELD program is designed to deliver this support.

MELD differs from many other self-help movements in that it teaches facilitators to be very skillful in managing the dynamics of the group process. In addition, the curriculum is orderly, academically sound, and timely. It provides an important focus for each session.

Finally, a site coordinator is employed to oversee the functioning of all groups at one location. The site coordinator recruits participants and facilitators, provides support and coordination for the facilitators, and ensures the effective functioning of MELD groups. In effect, MELD has identified and enhanced the strengths of the self-help movement while avoiding or overcoming the potential shortcomings of such groups.

What Does MELD Use for Its Curriculum?

Each MELD group chooses the topics it wants to cover from a list of more than 50 curriculum modules. MELD provides materials covering each topic for participant and facilitators. These materials are developed by MELD's curriculum specialists. Our writers are assisted by an academic advisory committee consisting of University of Minnesota professors (Willard W. Hartup, Ph.D.; Harold R. Ireton, Ph.D.; Robert Leik, Ph.D.; Robert Bensel, M.D.; Dr. Marvin Ack), by professionals working in relevant fields, and by parents who serve as advisors. The materials are written from a nonsexist, nonracist, eclectic viewpoint. They present a broad range of relevant information for each topic so that parents become familiar with many attitudes and options and can select those that seem most useful to them as individuals. MELD's goal is to help parents learn to make decisions carefully as they identify their own beliefs and desires.

The material for each topic includes suggestions for academic and experiential learning. For example, when exploring the effects of television viewing on individuals and families, parents read summaries of research findings and are encouraged to monitor their own viewing habits. Facilitators draw from many sources for the presentations of information. In addition to guest speakers, group members with relevant knowledge lead sessions. Thus, a MELD member who works as a speech therapist might describe language development in infants.

Each curriculum module is designed to present helpful information in a highly accessible manner. Parents read no more than 10 to 15 pages every two weeks. A wide variety of resources (individuals, books, articles, projects, etc.) may be used to learn more about each topic.

What Training and Support Do Site Coordinators and Facilitators Receive?

What Training and Support Do Site Coordinators and Facilitators Receive? MELD's success is greatly dependent upon the site coordinators and facilitators. These people are carefully selected for their suitability to our program. they receive preparatory training, in-service training, and continuing support from the MELD staff. This helps to maintain a consistently high level of quality in our program.

attend yearly seminars that provide opportunities for further learning and the sharing of support. Facilitators begin their training with an intensive weekend session. They learn to work as part of a three- and four-person team. They become familiar with group dynamics and the development of a supportive group. They also learn how to present information effectively, how to recogize when outside referrals are appropriate, and how to make such referrals. Facilitators continue to attend regular training session throughout their participation in the MELD program.

How Is MELD Funded?

The approximate cost in 1981 to deliver the MELD program was slightly more than $100 per participant per year. Since this represented up to 60 hours of contact time during the year, MELD is an inexpensive program. The site coordinator's salary is the major expense.

MELD has developed its funding base carefully and has not asked for federal assistance. A variable fee is charged for participation in our groups. Financial support has been received from local and national foundations, including the Lilly Endowment, Inc., Carnegie, Bush, Dayton-Hudson, McKnight, Mardag, Bremer, Cosgrove, the Minneapolis Foundation, Ripley, and the Northwest Area Foundation. Numerous corporations also contribute to our work. Among them are Levi-Strauss, St. Paul Companies, Green Giant, Dayton's, Northwestern National Bank, Northern States Power Company, and Target.

CONCLUSION

MELD's evaluation data document the success of the program. They show that parents can teach each other. MELD participants are encouraged to use each other as resources when appropriate. This lessens the unnecessary demands made upon professionals. Also, parents can support each other. They can develop friendships that lead to long-term support networks. The program shows that parents can assume much of the responsibility for managing their own groups. The peer, self-help approach enables parents to design their education to fit their own unique needs. Finally, experienced parents can be trained to facilitate parent groups effectively, providing new parents with support and information.

Since its beginning in 1975, MELD has provided an effective program:

- MELD promotes wellness, teaching prevention to parents rather than just dealing with problems after they appear.
- MELD is long-term. The two-year program provides the ongoing involvement needed to reinforce major change and growth.
- MELD is cost-effective. Trained volunteers are used to facilitate the groups.
- MELD serves fathers as well as mothers. Approximately 45% of the current group participants are men.
- MELD creates educated consumers who will support and use their community's services wisely.

While it is hard for any primary prevention program to measure the difficulty, stress, and expense that have been avoided, many MELD parents speak in strong terms about the effect MELD groups have had upon their lives. Positive results such as the following have been mentioned:

- phone calls that they do *not* make to their health care providers.
- the involvement of men in the care of their children.
- the deliberate planning they practice for their second pregnancy.
- comfort and confidence are gained from their peers.
- they experience new growth for themselves.
- increased closeness develops between partners.

In short, MELD strengthens families by providing the information (MELD's address is 123 East Grant Street, Minneapolis, MN) and support men and women need to become competent, confident parents.

11

Transforming Early Parenthood to Promote Family Wellness

Thomas Gordon

Without minimizing the importance of the role of parents during the infancy period, I see the 10 years following infancy as the most critical period for parenthood. During these years the problems children present seem always to be new and more difficult. From being an almost completely helpless and dependent organism requiring nearly full-time attention and total need fulfillment from the parent, the infant gradually changes into an active "youngster" with emerging capabilities of meeting his or her own needs and behaving independently.

As a result of these developmental changes in the child, parents change in the way they perceive the child and in the kinds of expectations they have for how the child should or should not behave.

With infants, most parents are inclined to allow them "to be what they are." Whatever infants do is seen as natural and normal; parents are quite accepting of most their behaviors, more than willing to assume the role of "giver," "protector," "observer," or "caretaker." By and large, parents take their clues from the child and assume the role of a *sensitive responder.*

As infants become "toddlers" and as babies become "youngsters," parents change to a different role. Now they begin to have expectations—they want children to do more things for themselves, they become unaccepting of a lot of behaviors, they try to control the child in certain ways by rewarding behavior they like and punishing behavior they don't like. After the infancy period, the typical parent turns into an active change-agent, a controller, a behavior modifier. From the previous role of sensitive responder, the parent inexorably takes on the role of *controller.*

I have come to believe that this shift in the parent role is a critical factor in influencing the psychological health of children. In fact, from my own experience as a parent, from my professional work with very large numbers of parents, and from my reviews of many research studies, I have become convinced that this change from *responder* to *controller* is reponsible for much of the serious and widespread damage that has been done to the psychological (and sometimes physical) health of children.

Consequently, I have serious doubts about seeing any significant improvement either in the wellness of children or in the wellness of families in our society unless and until there occurs a *radical transformation of parenthood,* especially during the critical 10-year period after infancy and prior to adolescence.

Is such a radical transformation possible? Without being much more than unconsciously aware of it until recently, I have been personally and actively involved in an effort to bring about such a transformation of parenthood. With the help of a handful of colleagues who have joined me along the way, I have been devoting almost all of my professional life for nearly 20 years to transforming the way parents relate to children.

Through the vehicle of an educational program originally called Parent Effectiveness Training (PET), now revised and renamed Parent Effectiveness, I have been offering parents a different model. The course is delivered to the public by a network of several thousand specially trained and authorized "instructors" who recruit parents in their own communities in classes of no more than 30 participants who attend a three-hour session one night a week for eight successive weeks.

This cadre of instructors has taught well over 600,000 parents in every state in this country, in all the provinces in both Canada and Australia, and in various cities and towns in Mexico, Puerto Rico, South Africa, Germany, France, Belgium, Holland, Spain, Switzerland, Denmark, Sweden, Norway, Finland, and Japan. In non-English speaking countries the course is taught in the language of the foreign country, using texts and workbooks translated from English.

Despite the widespread acceptance of Parent Effectiveness in a variety of different cultures, I have not thought about this course as a "transforming" experience for parents until recently. Instead, I have described it as training for increased parent "effectiveness" or for making parenting easier or more joyful. Parents are promised they will learn better communication skills, or increase their competence in resolving parent-child conflicts. Even among professional colleagues, Parent Effectiveness is always described as one of the various models of "social skills training" or "interpersonal skills training." I now see these descriptions as incomplete and inadequate—they fail to represent accurately what Parent Effectiveness asks of parents and the degree to which it has transformed parenthood for so many of them.

More than just skill-training to "improve," or "enhance," or "simplify," or "enrich" parenting, our program holds up to parents an entirely different model, a different role, a different way of being in relation to children.

To make this transformation, as some certainly have done, parents experience "180°" shifts in certain attitudes; they assume a completely new and different posture regarding discipline and parental authority; they find themselves speaking a new language that in time replaces the traditional and universal *language of power* used in parent-child relationships; and they take on a new definition of their role, both with their children and in their family.

My objective in this chapter is first to describe the key components of the Parent Effectiveness model that require these radical transformations. Finally, I will point out how and why the new model of parenthood will increase family wellness.

CHILDREN DON'T REALLY "MISBEHAVE"

I don't think I have ever met a parent who did not begin to employ the concept of "misbehavior" as their children moved from infancy into childhood. In fact, I believe this way of thinking about young children is universal among parents. The concept of misbehavior is also commonly employed by professionals who write books for parents. To my knowledge, the model of parenting employed in Parent Effectiveness is unique in repudiating and discarding the concept of misbehavior.

Strangely enough, the term is almost exclusively applied to *children*—seldom to adults, friends, or spouses. We never hear anyone say:

"My husband misbehaved yesterday."

"One of our guests misbehaved at the party last night."

"I got so angry when my friend misbehaved during lunch."

"My employees have been misbehaving lately."

Apparently only children are seen as misbehaving—no one else. Misbehavior is exclusively *parent language*, tied up somehow with how parents have traditionally viewed their offspring. Why is it used?

Parents say a child misbehaves when some specific action is judged as contrary to how the parent thinks the child should behave. Misbehaving, then, is clearly a value judgement made by a parent, a label placed on the child. Misbehavior is actually a specific action of the child that is seen by the parent as producing some sort of undesirable consequences for the parent. What makes a child's behavior misbehavior (bad behavior) is the parent's perception that the behavior is (or might be) bad for the parent. The badness of the behavior actually resides in the parent's mind, not the child's.

A more accurate description of what happens is as follows: Some behaviors will be seen as bad for the parent—in other words, it is the parent (not the child) who feels and creates the badness and the parent "experiences" the badness while the child does not. Even more accurately, it is the *consequences* of the child's behavior that are felt to be bad (or potentially bad), not the behavior itself and not the child.

When parents grasp this critical distinction, they experience a marked shift in attitude toward their children. They begin to see all actions of their children as simply behaviors; and, like all other creatures, children engage in behaviors for the purpose of getting their needs met. When parents begin to see a child as a person engaging in behaviors to satisfy normal human needs they can hardly evaluate any of these behaviors as bad. Rather, they come to judge all behaviors as adaptive and purposeful in that they are serving the essential function of need fulfillment.

Seeing that children don't really misbehave but only behave to satisfy normal needs does not mean, however, that parents will feel accepting of all behaviors of their children. Nor should they be expected to, for children are bound to do certain things that produce consequences that are unacceptable to parents—that just happen to interfere with the parents' "pursuit of happiness." But in those instances, when a child's particular way of seeking his or her own need satisfaction happens to produce unacceptable consequences for the parent, the child is not a misbehaving (or bad) child. The child is not trying to do something *to the parent*, but rather is only trying to do something *for himself or herself.*

Only when parents in our classes make this important "paradigm shift"—changing the locus of "badness" from the child to the parent— can they appreciate the logic of the "I-message," one of the basic communication skills we teach in Parent Effectiveness. An I-message is a nonblameful, nonevaluative message that tells the youngster merely what badness the parent is experiencing in response to some behavior of the child, as in the following examples:

"When the TV is on so loud, I can't carry on a conversation with your mother."

"I'm afraid I won't be able to enjoy the flowers I planted if they're trampled on."

"When I have to wait so long for you to get ready for school, it makes me late for work and my boss gets mad at me."

One of the educational objectives of Parent Effectiveness is to encourage parents to adopt I-language as an alternative to traditional "you-language." You-messages contain heavy loadings of blame, judgment, evaluation, and criticism. They are the expressions of a parent who sees the child as misbehaving, as in these examples:

"You ought to know better than to do that."

"You are a bad boy."

"You are driving me crazy."

"You are eating like a pig."

Apart from serving to keep the responsibility with the parent (it's the parent who obviously "owns" the problem), I-messages are more likely to make children want to modify their behavior out of consideration for their parents. If kids are not put-down or blamed for their behavior, they are much more willing to respond helpfully (modify their behavior) when they're told their parents have a problem with something the child is doing and are appealing for help from the child.

Not so with you-messages. They tend to make children defensive and resistive to change. A you-message is not an appeal of the parent for help, it is a put-down of the child. This is why you-messages are so damaging to children's self-esteem and why they often provoke youngsters to strike back with you-messages of their own, thus causing the situation to escalate into a verbal battle that brings hurt feelings, tears, slammed doors, or threats of punishment.

Dropping you-messages and learning to use I-messages, however, is merely the implementation of a prior *attitudinal transformation*— a radical change in the way parents come to perceive their children's behaviors, and in the meanings they attach to such behaviors. More than acquiring a new "skill," parents make a major perceptual transformation.

BEYOND DISCIPLINE AND CONTROL

In every country where Parent Effectiveness has been introduced, we have encountered almost total consensus among parents on the issue of discipline. With rare exceptions, parents in all of these countries are unanimous in their belief that after infancy children need to be disciplined and it's parents' duty to do it.

No less amazing to me than this cross-cultural like-mindedness among parents is the lack of clarity we have found in the way parents think and talk about discipline. Most discussions on the subject reveal that parents by and large are entangled in a jungle of muddled meanings.

Bringing more clarity and deeper understanding about "disciplining children" ranks high among the educational objectives of Parent Effectiveness. The results of our efforts have been more than rewarding: We see most parents undergoing another kind of radical transformation. Though not without considerable personal struggle and strong resistance to the new, many parents change their traditional role of parent-as-disciplinarian.

Probably the most common confusion results from the failure of parents to understand the difference between two radically different kinds of discipline: self-discipline and externally imposed discipline.

While everyone claims to value self-disciplined children, few people understand that with a self-disciplined child the responsibility for the control and direction of his or her behavior resides in the child. With the second type of discipline—that exercised by the parent—the responsibility for the control and direction of the child's behavior resides in the parent. A fundamental difference: inner control versus external control, locus of responsibility within the child versus within the parent.

The conventional wisdom, of course, is that parents must assume responsibility for controlling their children, especially during the 10 years after infancy. To be able to do this effectively, parents are told they have to "exercise their authority." It follows from this that the structure of families must be hierarchical with respect to "authority"—parents on top with the most, kids on the bottom with the least. (Some parents and professionals put father on top and mother below, much to the chagrin of advocates of equal rights for women).

It is not understood by most parents, however, that placing oneself on top of an authority hierarchy doesn't automatically endow one with the ability to control others, as we know from studies of bosses in business and industrial organizations. Controllers need power, derived from two sources: (1) possessing the means to satisfy the controllee's needs, and (2) possessing the means to deprive the controllee of need satisfaction or to inflict pain. Parents obviously have a lot of both kinds, and they employ them frequently. They reward behavior they want repeated (reinforced) and punish behavior they want discontinued (weakened).

For centuries (with little modification) this model of parenthood has designated the parent as the controller (disciplinarian) who derives power from rewards and punishment and dispenses rewards and punishments in such a way as to strengthen behaviors judged by the parent as "good" or to get rid of behaviors judged by the parent as "bad."

Few parents have more than a superficial understanding either of the way this power model actually works or of its effect on children. Here is a partial list of what we have found most parents don't know about rewards and punishment (behavioral control):

(1) For rewards to work effectively, children must be kept in a continuous state of *dependency*—unable to get the rewards except from their parents.

(2) For punishment to work effectively, children must be kept in a continuous state of *fear*—always afraid the parents will in fact inflict the pain or deprivation they threaten to use. Children must be kept "locked in the relationship"—unable to escape from the punisher.

(3) As a result of the above two conditions, rewards and punishments become increasingly less effective in controlling children's behavior as they grow older and learn that they can get most rewards on their own and can effectively avoid punishment by not being caught or by escaping (e.g., leaving home).

(4) Using rewards to control even a single discrete behavior takes a lot of expertise and time. It requires very complex schedules of dispensing the reward, requires rewarding immediately after the behavior, and requires that the controllee be in a state of need deprivation—for example, if food is the reward, the child must be kept hungry.

The more I have understood the complex technology of behavioral control with rewards and punishment, the more it appears an inappropriate model for parents: It requires the expertise possessed only by experimental psychologists, who have to have laboratory-like conditions and rigid procedures to make it work.

In our Parent Effectiveness classes parents complain about rewards and punishments not working. Usually when they discover that rewards are ineffective, they typically fall back on punishment. Starting with mild punishments or threats of punishment (that were often not carried out), most parents switch to more severe punishment when the mild ones fail. A very large percentage of these parents admitted to using some form of harsh physical punishment—spanking, hitting, slapping, kicking, punching, or beating.

Studies show that our participants in Parent Effectiveness are no different from other parents. Four different surveys have been reported in the literature showing how pervasive physical punishment is, both in the United States and in Great Britain (Blumberg, 1964; Bronfenbrenner, 1958; Erlanger, 1974; Stark and McEvoy, 1970). In these studies the percentages of parents saying they had used physical punishment ranged from 84 to 97 percent.

Tragically few parents show any awareness of the effects of physical punishment on children. They are shocked when confronted with the evidence from research studies on the effects of physical punishment:

- Low self-esteem (Coopersmith, 1967)
- Tendencies toward self-punishment, accident proneness, suicide intentions (Sears, 1961)

- Hatred toward parents, rejection of teachers, poor relations with classmates, quarrels with friends, shyness, worry and anxiety, guilt, unhappiness and crying, dependence on parents, unsatisfactory love affairs (Watson, 1934)
- Aggression and violence toward siblings (Straus et al., 1980)
- Delinquency and criminality (McCord, 1958)
- School vandalism (Hyman et al., 1975)

When parents in our classes grasp how punishment can damage children, they are usually more than willing to consider alternatives to power-based discipline.

In addition to the I-message alternative described earlier, Parent Effectiveness stresses modifying a child's environment in order to prevent or change unacceptable behaviors. The principle underlying environmental modification is simple: Instead of directing efforts at trying to modify the child by punishment, look for ways to modify some aspect of the child's environment, which might make the behavior acceptable to the parent or might change the behavior. A simple example: Instead of punishing a child for digging in your flower bed, designate a special place in the yard as the child's digging area.

Clearly, learning to replace behavioral modification with environmental modification requires a drastic transformation on the part of parents, involving a shift in both basic attitudes and behaviors.

Parent Effectiveness offers parents yet another alternative to discipline and control, and it too requires a radical shift in their attitudes and behavior as parents. It is universally accepted by parents, as well as by professionals who advise them, that children need limits and rules and that parents should not hesitate to set them.

Limits and rules are set by parents for an obvious purpose—to control certain specified behaviors of their children. In practice, however, they often don't accomplish this purpose; all parents complain about how often their kids test or ignore their parents' limits and break their rules. And when rules are broken, children often lie about it.

Parent Effectiveness proposes to parents that, while limits and rules are quite necessary in the parent-child relationship (as in all relationships), the critical factor is *who sets the limits and makes the rules.* We advocate giving children a voice in determining what the limits and rules shall be. Parent Effectiveness is advocating and teaching "participatory democracy" in the home or family government "with the consent of the governed"—basic principles that are totally consistent with the political philosophy of a democratic nation. However, when parents unilaterally make rules for children and enforce those rules with threats of punishment and actual punishment for disobedience, they are using the methods of autocracy and tyranny: "subjects" are dictated to, told what to do, coerced, compelled, and subjugated by those "in power" who "rule," "lay down the law," and "give the orders."

Parent Effectiveness, obviously, is asking parents to make a radical transformation in something as fundamental as their political philosophy—from their traditional autocratic philosophy to a democratic philosophy. To help parents implement their new philosophy we provide them with a specific set of procedures by which a parent (or parents) join together with a child (or children) in a "legislative" process (we call it a Rule-Setting Meeting) for the purpose of reaching consensus on the limits and laws by which their relationship (or family) will be governed.

Can parents be persuaded to give up what most feel is their *right to govern* their own children? Many are willing to try the democratic approach, especially after they understand that the only alternative to autocracy is *not* anarchy, which they fear. When they hear about families that have switched from autocracy to participatory democracy and end up not only having rules and laws that are honored by all family members but also having even *more* rules and laws than before, many parents are willing to give the new law-making procedures a try.

TOWARD JUSTICE AND FAIRNESS IN FAMILIES

Parent Effectiveness challenges parents with the opportunity to make a major transformation in their attitudes about justice and fairness in parent-child relationships. Many parents accept this challenge and successfully achieve a transformation in the way they deal with family conflicts.

In relationships, in groups, and in nations, rules and laws serve the function of preventing or avoiding conflicts. Obviously, they don't always succeed, for conflicts do occur over the interpretation of rules and laws. Conflicts between people or groups of people also occur with high frequency when there are no existing rules or laws covering the issue around which a new conflict emerges, as in the case of a conflict between a parent and teenager over buying a motorcycle. This means that conflicts in families are inevitable, and so they have to be resolved somehow.

Within the rather large population of parents whom we enroll in our Parent Effectivness course, we have found that well over 90 percent approach conflict-resolution with what we call a "win-lose" attitude. They feel that the resolution of conflicts inevitably will result in someone emerging the winner and the other the loser. If in resolving a particular conflict, the parent wins and the child loses, we call that Method I. When the child wins and the parent loses, that is Method II.

In the hypothetical conflict over whether the teenager buys a motorcycle, if the parent should say, "I will not let you have a motorcycle because they are too dangerous, and I don't want to hear any more about it," that would be conflict-resolution by Method I. The parent is happy with the solution but the youngster is not, so the solution will feel unfair to him and the child will see it as an injustice. On the other hand, if the teenager should say, "I'm going to buy a motorcycle no matter what you feel," that would be Method II with the youngster winning and the parent losing. Now it would be the parent who feels that the solution is unfair and an injustice.

Parent Effectiveness rejects this "either-or" thinking and asks parents to resolve all parent-child conflicts by Method III, the No-Lose (or Win-Win) approach. This method, judging from the initial reactions of participants in our classes, is perhaps the most "revolutionary" idea in Parent Effectiveness. It asks parents to show deep respect for the needs of their children and to accept that children have equal rights to getting their needs met. Parents are asked to forego using power, even though they obviously possess a lot of it when their children are young. For a few parents, however, the No-Lose method means they must stop being "permissive"—reluctantly giving in to all the demands of their children. These parents have to become more *assertive,* more respectful of their own needs, unwilling to be the victims of their children's winning. The No-Lose method also requires that parents take a lot more time to work out conflicts and find mutually acceptable solutions. They need to start listening more often and more accurately in order to understand what their children's needs are. And, one of the most difficult shifts to make is changing their perception of children as "minors," inferiors, underlings, subordinates, and second-class citizens in the family. Essential, of course, is making a commitment to pursuing and achieving *equity* and *fairness* in the family—"with justice for all."

My experience convinces me that unless this commitment is made, none of the so-called "interpersonal skills" will bring about much improvement in parent-child relationships. But parents we know who have made this commitment report significant improvements in their family relationships, some describing the changes as "revolutionary."

THE ANTECEDENTS OF FAMILY WELLNESS

Until now, I have not tried to identify or define any of the conditions I feel are necessary to produce family wellness. Rather, I have advanced a point of view and a personal belief that it will not be possible to achieve significant or widespread family wellness in society unless we first effect a radical transformation in parenthood. I have come to see that Parent Effectiveness is a program that teaches a particular "model" of parenthood that requires such a transformation in both attitudes and behavior.

Implicit in the Parent Effectiveness model of parenthood are certain assumptions about the conditions and antecedents of family wellness—specifically, assumptions about what kinds of parent-child interactions will most likely produce the necessary conditions for wellness. Now these assumptions will be made more explicit, as I identify some necessary conditions for personal and family wellness.

Need Satisfaction

To be physically healthy, organisms must have their physical needs met. Human beings have psychological needs as well as physical needs: for safety and security; for affection, love, and social interaction; for achievement and accomplishment; for self-actualization. It follows that for human beings to be "well," they must be successful in getting these psychological needs met. Family wellness is only an abstraction for the individual wellness of each human being who is a member of the family. A necessary condition for family wellness therefore, is maximum opportunity for both parents and children to achieve satisfaction of their needs. This is the core idea of the No-Lose method of conflict resolution as well as its principal purpose—to find solutions that meet the needs of each person. No one must remain deprived, frustrated, or feeling like a loser.

Discipline is an attempt to control, and control requires the exercise of power. Parents usually rely on punishment as their source of power. It follows that, because punishment by definition is a deprivation of some need, disciplining children is damaging to their psychological health (and, if severe enough to injure, their physical health too). Because the Parent Effectiveness model eliminates all punishment in the parent-child relationship, it will promote greater health.

Self-Esteem

High self-esteem has been frequently shown to be a correlate of positive mental health. And children's self-esteem is thought to be strongly affected by the kinds of communication they receive from "significant others" in their lives. The you-language used by most parents when behavior is unacceptable is often blameful, critical, deprecating, berating, belittling, and derogatory. Such messages inevitably chip away at a child's self-esteem. The Parent Effectiveness model advocates that parents learn nonevaluative "I-messages" which carry far less risk of damaging a child's self-esteem.

Problem-Solving Competence

Life is often harsh and always complicated. Both inside the family and in the child's world outside the family, he or she inevitably encounters difficulties and problems in getting essential needs met. The Parent Effectiveness model advocates involving children at all ages in the problem-solving process—to make rules and policies, plan special events, and resolve all conflicts. Parents give up being solution givers, decision makers, and lawgivers; instead they bring their children into the decision-making, problem-solving, and lawmaking process as full and equal participants. As a result children learn firsthand and get a lot of practice in effective problem solving.

Fate Control

The feeling of losing control of one's destiny has often been found to be a correlate of poor mental health and is particularly associated with depression, anxiety, and stress, At the heart of Parent Effectiveness is the value of self-control (inner control) versus external control by authority. External control produces dependency and other-directedness; inner control brings greater independence and inner-directedness. The healthy person has been allowed to develop self-control and hence will feel much more in charge of and responsible for his or her destiny. As Stanly Milgram concluded from his ingenious study of obedience to authority, "The disappearance of a sense of responsibility is the most far-reaching consequence of submission to authority" (Milgram, 1974).

Freedom from Fear

Power-based, punitive discipline generates fear. Punished dogs become cowed and nervous—and so do some children. Living in a climate of constant potential danger is damaging to people's psychological health, as we have learned so well from studies of Vietnam veterans. Children of parents who use the Parent Effectiveness model have nothing to fear within the family. Not only are they free of the fear of punishment, they are also free of the fear of "losing."

Freedom from Hostility and Resentment

Sick people are often angry people, turning their hostility either inward and hating themselves or outward and hating others. Anger and hostility are frequent coping mechanisms of "have-nots," consistent "losers" who have been deprived of opportunities to get their needs met. The No-Lose method of conflict-resolution in the Parent Effectiveness model greatly decreases the probability of kids feeling like losers, have-nots, or second-class citizens. Satisfied, need-fulfilled children seldom become angry, hostile, or retaliatory family members or members of society.

I am certain that this is only a partial list of the antecedents of individual wellness and hence of family wellness. Others can be added now and still others will be added in the future as we acquire even greater understanding of the complex dynamics of human relationships.

REFERENCES

BLUMBERG, M. (1964) "When parents hit out." Twentieth Century 173: 39-44.

BRONFENBRENNER, U. (1958) "Socialization and social class thoughout time and space," pp. 400-425 in Readings of Social Psychology. New York: Holt, Rinehart, and Winston.

COOPERSMITH, S. (1967) The Antecedents of Self-Esteem. San Francisco: Freeman.

ERLANGER, H. (1974) "The empirical status of the subculture of violence thesis." Social Problems 22 (December) : 280-291.

GORDON, T. (1975) Parent Effectiveness Training. New York: New American Library.

HYMAN, I., E. McDOWELL and B. RAINERS (1975) "Corporal punishment and alternatives in schools." Inequality in Educations 23: 5-20.

McCORD, J. and W. McCORD (1958) "The effects of parental modes on criminality." J. of Social Issues 14: 66-75.

MILGRAM, S. (1974) Obedience to Authority. New York: Harper and Row.

SEARS, R. (1961) "The relation of early socialization experiences to aggression in middle childhood." J. of Abnormal Social Psychology 63: 466-492.

STARK, R., and J. McEVOY, III (1970) "Middle class violence." Psychology Today, 4: 52-65.

STRAUS, M., R. GELLES, and S. STEINMETZ (1980) Behind Closed Doors: Violence in the American Family. New York: Anchor Books.

WATSON, G. (1934) "A comparison of the effects of lax versus strict home training." J. of Social Psychology 5: 102-105.

12

Preventing Parent-Adolescent Crises

David Catron
Sarah Catron

During the turbulent 1960s and in more recent years, a great deal of professional and media attention has focused on what seemed to be an increase in the intensity of conflicts and crises between adolescents and their parents. Articles in popular magazines and newspapers, motion picture themes, and television programs presented a picture of generations alienated from each other due to radically different life-styles, attitudes, and values.

Parent-adolescent crises and conflicts are not new. What appears to be a relatively recent phenomenon actually has a long history. For example, the Biblical story of the prodigal son who rebelled against his father, ran away from home, and squandered his inheritance would be regarded as a major parent-adolescent crisis, even by contemporary standards.

Parent-adolescent crises and conflicts have been regarded as inevitable. This inevitability has been variously attributed to different life experiences of the two generations (Davis, 1940), necessary rebellion of the adolescent in order to achieve a sense of personal identity (Pitts, 1964), and a shifting of power and resources within the family (Richer, 1968).

Even beyond the recognition that parent-adolescent conflict has been around a long time and that it may be inevitable, there has also been a generally held notion that conflict is negative and undesirable. It has been regarded as somewhat like an occasional illness—inevitable, but unfortunate. In fact, most conflict within families has tended to be regarded as negative, as a disruption or imbalance in what was expected to be a conflict-free situation. The goal, therefore, has often been to prevent, avoid, or smooth over areas of conflict as quickly as possible.

CONFLICT VERSUS CRISIS:
WHAT IS THE DIFFERENCE?

Conflict can be defined as a fight or struggle, a disagreement or quarrel, a clashing of opposed principles, or strife and discord. In parent-child relationships, conflict might be used to describe the situation in which either the parent or adolescent is dissatisfied and attempts to make some change which is resisted by the other (Scanzoni, 1979).

A crisis is more serious. A crisis exists where there is a threat to the relationship, when there is danger that the parent-adolescent interaction will be seriously disrupted. When unresolved conflict leads to chronic anger, resentment, hostility, coercion, or violence, or when either parent or adolescent refuses to interact with the other, a crisis in the relationship exists. Crisis is conflict carried to extremes. When conflict becomes pervasive and surrounds the relationship like a fog, the relationship is in jeopardy and a crisis condition prevails.

We are thus making a distinction between conflict and crisis primarily in terms of its threat to the continuation of the relationship. It is our assumption that conflicts are a normal, inevitable, and even essential part of the parent-adolescent experience. In fact, absence of any conflict may indicate alienation or domination. Further, these conflicts are not necessarily negative and can, in fact, lead to a strengthening of parent-adolescent bonds.

In contrast to conflict, most crises are *not* inevitable. Severe disruption of a relationship is generally not desired by either the parent or the adolescent. Since crises represent a threat to the existence of the relationship, we propose that crises should be prevented whenever possible.

Having taken a stand for the inevitability and potentially positive outcomes of parent-adolescent conflict, let us hasten to clarify that we do not imply that all conflict is healthy or suggest that "the more the merrier." Although it seems evident that there is some conflict present in most parent-adolescent situations, it is also evident that there is wide variation within families in the amount of conflict, the conditions which account for the conflict, the way it is managed, and the levels of satisfaction with the outcomes.

Our approach to prevention of parent-adolescent crises will be through an examination of factors which contribute to conflicts, and a consideration of ways through which conflicts can be more effectively managed and resolved.

CHARACTERISTICS OF PARENT-ADOLESCENT RELATIONSHIPS

Regardless of the wide diversity between families, there are some common themes that characterize all parent-adolescent relationships. In every case, the child began his life in a totally dependent state and gradually moved toward independence. As he or she gained mobility and maturity, he or she moved away from a high level of dependency toward relative autonomy and independence. This change is a gradual process, but the rate of change accelerates during the adolescent period. Also, during adolescence, children have increased opportunity for independent action as they move away from the watchful eye of their parents.

When the adolescent was a child, the parent typically made most of the decisions for the child. Indeed, the culture expected the parent to make these decisions and held the parent responsible for the results. During adolescence, however, parental dominance is normally challenged by the young person; in American society, excessive parental dominance is expected to terminate.

Even from the time a child is first anticipated, a prospective parent knows and expects that at some point the child will function independently. Generally, American parents recoil at the prospect of a 30-year-old person continuing to be dependent on his or her parents. Most parents would not choose for their maturing child to remain in the home indefinitely. At the same time, an adolescent also expects— and usually eagerly anticipates—the time when he or she will be out from under the tutelage of the parent.

In the big picture, it therefore appears that both parents and their adolescent children in our culture agree that the child will ultimately establish himself or herself as independent of the parent. However, parent-adolescent differences arise over the issue concerning *what* changes should be made, *when* they should begin, and *how fast* they should take place. During this transition period, patterns of interaction that began from positions of inequality must now be transformed into interaction based on greater equality. Unilateral decisions must now yield to joint decisions and, in the process, some amount of disagreement and conflict is inevitable.

FACTORS THAT INFLUENCE THE PARENT-ADOLESCENT RELATIONSHIP

CHANGING SOCIAL NORMS CONCERNING PARENTAL AUTHORITY

One of the changes which has occurred within the past few decades has been the emerging recognition of the rights of children within the family. The old adage that "children should be seen and not heard" is much less frequently quoted or practiced.

Another change has been the reduction of authoritarian practices that were once commonly used by parents. Although parental authority is generally expected to decrease during the child's adolescent period, there is considerable variability among parents in the amount of authority that is considered to be legitimate. In addition, parents vary in the amount of compliance they expect from their adolescent. In the past, fathers made the rules and compliance was assumed. In recent times, as Thomas Gordon points out in the preceding chapter, such an authoritarian stance has begun to yield to a more democratic position.

There is currently no general agreement about how much voice or control adolescents should have in determining their own affairs or how quickly such control should be granted. Some parents encourage children to make their own decisions as soon as possible, while other parents want compliance to parental wishes for as long as possible.

Parents feel unsure about how long they are accountable. The strong societal emphasis on parental responsibility has caused some parents to continue to feel responsible for the behavior of their adolescent children even past the time when they have little, if any, control.

If there is agreement between the parent and adolescent on the amount of control that the adolescent should have, then conflict may be minimized. However, if the child wishes to have more control than he or she is allowed, or if the parent desires the child to assume more responsibility for his or her behavior than the child wants, conflict will likely emerge.

DIFFERENCE IN PERSPECTIVE BETWEEN PARENTS AND ADOLESCENTS

During this time of transition in parent-child relationships, parents and adolescents understandably view issues from different perspectives. Adolescents tend to focus on areas where they wish to reduce the limits placed on them by parents, such as schedule regulations, hair styles, clothing, and so on. Adolescents talk about rights and freedom while parents talk about responsibility. From the parents' point of view, freedom is not a right but a privilege, conditional on responsible behavior. Thus, parents usually demand evidence of maturity and of the ability to handle additional privileges before yielding further control. Such evidence comes from areas such as school performance and being responsible in household chores and personal grooming.

THE JAGGED EDGE OF MATURITY

As mentioned above, one of the major concerns that parents have is with the development of responsibility in their adolescent children. Yet, the development of responsible behavior is often a process of "two steps forward, one step backward." Parents would like their adolescent to display mature behavior without deviation, but such expectations are rarely met; consequently, conflicts arise.

DEVELOPING IDENTITY

In spelling out the eight stages of human development, Erik Erikson (1963) listed the "identity crisis" as being one of the major developmental tasks facing adolescents. During the adolescent period, the young person wrestles internally with the classic questions of "Who am I?," "Where am I going?," and "What do I believe?" Because the adolescent is so overwhelmingly preoccupied with the spin-offs associated with trying to establish this sense of selfhood, it is particularly important that parents recognize and understand this process. The many physical and psychological changes that occur during adolescence contribute to the lack of ease of the typical young person during this time.

In order to establish a sense of personal identity, the adolescent must form an identity that is separate from—although still a part of—the family. During childhood, identity tended to be closely associated with the family and was primarily that of being the son or daughter of one's parents. Activities and values tended to be those of the family. During adolescence, this close association with the family is frequently challenged, sometimes leaving parents feeling rejected (if not attacked). Family identity may even be viewed by the adolescent as a threat to individual identity. Family values, activities, rituals, or things the family has "always" done may be resisted, resulting in conflicts if parents insist that their adolescent continue to participate.

From a personal perspective, we have felt some disappointment when our teenagers used their increased freedom to reject some of our traditional family events, like fixing popcorn together on Sunday evenings. Fortunately, we have also survived their adolescence long enough to experience the joy of seeing them anticipate being with the family for special events now that they have moved through the major period of this identity crisis.

PEER GROUPS

Few parents of an adolescent child are unaware of the powerful influence of peers during the years of adolescence. The peer group frequently appears to have more influence on the behavior of the adolescent than does the parent. Peers serve as a comparison group for the adolescent in judging whether his or her parents are "fair" or whether he or she has been granted the appropriate level of rights and privileges. The claim that "everybody else does it" is a strong argument often used by adolescents and is hard to counter by parents who seldom know the limits set by other parents. Adolescents hold up the peer group norm to their parents but the parents typically have no comparable parent group norm to guide them.

Parents are also influenced by their own type of peer or reference group, whether they are aware of it or not. Typically parents respond from some concern about what they think others would say about their decisions. Thus, the interaction of both parent and adolescent is influenced, to some extent, by the concern each has for the reaction of his respective peer group.

"FROZEN IMAGES"

Frequently, both parent and teenager may regard the other as being in a static condition rather than in a dynamic process of change. Whenever an adolescent acts irresponsibly, that action tends to become a part of the parent's "frozen image" of his or her child. Reciprocally, the adolescent may view the parent as reacting in exactly the same controlling manner as when the child was younger. Frozen images tend to be those of the parent viewing the child as immature or dependent and of the child viewing the parent as restrictive. Such images are expectations founded on outdated behaviors that may no longer be appropriate. Frozen images, like stop-action photography, fail to take into account the gradual dynamic changes that are taking place in the developing lives of both adolescents and parents.

WAYS TO PREVENT CRISES IN PARENT-ADOLESCENT RELATIONSHIPS

Let us now examine some of the ways through which conflict might be more effectively managed and resolved, thereby preventing crisis situations. Out of our own personal experience and study, we have formulated several general principles that seem to be consistent with research findings and with theories of development and family interaction. These proved to be viable guides as we lived with our own teenagers. We offer these principles not as magic formulas but rather with the hope that they may be useful to parents in keeping conflicts with their adolescent children from growing to crisis proportions.

RESPECT WHAT IS IMPORTANT TO THE OTHER PERSON

No two people have exactly the same set of values, preferences, or choices. As mentioned earlier, parents and adolescents often hold different views of issues and they also differ as to which issues are important to them. These differences become quite evident as the young person begins to assert his or her individuality and to establish an identity that is separate from that of the family. It is important that parents recognize these differences and treat them with respect.

When parents respect what is important to the adolescent, they treat him or her as a person and affirm the adolescent's right to make choices. Showing respect does not mean that we necessarily agree with his or her choice, and there is no reason to pretend that we agree. What we can do is to acknowledge the choice and still express any concern we feel about it without responding in a belittling or attacking manner. Empirical studies show strong evidence that parental behavior that conveys to the child that he or she is basically accepted and approved as a person is conducive to positive development in the child (Rollins and Thomas, 1979).

An adolescent learns to trust his or her parents by the parents' demonstration that they consider the interests of the adolescent to be important and that these interests are taken into account in their decisions. If parents treat some preference or concern of their teenager as trivial or unimportant, the level of trust between them is diminished. It is desirable to treat with respect what is important to the other because that is the foundation on which trust between parent and adolescent is built.

Parents are likely to treat their adult friends with respect and, ultimately, parents probably want their relationship with their adult children to be similar to their other adult friendships. Consequently, the degree to which parents show respect for what is important to their adolescent child may be a measure of the degree to which they regard him or her as an adult.

PICK THE ISSUES

If we attempted to list all of the issues over which parent-adolescent conflicts could arise, the list would be almost endless. Even for an individual parent-child combination, there are many issues about which there may be differences and possibly conflict. These issues are not all of equal importance. Some could be overlooked without major difficulty. We recommend that parents think through the issues on which they are conflicting with their adolescent and identify those that are of genuine importance and those that might be bypassed. Otherwise, there is the risk of "criticism overload"—that is, the total parent-adolescent interaction may be dominated by conflicts over relatively unimportant matters.

STICK TO THE ISSUES

Parents are prone to overgeneralize. If our adolescent demonstrates one type of behavior, even briefly, there is a tendency to project similar behavior onto future situations and to imagine all manner of undesirable consequences. Speculations about the implications of behavior may sometimes be appropriate, but a problem can arise when we generalize from the content of a situation to the character of the person, particularly when this leads to labelling or name-calling. For example, not telling the truth may be a serious matter, but calling a person a liar is inflammatory and often contributes to a conflict situation that escalates into a crisis.

NEGOTIATE DECISIONS

To the adolescent, the *process* by which decisions are made and conflicts resolved may be as important as the actual decision itself. Also, whether a conflict becomes a crisis may be more closely related to how parents and adolescents treat each other during negotiation than to the differences themselves. The adolescent, because of a history of relative powerlessness in the relationship, is likely to be particularly sensitive to whether discussions are conducted fairly— without threats or coercion.

Negotiated agreements between parent and adolescent take more time and energy than unilateral decisions. To listen carefully to each other and to give serious attention to the other's requests or point of view require both "quantity time" and "quality time." By giving each other full attention and by taking seriously the concerns and feelings of the other, parent-adolescent communication will be enhanced and the negotiation process fostered. In decision making, nothing takes the place of good communication—and plenty of it.

PLAN TOWARD GRADUATION

Another way of reducing destructive conflicts and crises in parent-adolescent relationships is to plan together toward "graduation" from the active parenting role. Some parents feel that they will never be free of this role, especially when they feel the heavy financial obligations of college or other post-high-school training. Other parents may not want to let go: To turn their offspring completely loose and let them move out of the home into their own environment is sometimes difficult. Parents who have centered their lives around their children may find that having the children leave is tantamount to losing their reason for being.

During this transition period, adolescents usually want to be independent and to feel adequate and competent in taking full charge of their lives. As long as there is financial dependency and feelings of parental control, the adolescent will likely feel some sense of inadequacy.

Parents and adolescents need ways to move through this transition period as smoothly as possible. One alternative could be for parents and teenagers to talk and plan together about their mutual goals for the child's independence. This could encourage the adolescent to develop the responsibilities and abilities the parent expects and could encourage the parent to extend full recognition of maturity as soon as possible. Plans such as this have been proposed as a way to prevent parent-adolescent crises (Sanderson, 1978). Without some explicit plans or goals, parents and adolescents tend to become bogged down in immediate interaction problems and long-term mutual goals become obscured.

If long-range goals can be recognized, the intermediate stages that demonstrate progress toward those goals can be celebrated together. As we periodically measure and celebrate the gains in physical height on the door post, so we might recognize and celebrate growth toward autonomy. In our family, we created a "celebration and blessing" ceremony when our oldest child graduated from our care.

PRACTICE POSITIVE INTERACTION

Learning to send direct, positive messages to each other is one of the neglected areas in family life. As sender and receiver of such messages, there is typically some discomfort or awkwardness. In contrast, we are more practiced in saying critical things to one another than we are in saying positive things. Practice in affirming one another—with no strings attached—is needed in our homes (and elsewhere). We need to say, "John, I appreciated your help in cleaning

the car." Such a genuinely appreciative and nonmanipulative statement can be a way of affirming the adolescent in a specific area of
behavior, without pairing it with further expectations such as, "Now,
how about taking out the garbage?" Programs of parent effectiveness
and communication training have demonstrated that parents and
adolescents can learn and practice more positive and effective ways
of interaction with each other. We encourage and promote many
practice behaviors in our families. We practice soccer, multiplication
tables, and table manners, we need to practice making genuinely positive statements to each other.

ORGANIZE A PARENT SUPPORT GROUP

Parents need a supportive peer group, just as adolescents do.
Without such a group, parents often feel isolated and with few
resources to help them think through concerns about their feelings
and behavior in relation to their adolescents. A parent support group
might involve five or six couples who meet periodically to share
feelings, ideas, and alternatives about their experiences with their
teenage children. Such a group could provide encouragement to
parents by helping them see that they are not alone in dealing with
these issues. In addition, parents could learn alternative ways of
viewing and handling situations. They would then have perspectives
and choices that they could not have without the input of other parents.
When parents feel isolated, out of control of the situation, and know
of no other alternatives for dealing with their teenagers, feelings of
desperation and anger can result.

KEEP PERSPECTIVE: THE LONG LOOK

As we have lived in our household with three adolescents, one very
helpful experience has been to periodically back away from the daily
situations to give some thought to the goals or aims we have for our
children. In trying to formulate these goals, two questions were
especially useful in helping us look beyond our immediate situation.
We asked ourselves these questions:

(1) What kind of person would I like my adolescent child to
become?

(2) What kind of relationship do I want to have with my children in future years?

Specific goals for each child may vary. Among other things, however, most parents probably want their children, as adults, to be able to make their own choices, to think for themselves, to set and achieve their own goals—in other words, to become autonomous. In order to accomplish these goals, some deliberate and consistent steps are necessary. For example, if we want our adult children to be able to think and make choices for themselves, we must give them a chance to express their opinions and we must honor their right to hold an opinion that differs from our own. If we want them to be able to manage money wisely, we must help them learn during the adolescent years to take some of the economic responsibilities needed for their own maintenance.

In reference to our goal for the kind of relationship we wanted with our adult children, we were sure of one thing: We wanted to have a strong relationship with our children on an adult-to-adult basis. When strong emotions have been aroused, our behavior has been moderated by our concern for maintaining the relationship and our desire to work toward this goal. Awareness of this goal helped us choose not to use coercive methods or to strain beyond reasonable limits of our legitimate, but waning, parental authority.

CONCLUDING STATEMENTS

Crises in parent-adolescent relationships threaten the existence of the relationship. Effective resolution of conflict helps prevent the development of such crises. We have claimed that conflict is not necessarily negative in parent-adolescent interaction. We further believe that through resolution of conflict, there is potential for strengthening this relationship (Scanzoni, 1979). This is possible as the resolution of conflict can increase trust and create more solidarity in the relationship because both parent and adolescent have learned that they can arrive at mutually satisfying solutions that take the interests of both into account.

In this chapter, we have not mentioned the need to understand what parents are experiencing developmentally during the time when their children are adolescents. Their development is an important influence on parent-adolescent relationships. There has also been no acknowledgement that there are times when we, as parents, have neither the emotional nor the physical energy to interact with our adolescents as appropriately as we might wish. We do have confidence, however, that adolescents and their parents have enough resilience to be able to withstand many of their own mistakes as well as mistakes of the other. Of primary importance is that a strong foundation of confidence and trust be developed between parent and adolescent so that each is concerned for the other and each considers the interests of the other in their interactions.

REFERENCES

DAVIS, K. (1940) "The sociology of parent-youth conflict." Amer. Soc. Rev. 5: 532-535.

ERIKSON, E. H. (1963) Childhood and Society. New York: Norton.

PITTS, J. R. (1964) "The structural-functional approach," in H. T. Christensen (ed.) Handbook of Marriage and the Family. Chicago: Rand McNally.

RICHER, S. (1963) The economics of child rearing. J. of Marriage and the Family 30: 462-466.

ROLLINS, B. C. and D. L. THOMAS, (1979) "Parental support, power, and control techniques in the socialization of children," in W. R. Burr et al., (eds.) Contemporary Theories about the Family Vol. 1. New York: Free Press.

SANDERSON, J. D. (1978) How to Stop Worrying About Your Kids. New York: Norton.

SCANZONI, J. (1979) "Social exchange and behavioral interdependence," in R. L. Burgess and T. L. Huston (eds.) Social Exchange in Developing Relationships. New York: Academic Press.

13

Whole Family Enrichment

Margaret M. Sawin

Programs for the complete family, as a system, constitute the latest development in the field of enrichment and complement the other aspects of the field. As Mace defines it, the act of enriching is "to draw from inside what is already there, latent and hitherto unappropriated, and to allow it to function" (Mace, 1979).

The most extensively used model of family enrichment—the Family Cluster Model—is designed to enable families "to draw from inside what is already there" and be affirmed by other families as they do it. The process of mixing together persons of all ages while helping families to work on common tasks helps to make this possible. Moreover, such seems to be true of family enrichment programs in general, as mentioned by Space (1980: 10) in her "Review of the Research on Family Enrichment Programs":

It appears that many families in family enrichment programs are finding "something" that contributes to their feeling more positive about their family and individual lives.

Not only do families grow and use hitherto untapped potential, they also avert both minor problems and major catastrophes. They do so by becoming part of a sustaining group, committed together through mutual agreement, which helps the family cluster function like an extended family of caring and sharing members.

The concept of family wellness as set forth in this book has been described as "the state of being able to make full use of all available resources in order to live together in happiness, harmony, and changing growth."[1] This chapter describes how the family cluster, as it has been used with thousands of family units throughout the world, contributes to family wellness.

THE HISTORY OF FAMILY ENRICHMENT

Family enrichment had its beginnings with the Family Cluster Model, emanating from my doctoral research on personality characteristics of Sunday church school teachers (Sawin, 1969). The findings showed that these people neither wished to be involved in the nurturance of others nor wanted to have persons share affection and caring with them. Reflecting upon these findings plus those of other studies about Sunday church school teachers, I became aware that religious education needed different models from those of the traditional classroom model of the Sunday church school.

In 1970 I experimented in the First Baptist Church of Rochester, New York with a model of family enrichment that I named the Family Cluster. The definition evolved as I worked with the model for two years in an empirical fashion. Two other churches also utilized the model and helped with the task of replicating and refining it. The Family Cluster Model was used primarily as an alternative to the traditional religious education program in church schools.

We defined a family cluster as a group of four or five complete family units that contract to meet together regularly over an extended period of time to share educational experiences of living in the family relationship. A cluster provides mutual support, training in skills that facilitate the family living in relationship, and celebration together of their life and beliefs. A family unit is defined as any number of persons who live in relationship with one another. It can be a nuclear family, a one-parent family, a couple without children, or one or more persons who live in a household together (Sawin, 1979: 27).

In 1972 I first heard that Herbert Otto had developed a similar model on the West Coast and called it by the same name! Otto had recruited families through newspaper advertistements and by word of mouth; they usually met on a weekend. The mode of leadership was very different, and there was no sponsoring agency (Otto, 1971). Little has been written about Otto's model since 1976, and there seem to be few Family Clusters of that genre.

In 1970 Margaret Mead wrote an article for *Redbook Magazine* in which she advocated the need for "clusters" in neighborhoods, defining a cluster loosely as "a setting in which each family would retain its own identity but in which each would be an integral part of a larger group, all of whose members would carry some responsibility for everyone within it, adult or child, man or woman" (Mead, 1970).

It was clear that the concept of families helping families was starting to be advocated across the country. In 1975 the term "Family Cluster" became an integral heading in *The Reader's Guide to Periodical Literature* as people began to use the term generically to mean a group of families who meet together for any reason.

With the publication of *Family Enrichment With Family Clusters* (Sawin, 1979), the term "family enrichment" was identified and defined as one of the numerous enrichment fields. The book denoted and collated 28 various models of whole-family enrichment that were available at the time of writing. Most of them were developed from 1975 into the late 1970s. By the close of the 1970s, family enrichment was a firmly established field.

Today, the majority of family enrichment models are used in church settings and the greatest growth seems to be in that context. Some of it may be attributed to the fact that the church is the institution in our society that deals with complete families as part of its clientele on a very large scale; therefore, it is relatively easy to bring families together within a congregational context. As Sunday church schools are also on the decline, many churches are searching for other models of religious education.

THEORETICAL FOUNDATIONS OF THE FAMILY CLUSTER

The foundation of the model is the basic premise that the system of the family can provide its own intensive framework for growth when set within the wider support of the cluster. The cluster emphasizes the family's strengths, so its own interrelational system can be recognized and used as a springboard for further growth. Being in the cluster can teach a family new things about itself so that its own interpersonal network can be appraised and changed, if so desired. In a time of rapid social change, it becomes imperative that we find ways for people to adapt, to cope, and to live with value systems that differ from those with which they grew up. Our knowledge about family systems comes mainly from the field of family sociology, family therapy, and multi-family therapy.

The strength of the model derives from the fact that it is a small group that develops mutual support and gives feedback to family members. Richard Farson of The Family Service Association of America has said that a network of families would not only support each other in times of crisis but also "monitor each other's family lives" (Farson, 1969: 74). My experience has been that it takes families from four to six sessions to begin to learn trust with each other in order to share their real concerns as well as to give and accept honest feedback. Full functioning seems to develop from the four-teenth to the twentieth sessions. We can see that families need adequate time to achieve the kind of in-depth sharing from which new behaviors can develop.

The interrelational structure in a cluster is a "collegial" one, meaning that everyone is a teacher at times and everyone is a learner. This avoids the hierarchical structure that infers that only adults can teach. Families can observe other family units in various experiences of communication, decision making, and problem solving, and this provides modeling for managing some of the crucial elements of living within a family. Asking for feedback and providing it for each other become strategic processes within families as well as between families. They can then decide "intentionally" if they want to keep the behaviors resulting from past family influence or if they want to change some of their actions.

There is interfamily exchange as well as intrafamily exchange, which can help the cluster group become like an extended family. Families may continue socializing after the formal termination of the cluster. One of the original groups I started in 1970 has a reunion each year and the families still maintain other contacts with each other.

"The gem of the Family Cluster Model is the contracting . . . [which] helps determine the success of involvement on the part of all family members," writes sociologist Lucinda Sangree (1974). The original contracting is done with each family in their own home, in order to assess the willingness of every family member to be part of the group. Then there is a cluster group contract in which everyone has shared power in determining the group's decision-making process, its modes of interaction, expectations, and outcome. Each person signs the contract so there is strong sense of commitment as the cluster is getting started. When family clusters have not had successful contracting, there is usually a lack of commitment, and sketchy participation, on the part of some families.

Contracting teaches individuals and families how to be participants in making and sharing commitments. This is needed for living in our present confused society as well as for developing a new social order. Daniel Yankelovich (1981: 89) has written that "a successful social ethic demands that people form commitments that advance the well-being of the society as well as their own." The act of contracting benefits individuals, families, and the cluster "society" of which they are a part. Yankelovich foresees "that Americans are growing less self-absorbed and better prepared to take a first step toward an ethic of commitment" (1981: 89). Young people learn this in a cluster for the benefit of their present (as well as their future) family life.

The family cluster is a leadership model. The leaders plan from the expressed needs of the families and facilitate the process as they experience and share together. Training for leadership has been in effect since 1972 with the laboratory model, and a core of skilled leaders are involved in the leadership network. Information regarding training events is available from Family Clustering, Inc., P. O. Box 18074, Rochester, New York 14618, telephone (716) 244-0882 or 232-3530. Knowledge of group dynamics and leadership is drawn from social psychology to provide information for this area. The outcome of the model is change, followed by growth that leads toward fulfillment or actualization, as described by Maslow (1962: 23). Because the family has the greatest influence on its members, growth needs to be fostered within the unit as well as within individuals. In this way individuals can influence the family system and the system can influence individuals—thus reinforcing each other in growth patterns. The cluster group also becomes a system which lends its support to the change-growth process within the family and between family units. The family changes one aspect of itself, receives feedback from the cluster, and moves in the direction of growth important to its members, as well as to the system as a whole. A cycle of intentional growth is started which is the kind of growth needed in a world of rapid social change. Families are encouraged to build on their strengths, dreams, and hopes as springboards to further growth.

A systems approach to growth makes for more potency than an individual approach, as attested by the authors of the book *No Single Thread:*

> the systems approach was more apt to reveal the strengths of a family while the individual, 'composite' approach . . . more often highlighted the family problems [Lewis et al., 1976: 204].

It is as though the exponential influence works for positive growth. Humanistic and transpersonal psychologies contribute knowledge to this area.

The method of achieving growth is that of experiential education in which reflecting on one's experiences becomes the content or "heart" of the learning. The content-subject areas are garnered from families in terms of their hopes, concerns, strengths, problems, interests, and questions. This expression is enhanced through using subjective techniques (e.g., role play, use of clay, relational exercises, puppetry, finger painting, games, and songs). These are not only fun to do but also germane to the expression of family interests.

After participating in an experience designed by the leaders from family needs, the group shares in reflection. Learning comes from reflected experiences rather than didactic content. From this point the families may move into analyzing and discussing the ways in which they hope to transfer their new learnings to the family system at home. With all of the family members participating in the experience, the opportunity for "back-home realization" is greater.

The process of learning experientially is in contrast with learning didactically. Here, one's experiences are the valid content. Everyone has an opportunity to share and to reflect on each other's experiences; thus, everyone has an opportunity to feel important and included and to serve as teacher. Learning is confluent when both cognitive and affectional components are recognized. Douglas Anderson suggests that experiential techniques enable participants to tap into the metaphoric segment of their minds (in the right side of the brain) where images of the world are stored.

> For a person's response to change requires change in that person's world image. Since the world image is a right-brain creation, anyone

seeking to facilitate change must communicate to the person in right-brain language, that is, in metaphoric words . . . a family also has its own unique world images . . . through which it interprets the world and responds to it [Anderson, 1980: 4].

The knowledge for this phase of the philosophy is contributed by learning theory and educational psychology.

The interpretation of these experiences is accomplished through the medium of existential valuing or process theology, whereby lived experiences are interpreted in sacred terms or in "reverential thinking" (Yankelovich, 1981: 89). Since all of life's experiences can have sacred interpretations, every occasion becomes a setting for learning about one's life within the ultimate of a higher being. The area of transpersonal psychology suggests that there is a transcendent power known by varying terms (God, Spirit, Force, Energy) which substantiates each person's existence. Since the emotional cognitive factors of a person's belief system are first formulated within family interactions, it is necessary to work with the family system to develop a faith system of integrity.

Each individual is on his or her own life's pilgrimage and can share that journey with others. A Unitarian minister has been credited with saying, "A little child may not lead you, but it is wise to share your journey with him as he is on a journey too." The basic elements of belief—trust, autonomy, initiative, and integrity—are built out of the psychodynamics of interpersonal relationships which receive their greatest impact from the family. The knowledge for this area comes from process theology and transpersonal psychology.

The following five areas of knowledge contribute to the philosophical foundations of the Family Cluster Model:

(1) Family systems.
(2) Group dynamics.
(3) Growth/change potential.
(4) Experiential learning.
(5) Process theology.

It is the synthesizing experience of these five dynamics that gives the model validity and allows for its replication in diverse settings.

GOALS OF THE FAMILY CLUSTER MODEL

From its inception, basic goals were established as guidelines for the use of the model. The family cluster has been used in churches of all faiths and all sizes in the United States, Canada, Australia, New Zealand, and England, as well as in branches of the military. All in all, its validity has been confirmed as it has been replicated in a variety of locations.

One can study the influence of the model through noting how well its goals are reached in replication. Such has been shown in *Hope For Families* (Sawin, 1983), which includes 15 descriptive case studies of family clusters in diverse settings across the world that show how the goals were met.

These goals may be summarized as follows:

(1) To provide an integenerational group of family units in which children can relate easily to adults and adults to children. By the nature of the family make-up, many families have (at least) two generations within the household. Intentional bonding and mixing between generations is evidenced in early formation of clusters. Children have models from adolescents and from adults, while adolescents have models from various stages of adulthood.

A pilot experience was held in 1980 whereby senior citizens were intentionally incorporated into a family cluster with much success. We have a large number of single and widowed seniors in our country, and some of these could become teachers and learners for the benefit of all in a cluster.

(2) To provide a group which can grow in support and mutuality for its members. One area of sharing which is needed today is life cycle and family cycle sharing. By learning what life is like at various stages, families can see a new way through a "blocked passage." With the absence of the extended family, it is important that other people contribute similar information. In one cluster, a young couple had bought their first house, so the other families helped them to move and then to celebrate the establishment of their first permanent home.

(3) To provide a place where parents gain perspective about their own children through contact with other children and other adults' perceptions of their children. Likewise, children can gain perspective about their own parents through contact with other parents and other children's perception of their parents.

Families often ask, "Are there others like us?" And they are relieved to know that there are! Family life is so privatized in our culture that increasing contact with others must become a priority so that people can share more of their family concerns.

In a family cluster, children observe their parents struggle with their own interaction processes and with the difficulties of change. They become cognizant of differences in behavior as they see parents develop new patterns of relating. At the same time, children can observe other adults working on similar tasks and can note differences among adult styles of parental and family functioning.

(4) To provide an opportunity for families to consider experiences seriously related to themselves as individuals, as family members, and as group members. The opportunity for growth is multiple, so people are able to learn and to grow in a variety of ways. Often this happens during the meal or after the formal session is over, sometimes when the family is driving home in the car.

(5) To provide a group where there is opportunity for families to model for each other aspects of their family systems in communication, decision making, interrelating, problem solving, and so on. There are few places in our culture for complete families to observe other complete families and to discuss what is going on within them. One experience I have had often in a cluster is a one-parent family doing positive modeling for the others. Often the single parent has undergone therapy and is sure of whom he or she is; this carries over to the kind of modeling they can do—with their family and before others. Everyone has an opportunity to model—the complete family may present a skit, participate in a simulated family role-play, or be part of a game. The use of simulated (pretend) families enables children and youth to share their ideas with other persons and learn from them about family living.

(6) To provide a joint interaction between generations where adults can share their concerns regarding the meaning of life's experiences for them during a time of rapid social change and of changes in traditional values; children can deal existentially with their real world experiences, using the group as a place to check out those experiences with its support and in the setting of its value system. One of the most difficult subjects to discuss amicably is that of differing values between generations. Many adults feel isolated or "ganged up on," while adolescents feel that their parents just don't know what it is like to live

in their world of drugs, sex, pregnancies, competition, and so forth. Margaret Mead has commented that "all of us who grew up before World War II are . . . immigrants . . . in a new age" (1970).

In today's pluralistic world, families are thrust into so much change that they may not be aware of how to cope until they reach a crisis or "breaking point." Often they need therapy to help recover from the disaster. The parents generally had no such experience in their families of origin, and the children are caught between adult remembrances of the unrepeatable past and fantasies of the unpredictable future. There is desperate need for a neutral but respected meeting ground where varying values and concerns can be considered and from which intentionalized decisions can be made. Buckland suggests that when all the family members participate together in sharing of values, behavioral change is accelerated in the intended direction (1972: 153).

(7) To help families discover and develop their strengths through increased loving, caring, enjoying, and creating. Highly functional families already have many of these characteristics and can model them for others. Sometimes all a hesitant family needs is permission to try and a safe place in which to experiment in order to appropriate some of the above experiences.

One cluster studied principles of transactional analysis, and several elementary-age children commented in their evaluation that they learned how to give "positive strokes" to family members. It is now widely accepted that most family members have within them the resources they need to accomplish their goals and to make the changes they desire for betterment. What they need is the key to unlock those resources from blocked patterns; often membership in a cluster can provide this.

(8) To provide an opportunity for positive intervention into family systems so as to facilitate their living and growing together more productively. One of the skills taught to advanced family-cluster leaders is how to intervene in a family so as to facilitate productive family living within their system. A growing number of people in family enrichment are claiming that our chief need is to train people to be "family system directors." I foresee training components being built into family life education programs to train "family facilitators" or "family enablers" via the laboratory method.

ADAPTATIONS OF THE
FAMILY CLUSTER MODEL

Because the process mode of learning is based on the needs and wants of the families involved in the cluster, it is an easy model to adapt to any type of situation. This cluster format has been used in many different ways, among them:

Public schools which are interracially and interculturally mixed.

Expressions of holiday celebrations.

Family service and mental health agencies.

Camps and canoe trips.

Drug prevention bureaus.

Branches of the military.

With increased emphasis on the need for social reform, there is renewed interest in utilizing family units to help bring it about. The Family Cluster Model has been used in the Family-Power-Social-Change project of the World Council of Churches. Healthy families have shared their processes of well-being with dysfunctional families, thereby sharing better ways of living within a family system. Since families provide the "yeast" for behavior in societal institutions, it might be wise to strengthen family life in order to strengthen other societal organizations.

CONCLUSION

The impact of a family growth group can be summarized in the following poem:

Family Cluster
Different, Unified
Threatening, Affirming, Creating
Looks to Loving Enablers
Meaningful Happening.

NOTE

1. This statement appeared on the program of the national conference (Milwaukee, October 17-18, 1981) with which this book is associated.

REFERENCES

ANDERSON, D. A. (1980) New Approaches to Family Pastoral Care. Philadelphia: Fortress Press.

BUCKLAND, C. M. (1972) "Toward a theory of parent education: family living centers in the post-industrial society." The Family Coordinator 21 (April) 2.

FARSON, R. et al. (1969) The Future of the Family. New York: Family Service Association of America,

LEWIS, J. M., R. W. BEAVERS, J. T. GOSSETT, and V. A. PHILLIPS (1976) No Single Thread: Sociological Health in Family Systems. New York: Brunner/ Mazel.

MACE, D. (1979) "Marriage and family enrichment—a new field?", The Family Coordinator 28 (July) 3: 409

MASLOW, A. H. (1962) Toward a Psychology of Being. Princeton, NJ: D. Van Nostrand.

MEAD, M. (1970) Culture and Commitment. New York: Natural History Press, Doubleday.

———(1970) "New designs for living." Redbook Magazine, October.

OTTO, H. A. (1971) The Family Cluster: A Multibase Alternative. Beverly Hills, CA: Holistic Press.

SANGREE, L. (1974) "Report and evaluation of the Family Cluster laboratory process." (unpublished)

SAWIN, M. M. (1982) Hope for Families. New York: Sadlier.

———(1979) Family enrichment with Family Clusters. Valley Forge, PA: Judson Press.

———(1969)"A study of Sunday church school teachers' personality characteristics and attitudes toward children." Ph.D. dissertation, University of Maryland.

SPACE, J. (1980) "A review of research on family enrichment program." The Center for the Study of Helping Services, Graduate School of Education and Human Development, University of Rochester, NY. (unpublished)

YANKELOVICH, D. (1981) "New rules in American life: searching for self-fulfillment in a world turned upside down." Psychology Today 15 (April) 4.

Part IV

Special Services to Families

Here we look at some examples of emerging new preventive services to families, particularly in the areas of interpersonal communication and of conflict resolution. We then assess how far the goal of family wellness is being promoted in three vital fields: in the churches, the educational system, and the practice of family therapy.

14

Promoting Effective Communication in Families

Daniel Wackman

Communication is central to all human relationships. This truism is probably the most general statement that has emerged from the last century of work in the social sciences. More specifically, good communication makes it possible to build and sustain relationships, and bad communication results in the destruction of relationships. This principle is particularly applicable in settings involving high degrees of interdependence—physical, social, and emotional—and intimacy: conditions that characterize marriage and family relationships.

Yet knowing that good communication is important doesn't really help very much because human communication is amazingly complex. Nonetheless, work over the last 25 years has unraveled a good deal of this complexity, revealing many facets of communication that characterize both effective, relationship-building patterns of communication as well as destructive patterns. More important, during this same period a variety of approaches and programs have been developed to help people learn more effective ways of communicating.

APPROACHES TO COMMUNICATION TRAINING

The basic approach used for communication training for marriage and family has been the small group program. These programs have been designed for three different subunits of the family—the couple, the family as a whole, and parents.

Marriage Enrichment Programs

Marital communication programs have been offered typically as marriage enrichment programs, designed as educational experiences aimed at helping good marriages become even better. The programs vary along a continuum from highly affective, consciousness-raising experiences to cognitive and behaviorally oriented skill development. The largest marriage enrichment program—Marriage Encounter—is largely a weekend consciousness-raising experience. Although conducted in a group setting, activity is carried out by individual couples apart from the group. The weekend culminates in a religious ceremony where couples have a chance to renew their marriage vows, a highly emotional experience for most couples. Marriage Encounter groups are offered by two separate organizations—National Marriage Encounter and Worldwide Marriage Encounter—and together their programs have reached four or five times as many couples as all other marriage enrichment programs combined, a total of nearly one million couples.

Skill development programs are usually conducted over a several-week period, rather than on a single weekend. Couples participate in four to eight sessions, each lasting two or three hours. The program is spaced out over several weeks to enable couples to practice the skills they are learning between sessions. Couple activities usually occur in the group context, and the group is an important resource for the couple's learning. The largest skill development program is Couple Communication, distributed by Interpersonal Communication Programs, Inc., which has reached over 100,000 couples. The Conjugal Relationship Enhancement Program, developed by Guerney and his associates and distributed by the Institute for the Development of Emotional and Life Skills (IDEALS), is another multisession groups program for teaching skills.

A number of other weekend marriage enrichment programs utilize a dual emphasis on consciousness-raising and skill building. The great majority of the more than 20 programs of this nature have been developed by Protestant denominations and are offered mainly to members of the denomination. The programs reach a relatively small number of couples each year, usually less than 1,000. Programs of this type teaching more than 1,000 couples per year include ACME, Encore (distributed by the Aid Association for Lutherans), and the Seventh Day Adventist program. A list of marriage enrichment programs is included at the end of this chapter.

Although a wide variety of topics with many different labels are taught in these programs, most teach a core set of skills: empathic listening, self-disclosure, recognition and disclosure of feelings, and communication flexibility. Programs typically put primary emphasis on only one or two of these broad communication skills, and often teach very specific behaviors as a way of performing skills (e.g., I-statements, feeling statements, reflecting, check-outs, etc.). Programs also tend to emphasize the learning of ways to communicate in a collaborative way.

Results of research testing the impacts of the various programs indicate the following general patterns: (1) Most programs have a modest positive impact; (2) impacts of skill development programs are somewhat greater than those of consciousness-raising or mixed programs; (3) impacts are strongest on learning of specific communication skills and are less on relationship satisfaction; and (4) behavioral measures show a stronger impact than self-report measures (Giblin, 1982).

Family Enrichment Programs

Family enrichment programs are generally less skill-oriented than marriage enrichment programs. Instead, they typically teach families perspectives for viewing their own family and provide opportunities to experience themselves as a family unit. The Family Cluster Model, most fully developed by Margaret Sawin (1979), brings together four or five families with a leader for an extended period of time for shared educational experiences about a variety of aspects of family life (see Chapter 13 of this volume). Understanding Us, developed by Patrick Carnes (1980), is a somewhat more structured program, utilizing four sessions to bring together eight to twelve families to learn perspectives for viewing their family patterns and to experience these patterns in a series of activities. In both Family Cluster and Understanding Us, all members of the family attend the program.

A more skill-oriented program for families is the Family Relationship Enhancement Program developed by Bernard Guerney and his associates (Vogelsong and Guerney, 1980). The program teaches similar skills to those taught in the Conjugal Relationship Enhancement Program discussed earlier.

These programs have reached far fewer families than the marriage enrichment programs. The programs are much newer, having been developed only in the last few years, but also the logistics of bringing whole families together make recruiting much more difficult than with marriage enrichment programs.

Relatively few impact studies have been conducted of family enrichment programs (Giblin, 1982). However, results of these studies are generally similar to those found in the marriage enrichment studies: a modest positive impact with strongest impacts on specific communication skills and less impact on other measures of family change or satisfaction.

Parent Education Programs

Parent education programs have probably had the greatest reach of these family-oriented communication training programs. The two most widely distributed programs are Dr. Thomas Gordon's Parent Effectiveness Training (PET) program (see chapter 11 of this volume) rooted in the Rogerian tradition (Gordon, 1970), and Systematic Training for Effective Parenting (STEP), an Adlerian program (Dinkmeyer and McKay, 1976). Another program based on Rogerian principles is the Parent-Adolescent Relationship Development (PARD) program, developed by Guerney and associates (Grando and Ginsberg, 1976). All of these programs have a heavy emphasis on listening skills and on helping parents to understand the dynamics of power struggles between themselves and their children.

Studies of the PARD program reviewed by Giblin (1982) show generally positive results. However, in the 12 studies of PET reviewed by Cromwell (1982) most suffered from serious enough methodological inadequacies as to call the whole set of modestly positive findings into question. In the same review, no studies of the impact of STEP could be found. Thus, these two major approaches to parent education have not yet been shown to have any significant impact.

Other small group parent education programs utilize a discussion format (e.g., the Adlerian study group), but as these focus less on communication skill development than on learning about children and changing parental attitudes, they will not be discussed here. Other communication training approaches involving single couples or families or large groups of parents also exist. These will be mentioned as we discuss different forms for delivering communication training.

Other Emphases in Communication Training

Besides the skill development emphasized most heavily in small group programs, several other aspects of communication have been emphasized in communication training in marriage and the family.

ANALYTICAL PERSPECTIVES

Even in the most behaviorally oriented programs, some attempt is made to provide a perspective about how communication works in addition to teaching specific skills. Gaining this new perspective usually occurs in one of two ways.

First, attitudes, motivations, or the "spirit" involved in communication is discussed. Most often, this includes discussion of the attitude toward other people that a participant adopts or expresses in his or her communication. Most programs emphasize an attitude of respecting, caring for, and considering the other person, and show how the communication skills that are being taught express this attitude. Skill training programs also typically emphasize how a selfish or controlling attitude can result in misuse of the skills.

A second form of perspective-giving involves the presentation of models or frameworks to help participants become aware of broader patterns of communication. The purpose of teaching the models or frameworks is not only to help participants be better talkers or listeners but also to help them become better observers of their own and others' interactions. Learning perspectives is seen as particularly important in helping participants identify problem spots in communication and in taking steps to change the interaction when trouble occurs.

CONTENT/TOPIC-FOCUSED DISCUSSIONS

Content/topic-focused discussions identify various topics that are important to discuss in marriage or family life. One approach is to provide a topical list for participants to consider in reviewing different aspects of marital or family relationships (e.g., finances, housing, children, leisure, sex, etc.). In some programs (e.g., PREPARE, ENRICH) members of a couple may complete lengthy questionnaires and then receive a computerized profile of their responses to help them isolate areas for discussion (Olson et al., 1981).

A second approach is to provide a framework concerning significant dimensions of marriage or family functioning. Participants use the framework to identify specific issues or concerns in their own lives that need to be discussed.

Many self-help and on-your-own programs are structured around a series of topics that can be discussed in the home. Small group programs are also sometimes organized around a list of topics and provide participants with an opportunity to discuss them, either as a separate couple or as a family unit, or in a small group with other couples and families. Sometimes coaching is provided by the group leader concerning how to talk about the topic, particularly in those programs where skill training is the primary focus. Topical discussions provide the opportunity to utilize and build upon the skills taught in the program.

SITUATIONAL APPLICATION

This approach typically utilizes less active involvement by participants. It most often occurs in large group settings where a leader lectures about specific communication situations or problems occurring in marriage or family life. Major principles of communication are often presented, followed by advice concerning how to apply the principles in day-to-day family situations. The highly successful Bill Gothard Seminars and Dr. James Dobson's film series *Focus on the Family* are examples of programs using this approach.

The mass media also illustrate this emphasis, particularly women's magazines, newspapers, and books. Readers are given principles and tips for dealing with specific situations or problems in their marriage and family.

The media reach many more people than all of the other approaches combined. For example, there are at least a dozen magazines (with a total readership of more than 80 million people) that emphasize information about the American home and family: *McCall's, The Ladies Home Journal, Women's Day, Family Circle, Family Health, Good Housekeeping,* and the like. These magazines include regular columns about marriage and the family and special featured articles. Daily newspapers publish regular columns of advice regarding specific relationship problems sent in by readers (e.g., Dear Abby, Ann Landers). Increasingly, newspapers are publishing feature articles and even entire sections on the American family. The bulk of the readership of these materials is women.

Although the reach of these media is widespread, the information they present is neither systematic nor comprehensive. Furthermore, the advice that is given seldom occurs in a context conducive to learning. Consequently, the learning that does occur is probably quite transitory and has little longer term impact.

FORMS FOR DELIVERING COMMUNICATION TRAINING

The above review of the four aspects of communication training in marriage and family was intended to highlight the complexity of the basic task involved in improving marriage and family communication. Highlighting these four emphases is important for two reasons:

First, *the various facets of communication speak to the different needs people have* in learning how to communicate better in marriage and family life. People need to learn more than just skills, which are the primary emphasis of most group communication training programs. They also need to learn some perspectives for understanding communication. They need to learn ways of sorting out and dealing with the many topics involved in marriage and family life. And they often need specific advice for dealing with communication situations and problems occurring in their lives.

Second, *the different programming forms used in communication training have different strengths and limitations for learning.* Because of this, no single program or program approach is currently designed to provide training in all facets of communication. Let's discuss the programming forms used in communication training more fully.

The *small group program* discussed earlier is the dominant programming form. In these programs, a limited number of participants (usually 20 or less) meet for a number of sessions with a leader or leaders. Participants typically participate in structured experiences and group discussions. A variant of the small group programs, growing out of therapy experiences, involves one couple or family in a series of structured experiences organized by a leader (L'Abate, 1975, 1977).

Second, the *large group experience* can be used and can include many people (perhaps as many as several thousand) who listen to a lecture given either in person or via film or videotape. Sometimes an opportunity for small group discussion is provided in the context of the lecture series. The Gothard Seminars and Dobson Film Series mentioned earlier are examples of the large group form.

Third, the *in-home experience* involves only a single couple or family following a self-help program in their own home and on their own schedules. Typically materials are used to guide and structure the experience including books or booklets (Patterson and Gullion, 1968; Campbell, 1980) or audiotapes (e.g., Swindoll, 1979; LaHaye, 1980; Miller et al., 1982). A number of games have also been developed to help create structured learning experiences about marriage and family life and some that emphasize aspects of communication in particular (e.g., *Family Contract Game, Generation Gap, The Ungame*).

Finally, *individual experiences* involve only a single person alone, usually in his or her own home. Again self-help books, booklets, or audiotapes can be used to guide the experience, but the most common form of individual experience is simply reading a magazine or newspaper article.

As noted earlier, each of these different delivery forms has particular strengths, and limitations, for effectively distributing different kinds of communication training. For example, small group programs generally focus on the kind of communication training that they are best suited for, namely skill training with a secondary emphasis on perspective/giving and/or content. Large groups can best provide perspective and situational advice. In-home experiences can best provide a context for examining content issues with some potential for providing skill training and perspective if the experience is created in the form of a booklet, book, or audiotape series, or for advice if the experience is created in magazine or newspaper articles.

DEVELOPING EFFECTIVE COMMUNICATION TRAINING PROGRAMMING

Taking both the content and the form into account is essential when thinking about communication training because of people's participation patterns. Participation in a marriage or family program depends to a considerable extent on the issues or problems a couple or family is currently experiencing in their own life. Consequently, different couples or families may seek—or be receptive to—quite different facets of communication training.

Further, participation is influenced by the amount of effort required to participate in the program. In general, people prefer to spend as little effort as possible to receive the benefits of the experience, but they will expend considerable effort if they feel a need for the program. Since there are differences between couples and families in their preferences and situation, they may seek or prefer quite different forms of participation.

Both of these considerations relate to the issue of motivation for learning, which is at the crux of the problem of promoting effective communication in marriage and family life.

Motivational Issues

Most current programming involves having the participant come to the program in a church, school, or some other local setting. This creates a barrier because *many people simply do not want to come to small group experiences.* Additionally, when programs involve several members of a family, it is often the case that one or more members are reluctant participants or, at least, that motivations to participate vary considerably among family members. (This is also true when in-home experiences are provided; family members usually differ considerably in their eagerness to involve themselves.)

Even when all family members are reasonably interested in participating in a program, however, there is a second general motivational issue: *Different family members vary in the extent to which they take seriously what can be learned in the program.*

The fact that participants from the same family—as well as participants from different families—are likely to vary in their willingness to participate at all and in their level of participating during the programming experience has important implications for program development, both regarding the content of the program and its form of delivery.

Programming Content

A major motivation for participation for many couples and families is to be able to spend some time together. Many families simply find it difficult to do this as a couple or family. A marriage or family program can provide a context. This suggests that programs developed for people with this kind of motivation should *provide an enjoyable experience* which does not require excessively hard work. This is especially true when children are involved.

Another significant motivation for participation is that the family is experiencing a change which is creating some stress. Current research on adult and family development identifies a large number of *transitions in normal family development,* transitions that *provide a motivational basis for programming opportunities* (Levinson, 1978; Bardwick, 1979; Campbell, 1980). The engagement period, newlywed phase, birth of the first child, the adolescent stage, and so forth have all provided opportunities for successful specific programming. But additionally, it is possible to incorporate stage-specific issues with more general communication training (skill and perspective learning) to appeal to people with similar concerns and motivations.

The principle that people's interests influence what they learn carries another specific implication regarding programming: Participants should have some choice regarding what they can work on. Even in relatively structured learning experiences, *there should be enough flexibility for participants to have a choice as to what they wish to emphasize* in their own learning. As a corollary to this, since people also vary in their willingness to participate in different activities, programming should include several kinds of experiences (e.g., experiential exercises, group discussions, minilectures, readings, etc.) that provide opportunities for various forms of participation.

These principles apply to both group and in-home experiences, but in-home experiences have a particular difficulty that group experiences do not have—namely, providing feedback to participants. This is an especially difficult problem in programs that try to emphasize skill training where *feedback on performance can be very important.* However, by developing learning aids such as observer sheets, audiotapes, and the like, it is possible to help participants observe and reflect on their own experience and thereby provide feedback to themselves.

Programming Forms

A truism of modern life is that it is very hard to get any two people together for a series of experiences. When you try to get even more together, such as a whole family, it becomes ever more difficult. Thus decisions on the form of the programming experience are even more significant than programming content is in determining the ultimate impact.

The hectic pace of modern life suggests that *programming efforts should extend over a relatively short period of time.* Most successful programs involve only four or five sessions; those that extend much beyond four sessions either get few people signing up initially or have major drop-offs in attendance for later sessions. This pattern is also true for involvement in in-home programs.

In family programs, very few families attend all sessions as an intact group, especially when the family contains adolescents. The structure of programming should make it possible for family members to miss sessions, yet continue to be involved in the program as a whole. Written materials are helpful in this regard as well as some modest supplementary experiences to use at home. Guidance can also be offered to families to help them involve the missing members. At a minimum, *families should be encouraged to use their own creativity in involving all family members in some way,* even those members who never attend a session at all.

Many kinds of communication training can effectively utilize alternative delivery systems. Thus, it is possible to develop programming that will use multiple delivery forms. For example, a program might offer the option of a small group experience or an in-home experience, it might be designed as a one-session program, or, as another option, as a multisession program.

LEADERSHIP TRAINING

A final important issue in developing communication training programs concerns the role of the leader in the experience and the type of training needed for fulfilling this role. Early communication training programs typically involved highly intensive leadership training. Often this training was offered only to professionals who had had years of experience in counseling, group work, and so on. Over time, it became clear that this was a self-defeating strategy because it was very difficult for professionals to make a living by offering communication training for marriage and family.

Fortunately, the general communication skill level of many lay people increased substantially during the 1970s making it possible to shift the leadership base to those lay individuals and couples who had participated in the programs. An added benefit from this was that these lay people brought an excitement and dedication to the programs that professionals often did not have. Yet the intensive training process still continued. A problem now developing is that much of the current leadership training simply replaces the dedicated volunteers who have moved on to other activities.

As new programming develops, it is important to keep this pattern in mind. Two specific considerations are suggested. First, in designing the programming itself, *serious consideration should be given to structuring the program so that the leader's role is less demanding.* This is not meant to suggest that totally leaderless programs are preferable because, in fact, the effectiveness of most small group programs is highly dependent on a person or couple exerting effective leadership. Rather, what is being suggested is that the leader's functions be shifted away from the kinds of activities requiring intense leadership training (e.g., providing process feedback, providing conceptual input, etc.) to those activities requiring less leadership training (e.g., guiding exercises, managing group process, etc.).

Second, careful attention should be paid to developing teaching aids for use in the group such as audiotapes to present conceptual materials, worksheets for guiding observers, and so forth. Additionally, well-designed, easy-to-follow instructor manuals should be developed to increase the training that can be done on a self-study basis.

A CONCLUDING NOTE

Much of what I have said in this chapter is based on my reading of recent trends that have been occurring in the marriage and family movement in the United States. In effect, I am suggesting that continuing these trends in a heightened fashion carries a potential for improving communication in marriage and family life on a broad scale. Yet it is unlikely that any single group or organization will be able to have a major impact by itself because of the staggering complexity of our society.

Consequently, I would urge all who wish to develop communication programming to *think small.* Develop programs with limited objectives designed to appeal to limited segments of society. Above all, keep your expectations limited. From the limited efforts of many people can grow a truly significant national movement. In fact, it is happening right now.

LIST OF ORGANIZATIONS PROVIDING MARRIAGE ENRICHMENT PROGRAMS

ENCORE
Aid Association for Lutherans
Appleton, WI 54919

General Council Assemblies
  of God
1445 Boonville Avenue
Springfield, MO 65802

Association of Couples for
  Marriage Enrichment, Inc.
P.O. Box 10596
Winston-Salem, NC 27108

Christian Church (Disciples
  of Christ)
P.O. Box 1986
Indianapolis, IN 46206

Church of the Brethren
1451 Dundee Avenue
Elgin, IL 60120

Church of God
Board of Christian Education
P.O. Box 2458
Anderson, IN 46011

Ecumenical Family Ministries
8 Cobalt Street
Copper Cliff, Canada

Friends General Conference
1520 Race Street
Philadelphia, PA 19102

Institute for the Development
of Emotional and Life Skills
c/o Prof. Bernard Guerney
College of Human Development
Pennsylvania State University
University Park, PA 16802

International Marriage
Encounter, Inc.
955 Lake Drive
St. Paul, MN 55120

Couple Communication
Interpersonal Communication
Programs, Inc.
1925 Nicollet Avenue
Minneapolis, MN 55403

The Living Center for
Family Enrichment
3515 Broadway, Suite 203
Kansas City, MO 64111

Lutheran Church-Missouri
Synod
3558 S. Jefferson Avenue
St. Louis, MO 63118

Marriage-Family Encounter
Inc.
P.O. Box 20756
Bloomington, MN 55420

National Council of Churches
475 Riverside Drive (Room 711)
New York, NY 10115

National Marriage Encounter
7241 N. Whippoorwill Lane
Peoria, IL 61614

National Presbyterian Mariners
Box 1270
League City, TX 77573

Reformed Church in America
Western Regional Center
Orange City, IA 51041

General Conference of
Seventh-Day Adventists
6840 Eastern Avenue, NW
Washington, D.C. 20012

United Methodist Church
Marriage Enrichment Program
P.O. Box 840
Nashville, TN 37202

Worldwide Marriage Encounter
3711 Long Beach Boulevard,
Suite 204
Long Beach, CA 90807

REFERENCES

BARDWICK, J. (1979) In Transition. New York: Holt, Rinehart, and Winston.
CAMPBELL, S. (1980) The Couple's Journey. San Luis Obispo, CA: Impact
Publishers.
CARNES, P. (1980) Understanding Us. Minneapolis: Interpersonal Communication
Programs.
CROMWELL, R. (1982) "Primary prevention family-focused educational models
and programs: 'a state of the art paper.'" (unpublished)

DINKMEYER, D. and G. D. McKAY (1976) Systematic Training for Effective Parenting: Leader's Manual. Circle Pines, MN: American Guidance Service.

GIBLIN, P. (1982) "Meta-analysis of premarital, marital, and family enrichment research." Ph.D. dissertation, Purdue University.

GORDON, T. (1970) Parent Effectiveness Training. New York: Peter H. Wyden.

GRANDO, R. and B. G. GINSBERG, (1976) "Communication in the father-son relationship: the parent-adolescent relationship development program" The Family Coordinator 4, 24: 465-473.

L'ABATE, L. (1977) Enrichment: Structured Interventions with Couples, Families and Groups. Washington, DC: University Press of America.

———et al. (1975) A Manual: Family Enrichment Programs. Atlanta, GA: Social Research Laboratories.

LaHAYE, T. (1980) The Act of Marriage. Santa Ana, CA: One Way Library.

LEVINSON, D. (1978) The Seasons of a Man's Life. New York: Knopf.

MILLER, S., D. B. WACKMAN, and E. W. NUNNALLY (1982) Communication Skills for Couples. Minneapolis, MN: Interpersonal Communication Programs.

OLSON, D. H., D. G. FOURNIER, and J. M. DRUCKMAN (1981) Prepare/Enrich Counselor's Manual. Minneapolis, MN: Prepare, Inc.

PATTERSON, C. R. and M. E. GULLION (1968) Living with Children: New Methods for Parents and Teachers. Champaign, IL: Research Press.

SAWIN, M. M. (1979) Family Enrichment with Family Clusters. Valley Forge, PA: Judson Press.

SWINDOLL, C. (1979) Strike the Original Match. Portland, OR: Multnomah Press.

VOGELSONG, E. L. and B. G. GUERNEY, Jr. (1980) "Working with parents of disturbed adolescents," in R. R. Abidin (ed.) Parent Education and Intervention Handbook. Springfield, IL: Charles C. Thomas.

15

Training Families to Deal Creatively with Conflict

David R. Mace

The word "conflict" represents something that is usually avoided and feared in family relationships. Our culture has communicated to young people embarking on marriage that they should expect their shared life to be continuously happy and harmonious. Becuase they are "in love," they should automatically be motivated to please each other and to desire to meet each other's wishes. Even if they are sophisticated enough not to buy the "happily-ever-after" myth and are prepared for a few minor disagreements, the idea of confronting each other in open conflict with all the pain and disillusionment that this can bring is abhorrent to them. Of course they are aware that this can and does happen in some marriages, but they believe and hope that it will not happen to *them*. And they are resolved that they must do everything in their power to avoid it because the consequences could be quite disastrous. Even if they have had a few hassles in the course of the courtship, they feel pretty sure that when they really settle down in their own home they should be able to avoid that sort of unpleasantness.

So, when we talk about dealing "creatively" with conflict, most people would interpret this as being able to keep negative feelings toward each other under control, denying them expression, and learning some trick that will make them go away—perhaps never to return. The view widely held is that conflict is something extraneous to the relationship, an unwelcome and hostile interloper like the serpent in the Garden of Eden, that threatens to destroy the peace and harmony of a secluded place.

Though I personally once held these views, I have come to believe that they are simply not in accordance with the facts. I now see conflict as an inevitable concomitant of all close relationships and one that has the potential to make a vital contribution to the well-being of the persons concerned. I would even go so far as to say that apart from what conflict can contribute to the growth of love and intimacy, really satisfying and productive family relationships are unattainable.

That is what I believe. My task, in this chapter, will be to attempt to prove it. The basis of my proof will be partly the fact that it is theoretically convincing, and partly that in my own marriage—and in the relationships of other couples with whom I have been closely involved—I have seen it happen over a long enough period of time to have become convinced. In other words, it makes sense in theory and it works in practice.

HOW A MARRIAGE DEVELOPS

In order to simplify the discussion I will confine myself to *marital* conflict although the same principles apply in other family relationships. In fact, the resolution of conflict in the marriage is generally the key to the wider task of bringing harmony into the family.

We shall imagine a married couple, and for convenience we will call them John and Mary.

It all begins when John and Mary find themselves attracted to each other. This may happen very rapidly (love at first sight) or slowly over time (a friendship that ripens into love). Either way, its immediate or gradual result is that each feels an urge to get close to the other—physically, on the basis of sex attraction, and personally because they find that they are alike in some respects and complementary in others:

Both factors have been recognized as playing a part in the process of mate selection.

What is also true, of course, is that John and Mary are *different* in a number of respects. But that seems not to matter so much at this stage. What motivates them strongly is a feeling of wanting to be together.

At this point I will introduce Diagram 15.1—The Quest for Intimacy—adapted from one I used in an earlier book (Mace and Mace, 1974). The horizontal dimension represents time, and the vertical dimension represents space.

The desire of John and Mary to get close is shown by the arrows pulling them toward each other. Following the first pull of direct attraction, they agree to turn together toward the future in a continuing quest for increasing intimacy represented by the time line above the diagram. This begins in the courtship period, but should also continue into the marriage. The wedding is not shown on the diagram because it can take place at any point in the process; the couple's objective, both before and after the wedding, should remain the same so that the process is continuous. Their goal is the fullest possible intimacy that is consistent with the inviolate preservation of their separate personal identities. Marriage can never be a *union* of two persons although they may have temporary experiences, on both physical and interpersonal levels, in which they feel truly united.

Certain disturbing events occur as John and Mary move together toward increasing intimacy. Each of these events occurs in three stages, which are indicated in the time line below the diagram. Although the sequence is shown only once, it normally recurs again and again in the history of a close relationship.

THE NATURE OF THE CONFLICT

When John and Mary first become interested in each other, their attention is focused on what they have in common or on what is congruent in their relationship. But occasionally they become aware of the less welcome fact that they differ from each other in important respects.

During the courtship period, however, those differences tend to be suppressed. Eager to seem pleasing to each other, the couple conceal or restrain any negative feelings aroused in them. Indeed, in the joyful experience of coming close, at first the differences don't seem to matter very much.

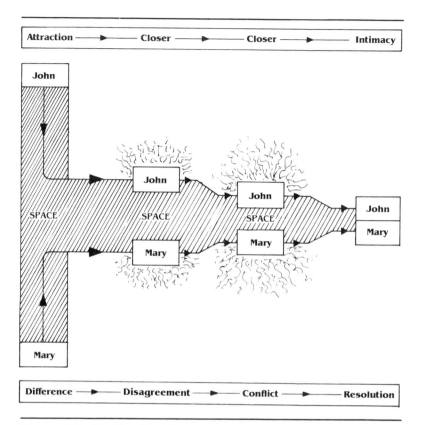

Diagram 15.1 **The Quest for Intimacy**

However, the differences *do* matter. This is particularly true of differences that place them in opposition to each other and, if emphasized, would bring about a clash of wills. It is an inescapable fact that in the relationship of any two persons the number of differences is so great that they could never all be counted or recorded. Some of these potential barriers to closeness will probably never lead to a head-on clash of personalities, but others will threaten this sooner or later and will have to be dealt with in one way or another.

What brings on such a clash is shown in the diagram. As John and Mary move closer into each other's lives, their individual living space is inevitably reduced. Of course that is what they are deliberately seeking. But what they may not realize is that when two people (however loving they may be) get crowded together in a diminishing amount of space, they inevitably begin to get in each other's way and to frustrate some of each other's wishes.

We can express this by saying that some of the differences between them surface and turn into *disagreements.* It is obviously impossible for any two people to want always to do the same thing in the same way at the same time. So, however tolerant they may strive to be, a point will come at which their closeness will become an irritant. And that is precisely the point at which conflict begins to appear.

We see, therefore, three successive stages. First, as their living space is deliberately reduced, difference between John and Mary develops into disagreement. Then, as disagreement continues and increases, we see it develop into conflict.

So, what exactly *is* conflict? The answer is very simple. Conflict is *disagreement heated up* by strong, negative emotion—and the name of the emotion is *anger.*

WHAT IS ANGER?

Like conflict, the word "anger" has come to have a bad reputation. It is commonly seen as a threatening, dangerous emotion that easily gets out of control. Some religious people even view it as a sinful condition which nice people should not experience. Or, if it *does* occur, it should be suppressed and not acknowledged.

This is an unfortunate misconception. Anger is not to be confused with rage and fury although the one can—and often does—lead to the other. The word anger, however, comes from the same root as the German word *"angst"* or our own word "anxiety." It means an experience of grief or pain—essentially a *hurt feeling.*

I would define anger as the first outpost of the defense system of the ego. Most of us wish to get along smoothly and comfortably with the other people in our lives if possible and that is what we try to do most of the time. However, inevitably there are occasions when this becomes impossible. Another person invades your privacy, lets you down, puts you down, exploits your trust, or disappoints your hopes. Then your ego suffers a sense of threat and you withdraw from the relationship and go on to the defensive. We all know that first pang of anger, the awareness that the situation has taken a turn that makes us feel threatened or displeased.

The onset of anger has to be immediate. Physiologically, it is the production of a surge of energy, in response to a danger signal. Strictly speaking, the anger is there before you have any control over it. But once you are aware of it, you have the power and the right to decide how to respond.

Anger need not, therefore, develop into an aggressive response. In fact, many of us learn to suppress it. Sometimes that is appropriate in that it is the best way of handling the situation. But if your relationship with the other person is one you want to develop positively, neither aggressive attack nor silent withdrawal will achieve your goal.

Anger may develop just as readily against your best friend as against your worst enemy. The desirable way to deal with it, however, differs fundamentally in these two situations. In the case of the enemy, your objective would probably be to drive him or her away. In the case of your friend, your desire is to bring him or her back to closeness.

In the relationship of John and Mary, therefore, we have two emotions operating. The one that is drawing them together as trust between them develops over time is usually called *love.* The one that tends to interrupt the process by pushing them apart is *anger.* Of course their desire for intimacy can easily persuade John and Mary that love is a good emotion and that when a contrary force interferes and pushes them apart this must be by contrast a bad emotion. But this is not really true.

Their anger, in fact, is protecting them from undesirable results that could follow if love alone could exercise its full force in drawing them together. This could lead to suffocating closeness of unhealthy interdependence that could be damaging to their separateness, which is vital for the preservation of the individual personhood of each. The exact degree to which John and Mary can effectively tolerate intimacy may not be the same as for other couples and may indeed change over time for them. The balance between separateness and togetherness is never constant—it fluctuates continuously.

What is important, however, is that this balance should be maintained. Only then can the relationship reach its maximum level of mutual fulfillment. And the mechanism for fine-tuning that vital balance is the interaction between love and anger. Far from being opponents, if given the chance, these two important emotions will cooperate as colleagues in enhancing the relationship.

OUR NEW UNDERSTANDING
OF RELATIONSHIPS

Once these basic facts are clearly grasped, the task before John and Mary is to work toward the achievement of this healthy balance. Unfortunately, this is not an easy task. During most of human history it has been considered impossible. Consequently, almost all our social and interpersonal systems have been structured on a vertical basis with one person in a position of authority and able to use power and the other person kept in a position of subservience by fear of the other's power. Until the advent of democracy, this was considered to be the only manageable way of structuring all human relationships—including marriage and the family.

Today, however, we are making new ventures in the development of horizontal relationships that, with due safeguards, can allow the persons involved a high degree of individual freedom while still maintaining the intimate relationship. Indeed, we are realizing today that this could open up the way to the achievement of productive close relationships on a scale hitherto unknown.

The relevance of this for family wellness will be obvious. However, there is little evidence as yet of any widespread readiness to take seriously the new insights that are being tested out in the field of marriage and family enrichment.

It was estimated by Lederer and Jackson (1963) that not more than 5-10 percent of marriages today are achieving their true potential. I would agree with this figure. And I have come to the conclusion that the quality of any marriage is largely determined by the "coping system" which the couple use in developing their relationship (see Chapter 8 of this volume). As has already been indicated, an effective coping system consists of three essential components:

(1) a clear commitment by both partners to the ongoing growth of the relationship;
(2) an open and effective communication system;
(3) the ability to use conflict creativity.

Given such a "coping system," the chances that most marriages could turn out to be satisfying to the couple should be very good; and lacking such a coping system, the chances of success would be equally poor. I recognize, of course, that for a marriage to be "successful" or "satisfying" would require that the expectations of the couple be in reasonable accordance with attainable reality.

LEARNING TO USE CONFLICT CREATIVELY

My remaining task is to indicate specifically how, in practical terms, John and Mary can take advantage of these new insights. In doing this, I will rely heavily on personal experience—my own and that of others who have shared their experiences with me.

The first step is, of course, for the couple to make the necessary commitment to growth with each other. The best way for them to do this is to participate in a marriage enrichment experience—a retreat or growth group. The value of this has been demonstrated again and again. The chances that any couple will make this kind of commitment to each other privately with a really firm intention to carry it out seem to be quite poor. While the self-help principle is impressive in theory, it fails dismally in practice. On the other hand, a situation in which a group of couples make this commitment *together* seems to be much more effective. The intention becomes far stronger when it has been shared with others—particularly others who have registered a similar intention.

However, we are not justified in assuming that participation in a marriage enrichment retreat will be sufficient for most couples. I am now convinced that what happens in such an event is only an *attitudinal* change, and that it is not likely to be sustained unless it is translated over time to *behavioral* change. Moreover, in this period of transition John and Mary will need the support of other couples just as much as they needed it at the earlier stage of attitudinal change. I would say that, to consolidate the growth process, continuing in a support group for at least a year would be highly desirable.

Following the commitment, the process of change will require that John and Mary develop and maintain the ability to *communicate* openly and honestly with each other. We have learned a great deal about communication in families in the last decade, and training courses for communication are now available in most parts of the country. Since this subject has been covered in the preceding chapter, I need say no more. I would add, however, that I doubt whether full use can be made of the newly available skills unless they are exercised on a daily basis. Specifically, I mean that John and Mary should make time for what I call daily "sharing time"—an occasion when husband and wife can spend at least 20 minutes opening up to each other their inner thoughts, feelings, and intentions. This need not be done elaborately. Basically, it is a process of "checking out" so that each knows where the other is. This has the very beneficial result of making sure that any confusion or misunderstanding that develops in the relationship cannot go unreported for a longer period than 24 hours.

The second important requirement for the "intentional marriage" (as we call it) is that any issue that threatens to be damaging to the relationship should be faced and cleared without delay. This applies particularly to the emergence of a conflict or, better still, to a disagreement that has not yet had a chance to grow into a conflict.

The slogan for John and Mary should be "Nothing on the back burner." Unresolved conflicts in close relationships can expand and gather to themselves a complex network of misunderstanding, of alienation, of inaccurate conclusions, and of unjust judgments. The sensible way to deal with such an emerging situation is to treat it as a crisis, which it is, and to clear the necessary time to work it through. I know well that this is hard for people with busy schedules, but I am convinced that to *make* time to clear up a relational crisis is to *save* time in the end.

THE PROCESS OF NEGOTIATION

Dealing with conflict, when John and Mary sit down together, confronts them with the task of *negotiation*—a process in which ideally *every* couple should receive training. Let me briefly summarize how this is done.

If indeed a conflict has developed, then the anger must be processed first because in a state of anger there can be no effective negotiation. I would recommend any couple, in order to have a workable plan for dealing with anger, to make three contracts with each other:

(1) "I recognize that you will get angry with me from time to time, and it's okay for you to do so. But I want your assurance that when this happens you will *tell me about your anger* before you take any action."

(2) "When you are angry with me, I ask you to pledge that *you will not attack me.* If you do, that is likely to put me on the defensive, and I too will then become angry. We just can't afford to be both angry with each other at once."

(3) "When either of us is angry with the other and tells the other about it without attacking, we will both pledge to make time as soon as possible to sit down together and get behind the anger to the hurt feelings that have caused it. If it is too hot to handle at first, we will disengage and cool down before we begin to process it."

Once the cause of the anger is clearly understood by both partners, the underlying disagreement can be examined and resolved by *negotiation.* In any such exchange, three options are possible:

(1) Either John or Mary can go over to the side of the other and give up his or her earlier stance as a loving act of *capitulation.* To capitulate voluntarily as a gift of love is quite different from forced capitulation under coercion.

(2) They can try to find a meeting point where a *compromise* can be reached, each yielding some ground to accommodate the other. This is the age-old process of bargaining.

(3) They may have to settle for *coexistence,* an agreement to differ for the time being until there can be some change in the total situation. This can be done without bitterness if it is agreed that they will go on seeking an acceptable solution. Coexistence *must* be a possible option—otherwise the temptation to use power to "get it settled" becomes very strong. The use of power in a love relationship is always damaging, and the continuing use of power is always destructive.

The procedures I have explained can be learned by any couple willing to put in the necessary time and effort. Properly applied, those skills should enable John and Mary to use each conflict that develops between them as a means of growth for their relationship. There are plenty of enlightened couples who are now doing this and reaping the rewards in richly satisfying marriages. And the same procedures can be effectively applied to other relationships within the family. The procedures explained briefly in this chapter are presented in much more detail in the book listed in the reference list.

What if all these preventive resources, conscientiously learned and applied, fail to work? In that event, John and Mary should make an appointment without delay to secure the help of a qualified marriage counselor—just as they would call a doctor in the case of physicial symptoms that failed to yield to all available home remedies. Most communities today have competent marital therapists. Like physicians, they can do much more for you if you seek their help before your illness becomes chronic.

CONCLUSION

Sooner or later, I am convinced, we shall acknowledge the fact that all of us need to be trained for marriage and family living, just as we need to be trained for a career. We now know how to do this. I believe the right time is during the first year following the wedding, the period during which the complex interaction patterns between John and Mary are developed, for good or for ill. Not all marriages can expect to be successful in terms of today's high expectations, but with effective training I am convinced that the number of well families in our communities could be dramatically increased.

REFERENCES

LEDERER, W. J., and D. D. JACKSON (1968) The Mirages of Marriage. New York: Norton.
MACE, D.(1982) Love and Anger in Marriage. Grand Rapids, MI: Zondervan.
———(1977) How to Have a Happy Marriage. Nashville: Abingdon.
———(1974) We Can Have Better Marriages. Nashville: Abingdon.

16

Promoting Family Wellness Through the Churches

Leon Smith

The churches are well suited, both philosophically and programmatically, to work for family wellness. That is the thesis of this chapter, although some very critical questions surrounding this position remain to be answered.

In this chapter I use the "ideal" approach, emphasizing the churches' potentials for effective family ministry. It is my conviction that the true nature of any social institution lies in its highest possibilities. At the same time, I believe we must be realistic about the churches' shortcomings, and even about their detrimental influences on families.

Here, "the churches" means the mainline Protestant denominations, for these are the religious groups I know best. After nearly 20 years as a pastor in local churches in Georgia and New Jersey, I became in 1962 Director of Marriage and Family Ministry for the United Methodist Church in the United States, and served in that position for a further 20 years. I have also been active in the Commission on Family Ministries and Human Sexuality of the National

Council of Churches of Christ. In this latter group, I have worked closely with colleagues in the field of marriage and family life in the major denominations. To them I am greatly indebted for many insights and proposals in this chapter although I alone am responsible for the way in which they are stated here.

Obviously I cannot speak with any kind of authority for other religious groups. I have, of course, enjoyed the fellowship of professional colleagues whose affiliation was to Catholic, Jewish, Mormon, or other religious faiths. I have learned from them and from what I know of their activities on behalf of family life that there is every reason to believe that they also would give strong support to the movement to promote family wellness. Obviously, however, I have no right to speak for them on questions affecting policy, and I shall not attempt to do so.

THE FAMILY IS IMPORTANT

Effective family ministry begins with the churches' conviction that families are important. First, *the family is important to its own members*—providing food, shelter, clothing, and so on for their basic physical needs, and even more so as it helps to meet their individual and affectional needs as children, youth, and adults.

Second, *the family is important to society* as it is the primary unit of our social structure and performs certain essential functions for the society's general welfare: producing children and caring for them; helping children to mature as responsible members of society; providing for the needs of adults as persons in relationships; and feeding into the culture certain values that both undergird stability and stimulate creative change.

Third, *the family is important to God.* It is the basic structure of human relationships, providing community for individuality and given by God in creation for the welfare of all humankind. It is a channel for God's unconditional love (as fully as human beings can express it)— affirming, sustaining, sacrificing, forgiving, and redeeming—as an opportunity for the Kingdom of God to come on earth within families and in society.

FAMILY MINISTRY IS
UNIQUE AND COMPREHENSIVE

Family ministry is unique because of its focus. It is different from ministries to children, youth, or adults as individuals, important as these are. The focus of family ministry is on *families:* (1) on persons as family members; (2) on families as social units; (3) on environmental forces affecting families; and (4) on the potentialities of families. Let us consider these in more detail.

(1) *Family ministry focuses on persons as family members* with family concerns, not mainly on men and women as individuals but rather as husbands and wives or as fathers and mothers and as grandfathers and grandmothers. The focus is not primarily on boys and girls as individuals, but on boys and girls as daughters and sons, as brothers and sisters, as granddaughters and grandsons. It is not on youth as persons with all their concerns for growth, but on young people as family members in learning to affirm their sexuality, in moving out of their families, and in preparing for marriage, to name only a few. Again, it is not on young adults as single persons living alone or with others but as they relate to their families of origin or to the establishment of their own families.

(2) *Family ministry focuses on families as units.* Its main concern is with the immediate family as a small group of two or more persons related by marriage, birth, or adoption, usually bearing a common name and sharing one household, and living together in the intimate role-relationships of husband or wife, father or mother, daughter or son, and brother or sister. The family is a basic unit of society performing certain functions as a social institution—sustaining, creating, and transmitting a particular culture unique to itself and common to its own members.

The focus is on all kinds of families: husband-wife families with or without children, mother-child or father-child families with only one parent at home, sibling families living alone, three-generation families, larger families with aunts or uncles, or nieces or nephews or cousins; affluent families, deprived families; suburban or inner-city families; white, black, red, yellow, or brown families—all the varieties of families you can think of!

The focus on families as units is on families at all the eight stages of the family life cycle: (1) beginning families, (2) childbearing families, (3) families with younger children, (4) with elementary school children, (5) with teenagers, (6) families in the launching stage, (7) in the middle years, (8) aging families.

(3) Family ministry is concerned with the *environmental forces affecting families.* These are influences from outside the home that impact families for good or ill: cultural factors such as the moral climate of the community, racial attitudes, urbanization, depersonalizing influences of technology; social and environmental conditions—inflation, unemployment, housing, pollution, population policies; specific forces and events—television and other mass media, movies, magazines, war or peace; and the social structure—business, government, education, health services, as well as religion itself.

(4) The focus is also on *the potentialities of families:* not only on their problems but also on their possibilities, and not only on the family as an *object* of the church's concern but also as an *agent* of the church's ministries. Family ministry is not only the ministry of the church *to* families—to help them bring the gospel to bear on the issues and on the forces with which they struggle and on the developmental tasks they face at all stages of the family life cycle—but also the ministry of families *to their own members*—to help one another within the family in every area of life, and especially to improve Christian nurturing in the home throughout the lifespan of all family members. It includes also the ministry of families *through the church*—to identify themselves as children of God and members of the Christian community, and to join in meaningful participation in the life of the congregation and other expressions of the church. It is also the ministry of families *in the world*—to fulfill their mission by witnessing and serving in the community, state, and nation.

Admittedly, this four-fold focus of family ministry is overwhelming! But that is how important family ministry is, how all-encompassing family issues are, and how urgent it is for churches to give it a high priority. The churches need such a comprehensive view of family ministry to give perspective and structure to particular programs that are developed within this framework in response to emerging needs.

FAMILY MINISTRY AND FAMILY WELLNESS

The churches are in a good position to work for family wellness because of their purpose in family ministry: to help families in both church and community to realize the fullness of Christian family life throughout the life cycle.

Here we center on the immediate family as defined by most social scientists, the kind of family in which almost 90 percent of all children grow up today. The immediate family generally has six characteristics: (1) It consists of a small group of two or more people; (2) they are related by blood, marriage, or adoption; (3) they usually bear a common name and live in one household; (4) they live and share together in certain kinds of intimate role-relationships as husband or wife, father or mother, daughter or son, brother or sister; (5) it comprises a unit of society and performs certain functions as a social institution; (6) it sustains, creates, and transmits a culture unique to itself and common to its members.

This definition distinguishes the immediate family from alternative family forms. Since the latter are not families in the strict sense, it is more accurate to call these alternative forms "familial groupings." they are familial because they are family-like in that they provide living arrangements in which members seek to meet their family needs.

What is urgently needed today is that church leaders do not condemn and ostracize persons in alternative lifestyles, but instead make a serious effort to understand what they are rejecting in traditional families and to discover what they are seeking in their alternative forms so that effective family ministries may be developed to meet their needs as well.

Based on the above definition, Christian families have the following distinctive characteristics: (1) Their Christian family is made up of persons who respond in faith and love to God as revealed in Jesus Christ; (2) these family members are faithful in performing their various family functions, especially those involving the Christian meaning of marriage as a covenantal relationship and parenthood as a vocation; (3) because of their faith in Jesus Christ, family members share the common name "Christian" and are an integral part of the

Christian community, the "household of faith"; (4) the Christian sees God at work in the interpersonal relationships of the family, offering the kind of understanding and love that creates unity and providing constructive ways of dealing with difficulties; (5) as belonging to a unit of society, members of a Christian family seek to fulfill their common discipleship by doing God's work in the world today; (6) finally, the Christian family sustains, creates, and transmits a culture informed by Christian values and tradition.

THEOLOGY OF MARRIAGE AND FAMILY

A further indication that the churches are suited for family wellness lies in their philosophical position. Although further work is needed, biblical and theological statements provide a strong base for family wellness. Many scripture passages can be quoted to emphasize the value placed on wellness. Perhaps chief among these are the words of Jesus: "I came that they might have life, and have it abundantly" (John 10:10, RSV).

Other references relate to the healing ministry of Jesus such as the woman who said, "If I touch even his garment, I shall be made well" (Mark 5:25-34 RSV). The theological concept of salvation is interpreted as wholeness of life, as being saved from sin, decay, and death, to forgiveness, health, and life, both now and in the hereafter.

Based on the above positions, most churches have official statements affirming the value of family life. An example is the United Methodist statement which reads:

"We believe the family to be the basic human community through which persons are nurtured and sustained in mutual love, responsibility, respect, and fidelity. We understand the family as encompassing a wider range of options than that of the two-generational unit of parents and children (the nuclear family); including the extended family, families with adopted children, single parents with children, couples without children. We affirm shared responsibility for parenting by men and women and encourage social, economic, and religious efforts to maintain and strengthen relationships within families in order that every member may be assisted toward complete personhood."

Note also the paragraph on marriage:

"We affirm the sanctity of the marriage convenant which is expressed in love, mutual support, personal commitment, and shared fidelity between a man and a woman. We believe that God's blessing rests on such a marriage, whether or not there are children of the union. We reject social norms that assume different standards for women than for men in marriage." [The Book of Discipline of the United Methodist Church, 1980: 89].

In addition to biblical references and official statements, today we very much need a theology of marriage and family to give motivation and direction to family ministry. Although professional theologians carry a major responsibility for this task, each person is responsible for doing his or her own interpreting.

A COMPREHENSIVE PROGRAM WITH SPECIFIC TARGETS

The churches are well suited to develop family wellness also because of programming possibilities as they focus on persons as family members and on families as units. As noted above, most churches are concerned about all kinds of families and all areas of family life—not just the "spiritual," as some might think. Further, most people expect their church to provide help with family life at all of the three levels of prevention. In fact, more people seeking help turn to a clergy person than to anyone else.

However, the churches need to translate their concerns into ministries so as to meet the expectations of their members. What is required is a comprehensive program with specific targets (Smith, 1975: chap. 5).

One approach is to develop ministries around certain family concerns, such as Communication in the Family, the Meaning of Sexuality across the Lifespan, Human Growth and Self-Esteem, Preparing for Marriage, Marriage Enrichment, Parenthood, Moral and Spiritual Values in Christian Nurture and Decision Making.

Another and more comprehensive approach is to define developmental tasks throughout the family life cycle. At each stage of the family cycle 10 developmental tasks may be identified and approached in the light of the Christian faith:

(1) Religion: Developing and sustaining a Christian way of life in the family, including religious rituals, the family's participation in the life and work of the church, Christian nurture, and family worship.

(2) Physical Maintenance: Providing the necessities of food, clothing, shelter, medical care, transportation, and so forth.

(3) Money: Earning and spending the family income, and management and use of possessions and resources in a world of scarcity.

(4) Management: Governing and managing the family—authority, responsibilities, and accountability.

(5) Communication: Establishing and maintaining creative systems of intellectual and emotional communication—verbal and nonverbal— and handling differences and conflict.

(6) Personal Needs: Meeting the needs of individuals (children, youth, adults, and the aging) for socialization, affection, and companionship, including satisfying sexual relations of husband and wife.

(7) Children: Deciding whether to have children, planning for them, rearing and launching them, and establishing relations with them as adults.

(8) Relatives: Adjusting to each other in the larger family including in-laws and establishing one's own independence.

(9) Friends: Creating and sustaining friendships, including business associates and children's friends.

(10) Community: Participating in various community activities, organizations, and movements, and facing the community's influence on the family and family members as well as the family's responsibility to society.

One advantage of following the family life cycle approach in planning family ministries is that the stages correlate closely with the age groupings of the church school. This correlation has positive implications for planning, promotion, and follow-up of specific programs. Another advantage is that families in a particular stage may be served at a given time. A guideline to follow is to discover the needs of families and to plan ministries in response to those needs. Another is to center on only one stage of the family cycle at a time. The more specific the program, the more helpful it is likely to be.

However, some criticisms of family programs in the churches have suggested that more should be done to provide opportunities for whole families to be *together* in religious activities. Indeed, there is growing interest in intergenerational programs of all kinds. Nevertheless, as a matter of convenience for teaching and other purposes, families are often fragmented—children are separated from their parents, husbands from wives, young children from teenagers, grandparents from grandchildren. Often the family members are not together even in public worship. The emphasis made by Dr. Margaret Sawin in the Family Cluster movement which brings all family members together as one unit, is greatly needed (see Chapter 13 of this volume). It is sad indeed for a church to offer no ministry to united families other than an occasional family night supper.

HEALTHY FAMILY FUNCTIONING

Family wellness as primary prevention is described in detail elsewhere in this book. Nevertheless, I want to emphasize some aspects of healthy family functioning that I see as being of special concern to churches that follow the developmental approach to families as units.

Families function well (1) when the instrumental needs are met, such as the basic needs for food, shelter, clothing and health care; (2) when the expressive needs of all family members are met by each member being supported in developing a healthy sense of self-esteem and full development as a person-in-relationship who is contributing to social well-being; (3) when the family has a sense of solidarity and the experience of working together as a unit; (4) when the unit, as well as individual members, contributes to the general welfare of society.

The family is not an end in itself, but it fulfills some unique purposes in meeting the needs of persons and in serving society. Churches must not make an idol of families. At the same time, they need to be careful not to exploit families in order to meet their own institutional needs. Most of the churches, it seems to me, have given so much emphasis to the expressive needs of family members that they have neglected the instrumental needs. Except for a few cases (mostly in mission work) they have taken these basic needs for granted. And not being alert to these needs *in the light of the Christian faith* has sometimes had the effect of leaving families to follow the cultural norms such as "get all you can," and to indulge in conspicuous consumption. The struggles brought on by inflation, unemployment, and recession in a world of hunger and scarcity may force churches to rethink this vital area of family ministry.

At the same time churches must continue to help families meet their expressive needs; especially to develop those inner resources—knowledge, skills, attitudes—that contribute to interpersonal competence. Churches are concerned to help families learn and use the family processes that are necessary for good family functioning. Among these are open communication in sharing, listening, and responding; skills in acknowledging, expressing, and constructively using negative feelings such as guilt and anger; shared decision making that appreciates each person's worth and contribution to the process; affirmation and celebration of each member, and of the family as a unit; and having fun together.

MINISTRIES IN MARRIAGE

In their family ministries most churches have put so much emphasis on the parent-child relationship that they have neglected the husband-wife relationship. We need to reaffirm this as the primary family relationship. For the quality of the marriage (or the lack of it) provides the environment—the atmosphere or climate—of the entire family. Recognizing marriage as the foundation of the family calls for a reordering of our priorities in family ministry. This does not mean neglecting parent education, but it does mean putting a major emphasis on marriage—on preparing for marriage as well as on marriage enrichment and marriage counseling.

What our churches need and are in a good position to develop is *a full marriage program.* This needs to begin in early childhood, helping each child to have a sense of self-worth and of being proud to be a boy or a girl, affirming the body as a good gift of God. It needs to move through all stages of boy-girl relations and include a thorough program of marriage preparation as part of a comprehensive marriage ministry throughout the family life cycle (Smith and Smith, 1982).

Couples should be encouraged to see their pastor as soon as they are engaged, either formally or informally. They can be invited to join a *marriage preparation group* such as a premarital communication lab. Or they may become a part of a couples' sharing group in which two or three couples about to be married meet with an equal number of married couples for two or three evenings. Couples can be invited to read and discuss some good books on marriage from the church library or from the pastor. The pastor may require several *premarital counseling sessions,* perhaps two with the couple together and one or more with each privately. The pastor can conduct the rehearsal so as to prepare for the wedding as a celebration in worship and commitment. Many pastors encourage a final "postwedding" interview from one to six months after the wedding. Couples may be expected to take part in a *marital growth group* about a year after marriage or a weekend retreat followed by a marital support group. Programs of this kind are described in earlier chapters of this book, so they need not be further elaborated here.

AFFIRMING ONE'S BODY AND ONE'S SEXUALITY

Another necessary element of family wellness is the affirmation of one's body and one's sexuality as "a good gift of God," accepted and enjoyed responsibly, not rejected or abused. Some churches say that they

"believe persons can be fully human only when that gift is acknowledged and affirmed by themselves, the Church, and society. We call all persons to disciplines that lead to the fulfillment of themselves, others, and society in the stewardship of this gift. Medical, theological, and humanistic disciplines should combine in a determined effort to understand human sexuality more completely."[2]

Education in sexuality is a joint task of church, home, and school. In each setting, sex education is best done in the context of family life. Churches have an opportunity to assist parents in being the best possible sex educators with their own children.

SUGGESTIONS FOR IMPLEMENTATION

Pastors and other professional church leaders need to be helped to understand the value of families and the importance of family ministry, so that they are emotionally committed and highly motivated to work for family wellness. The place to begin is with one's own marriage and family life (when the person is married).

These church leaders also need professional training in family life. This training can equip them to be effective "family ministers" in the regular work of the church, using such varied occasions as membership training or funerals as family ministries as well as in special services to families such as marriage enrichment or counseling.

Churches need to make optimum use of their members in family ministry. These efforts include involving family members in assessing their own needs and in developing ministries to meet those needs as well as in finding ways to make full use of professionals and other trained persons in family ministry.

Programs can be developed to facilitate families helping families directly. This helping may be in meeting the instrumental needs as well as the expressive needs of families—from swapping skills in home repairs to family clustering.

Churches can help families evaluate their lifestyles and assess their impact on the community. Families need to become aware of the implications of their lifestyle for community values and resources. This may be as important and pervasive as the kind of food we eat, the fuel we use, or what we invest in a wedding or a funeral.

Families may be challenged to get involved in programs of peace and justice in the community, the nation, and the world. Family wellness necessitates moving beyond one's own family to concern for others and for systems and structures as well as for individuals and groups of people.

Local churches need to cooperate with other religious groups and family serving agencies in the community in developing those programs that can be done best through ecumenical approaches such as in helping couples prepare for marriage or in providing training for marriage and family enrichment leaders. Even though local churches are likely to be the units that develop family ministries, these churches need the help of highly trained family professionals and well-developed family life resources from the denominational level.

Throughout the nation there is increasing concern for the quality of family life. In most of the churches there is a rising interest in giving a high priority to family ministries. More and more church leaders are speaking up for families, yet most of the churches are not supporting their words with actions. In fact, with the present economic pressures, many churches are cutting back on staff and resources for marriage and family life. The most critical question of all is whether the churches are willing to make the commitments of time and resources to translate into reality such ideals of family ministry as I have tried to describe in this chapter.

NOTES

1. This section and much of this chapter is adapted with permission from *Family Ministry: An Educational Resource for the Local Church* by Smith (1975).

2. From *The Book of Discipline of the United Methodist Church* (1980: 90). One of the best books on this subject is James Nelson's *Embodiment* (1978).

REFERENCES

McGINNIS, T. C. (1976) Open Family Living: A New Approach for Enriching Your Life Together. New York: Doubleday.

NELSON, J. (1978) Embodiment. Augsburg.

SMITH, L. (1975) Family Ministry: An Educational Resource for the Local Church. Nashville: Discipleship Resources.

———and A. SMITH (1982) Preparing for Christian Marriage: Pastor's Manual. Nashville: Abingdon.

The United Methodist Church (1980) The Book of Discipline of the United Methodist Church.

17

Promoting Family Wellness Through the Educational System

Bernard Guerney, Jr.
Louise F. Guerney
Janet M. Sebes

It was a very warm and hazy day. The soft buzzing of a honey bee was cadenced like a lullaby. The boy's chin fell slowly from against the tree onto his chest, and his drooping eyes fell fully shut. The book which had been propped on his upraised knees—Hugh Lofting's *Voyages of Dr. Dolittle*—slid down on his thighs and a few pages flipped over, driven by the gentle breeze. The buzzing lullaby grew louder, its rhythm became more irregular, its sounds more distinct. It then became clear to the motionless boy that the bee was not humming but in a strange rhythmical way was actually *talking*. As he became used to the strange rhythm, and after he realized that most of the "z-z" sounds should be taken as "s" sounds, the boy found he could understand everything the bee was saying! But he didn't much like what he heard:

"You laz-zy good-for-nothing boy, waz-zting z-zuch a beautiful z-zummer day!"

"Forgive me, Mr. Bee," he said, "but don't you think you're being— sorry, no pun intended in that—rather harsh in judging me lazy so quickly. After all, we've only just met. In fact, we haven't really met at all—my name is Billy, and yours is . . . ?"

"Mr. Bee will do juz-zt fine. I don't have time to waz-zte on formalitiez-z. I've got all z-zortz-z of work to do today. In fact, I don't know why I'm taking the time to talk to you. Except that I z-zaw you reading Dr. Dolittle and I met him once. I was very imprez-zed. In fact, it was from him that I learned that people read and write. Bez-zidez-z, you're z-zitting practically on top of the flower from which I had come to get nectar."

"Well," said Billy, "Dr. Dolittle is my favorite fictional character, and I'm honored to meet a friend of his. Would you tell me now, why do you say I'm lazy? Don't you think it's okay for a boy my age—I'm not even in my teens—to spend some time relaxing, enjoying nature, and reading a good book? Don't you do such things?"

"I don't *enjoy* nature," said the bee, "I *am* nature. And it's not natural to read. But itz-z all very well, I'd z-zay, for you to read a book if that's what gives you a buzz, but you should read late in the evening or on a Z-zunday. Now it'z-z the middle of the day, in the middle of the week. You should be doing az-z I'm doing—or waz-z doing 'til you got in my way. You should be out working, helping your mother and father earn a living. In a beez-z lifez-zpan, I'm far younger than you are; z-zo I don't z-zee that being a young boy haz-z anything to do with it."

"Oh," said Billy, "I think I understand why you feel as you do. As you said, you *are* nature. So work comes to you naturally. You know how to work without having to be taught. I guess this will seem very, very strange to you, but I *don't know* how to help my family earn a living. To prepare for the kind of work grown-ups do in my world, I have to go to a place—it's called a school—for many, many years to learn all kinds of things—especially reading, writing, and arithmetic— in order to do the kind of work that will earn a proper living. By the time I learn all I should know, I'll be just about old enough to start having children of my own."

"Well," said the bee, "I think I do understand better now. Your world certainly iz-z vaz-ztly different than mine. Imagine, having to z-ztudy to do z-zomething az-z natural az-z work! I do take it, though, from what you z-zay, that work iz-z one of the most important thingz-z in your world, az-z it iz-z in mine. We have a philoz-zopher-z-zien-tiz-zt, Z-Zigmund z-zomebody-or-other (for z-zome rez-zon I find his first name much eaz-zier to remember than hiz-z last) who conz-zidered happinez-z and competenz-z in work and love the two most important thingz-z in a beez-z' life. I must z-zay I've never found a bee who diz-zagreed with him. Iz-z finding and keeping love—having a loving family life—a key to making life worthwhile in your world too?"

"Oh, it certainly is!" said Billy. "I guess I care about that a whole lot more than I care about learning to work well!"

"How iz-z it, then," said the bee, the bottom of his antennae drawn together on his forehead in a puzzled frown, "that I heard you mention reading, writing, and arithmetic—whatever that might be—but I didn't hear you z-zay anything about learning how to be caring and loving toward your family or, for that matter, your friendz-z and fellow workerz-z? Are people like we bees are when it comes to love? Our mother, the queen, knowz-z exactly how to behave to make uz-z feel happy and loved. And we know from birth exactly what to do for her to show her how much we love and care about her. Iz-z it that way with you too—inz-ztinctive? Or did your mother, and will you, have to learn to show your care and your love? Iz-z that z-zomething that you alz-zo z-ztudy for many. . . . ?"

At that moment the bee jumped fully five feet up in the air and then headed straight away toward the distant trees. In just a couple of seconds he was but a speck, and in another he had completely disappeared from the boy's view. The boy had by then jumped to his feet and was rubbing his eyes. The book had tumbled to the grass. The cause of all the alarm was a shriek that came from a woman shaking a broom at Billy from the back porch of the boy's house:

"You lazy good-for-nothing boy, wasting such a beautiful summer day!" she said shaking the broom at him. "Get over here this instant or I'll give you a lesson you won't soon forget!"

"I'm coming, Mom!" said Billy. As Billy started for the porch, he wondered if the bee would ever come back to hear the answer to the question he was asking. Then he thought that probably the bee had already gotten the answer.

Knowing how to love children, parents, and fellow humans is unfortunately not instinctive for humans. Even the once unquestioned interactions of newborn and mother are now known to be the outcome of a delicate fragile process of early socialization that can easily be disrupted if the proper conditions to nuture the process are not present. Yet, as Bronfenbrenner (1979) said,

> A young person can graduate from high school at age 18 never having done a piece of work for anybody else, never having held a baby in his/ her arms for more than a minute, never having cared for someone who is old or ill, never having had to comfort the lonely. The result is a genera-tion of helpless misfits who do not know how to live with other human beings [pp. 35-36].

In addition to the interpersonal competencies specified by Bron-fenbrenner, there is the vast area of socialization of the individual to full participation in a democratic society. In fact, that is the raison d'être of the school system: "Public schools were established in order that all citizens should be made active and enlightened citizens in . . . government of the people, by the people, and for the people . . . " (Tippett, 1936). The central supporting psychoaffective pillar of democracy is compassionate empathy: the recognition that another's views may be as valid, perhaps even more valid than one's own, and therefore the desire to fully experience ideas and values from others' perspectives. We now know that this is an attitude, a skill, which can be taught. The school is a proper place to teach it along with other affective and interpersonal skills.

Even effective vocational preparation per se now requires the teaching of affective and interpersonal skills. Technological, scien-tific, managerial, and skilled labor requires such skills more than ever before. Such endeavors now are predominantly matters of team effort, and working effectively on a team requires affective and interper-sonal skills. Also, in today's work world, the provision of services occupies a greater place proportional to the production of goods than in the past. Good service-providing requires high levels of psycho-social skill.

One last point: The day of reading and talking computers that can translate voice to print and print to speeded-voice is dawning. When it arrives, psychosocial skills may be far more essential to almost everyone than the ability to read and write! It is not too early for the schools to begin planning to give even *more* emphasis to psychosocial skill training—for teachers as well as students—than to traditional cognitive subject matter. And what would be wrong with that? What good is it if students learn technical skills if these end up being used in the service of conflict and atomic annihilation?

With that we rest our case for the legitimacy of a prominent place in the public schools for affective education and psychosocial skill training. The next questions are: What psychosocial skills, in general, are the schools now teaching? And—more important, because for the foreseeable future the family will continue to be the institution in which individuals learn either compassion and love or intolerance and hatred—what psychosocial skills are the schools teaching that directly promote *family wellness?* Space limitations prevent detailed, exhaustive answers to these questions. However, in broad perspective we can answer as follows.

FAMILY-SCHOOL RELATIONSHIPS

The interdependence between school and family in the socialization of children has long been recognized. Much has been written about the invaluable contribution of family to children's academic progress and attitudes toward learning and, conversely, the value of teachers' interest and intervention in the families of their pupils. Methods of involving parents with formal education through PTAs, parent advisory committees, Home-State programs, and the like have been developed which serve primarily to upgrade formal education. Schools also have helped the family by providing health and safety programs, nutritious lunches and breakfasts, clothing exchanges, supervised programs for children who must arrive early and/or stay late, and so forth. Such direct support is critical to families, but contributes little to increasing the internal strengths of families. Rarely has the goal of any of these programs been a full sharing of mutually defined responsibility for the life education of children. Recognition of this broader goal as legitimate is developing slowly and unevenly, ebbing and flowing with changes in the economic and political climates. Nonetheless, recently steps have been taken in hundreds of instances to provide programs that educate students in personal and interpersonal competencies and for assuming adult roles in the family context. In selecting the types of activities undertaken by schools for mention in this chapter, we have chosen only those which have the potential for altering cognition, attitudes, and/or behavior in such a way as to result in higher levels of social competence and, directly or indirectly, of family functioning.

PROGRAMS FOR PERSONAL DEVELOPMENT

Value Clarification and Decision Making

Perhaps the most minimal departure from standard academic training are the programs designed to enhance personal competence. Many of these programs stem from concern about the abuse of drugs and alcohol or inappropriate ventures into sexual activity. Some of the drug abuse prevention programs have the goal of primary prevention, and thus are offered even at the elementary school level; these focus on root issues of values clarification and/or decision-making skills without referring to any specific problems. Some sex education programs are offered at both secondary and postsecondary levels that emphasize not mere biological facts or contraceptive methods but the responsibility assumed with sexual activity and also explore the effects of sexual behavior on relationships, as well as the impact of early pregnancy and parenthood on teenagers, their children, and their parents. Sex education programs remain among those most vulnerable to community fears that alien values will be communicated to the students.

Self-Awareness, Self-Esteem, and Self-Expression

Programs for increasing self-awareness and self-expression contribute to individual development as well as to interpersonal relations and can be conceptualized in terms of either. Such programs may be taught by teachers or by pupil personnel staff (e.g., guidance counselors). One of the most exciting areas in developing individual potential are the new programs aimed at developing feelings of self-esteem in students. In addition to writings that outline teacher behaviors that enhance self-esteem, there are program packages for the children themselves. One such program trains children to value individual group members whose status is low. Contributions such children make to the group are cited. Group status has been shown to increase along with a concomitant rise in self-esteem. Programs for children as young as kindergarten—earliest among them are the Bessell and the Palomares Magic Circle—cover awareness of feelings and the building of self-confidence. The DUSO (Developing Understanding of Self and Others) program by Dinkmeyer also can be considered a self-esteem building program. The SEE (Self-Enhancing Education) project is another model program.

Project HELP, conducted by the Rhode Island Department of Education, is a unique program designed to help youngsters from grades three through six function independently in the home while left there alone. The project HELP curriculum is designed to teach life skills that enable children to become self-sufficient and to build self-esteem by showing them how competent they really can be on their own. Program developers see the need for developing self-competence in children for home life because of the many parents who are away all day working and the many single parents who rely on the children to take over many adult chores including childcare.

Indirectly, an understanding and valuing of self is believed to result from including an emphasis on children's feelings about themselves and about others, while at the same time being taught in traditional academic subjects. Of course, teachers need not limit themselves to certain specified occasions; they can incorporate concern for affective development into their daily teaching plans (as in "Confluent Education"). Interestingly, there is evidence that an emphasis on affective education with its concern for the development of self results in higher academic performance as well as individual and interpersonal esteem.

PROGRAMS FOR DEVELOPING INTERPERSONAL COMPETENCE

Many programs have been incorporated into the public schools that involve training in skills that improve the interpersonal competence of children in the school setting. Conceivably, because of the prosocial nature of these competencies, the children's families benefit as well as the school group even though direct efforts to transfer skills to nonschool settings are rarely included.

Communication, Interpersonal Problem Solving, and Discipline

The emphasis on actual acquisition of skills and their application to suitable situations through modeling, rehearsal, feedback, and generalization characterize interpersonal skills programs. Limited training in communication can be started at the preschool level and be continued in a variety of programs through high school. Children are trained to be self-expressive, appropriately assertive, and, at ages earlier than previously believed possible, to empathize with others and to communicate their understanding of others in effective ways. One of the most extensive interpersonal training programs to date is that developed by Spivack and Shure known as the Interpersonal-Cognitive-Problem-Solving Training Program (ICPS). Children are trained to deal with hypothetical and actual interpersonal problem situations involving classmates. Recent attempts to help students transfer such skills to sibling-parent interactions should make a real contribution to family wellness.

Following pioneer work by Turner, Guerney and Merriam have successfully taught teachers to teach democratic procedures for solving interpersonal problems and establishing self-control and classroom discipline to children as young as six. The Pupil Relationship Enhancement Program (PREP) includes generic communication skills and interpersonal problem-solving skills that can be adapted to all school-age groups from elementary through college years and is readily generalized to family relationships. Programs based on modeling (e.g., Borgen and Rudner's work) and other behavior modification techniques take a different approach with the same goal of teaching youngsters how to cooperate with their peers and to control aggressive and impulsive behaviors. Here, too, transfer to the home situation would be a logical next step.

Interpersonal Skills Training Programs with a Family Orientation

The Life-Skills Training Program of Gazda, the Structured Learning Program of Goldstein, the Relationship Enhancement programs of Guerney, the Cincinnati Social Skills Development Program of Kirschenbaum, and the Life Skills for Health Programs of the North Carolina Department of Public Instruction share the common and exceptional feature of including components directed specifically to relationships with the families of students among other interpersonal components. Through the use of role-playing and audio-visual teaching materials, they create family-like situations that facilitate transfer to the home settings. A unique skills-training program has been developed by Seidenberg for training siblings to communicate and solve problems in relation to each other. Together, older and younger sibling pairs attending the same school learn in the school setting how to interact at home through the use of role-playing and training exercises.

Programs for families in transition have found their way into secondary schools and even elementary schools in some enlightened communities. These programs are somewhat different than those directed toward the development of relationships and instrumental abilities in the intact family. They presume that a remarriage has taken place due to death or divorce and that the new relationships will be complicated by grief and/or continued interaction with the original family. Consistent with the understanding that this is not exclusively a prevention effort is the fact that the reported programs are conducted by guidance counselors or other mental health personnel as opposed to teachers. Social and/or sports activities are sometimes included creating a peer group and an atmosphere of normality about their family situations for the youngsters. Such programming in the school day appears to represent a genuine out-reach effort on the part of the schools to meet a need of families.

Such is the case also with programs designed to help children deal with separation and grief. While, again, these efforts might be classified as secondary rather than primary prevention, it is just as legitimate to conceptualize them as creating wellness in the newly changed family grouping.

Programs with a Future Family Orientation

There are many marriage preparation courses in high schools teaching young people about the marriage relationship along with consideration of instrumental marital behaviors (e.g., finances and housing). While many of these are essentially cognitive in their approach, unique exercises are often introduced to make the courses experiential and dynamic. Mock weddings, family budgets, and the use of an egg that must never be left behind, and, of course, never broken (to demonstrate the diligence and care necessary in meeting family responsibilities) are among the more original. While "marriage and family" courses have been traditional offerings for many years in most colleges and some high schools, it is only recently that efforts to use experiential teaching and skills-training have been reported. The experiential and skills-training approach is vastly different from studying marriage statistics and facts about pregnancy and child development.

Though far from universal, courses on parenting information and/ or skills are frequently offered. Probably most broadly disseminated is the "Education for Parenthood" program sponsored by the U.S. Bureau of Education. This program contains cognitive, affective, and behavioral components with observation and active involvement of teenage youngsters with preschoolers in nurseries or day-care centers. Film strips of children and their families are used to discuss child development and parent-child interactions. While oriented toward adult responsibilities, the course does not emphasize projecting one's self into the future. Responding as a teenager to the wonders of little children and their problems and limitations provides the basis for both the cognitive and behavioral aspects. Feedback on practicum experiences is provided.

Many schools offer their own versions of Education for Parenthood including parenting courses and practicum components via small child study laboratories. Community preschool children attend for a minimal fee and are cared for by the students under the supervision of the laboratory teacher. Feedback and discussion of developmental principles round out the course. Schools lacking a self-contained child laboratory often arrange to have students volunteer in various community settings. A practicum course entitled Sensitivity to Children (offered by Stollak) in which undergraduates are trained to conduct play therapy sessions has been extremely successful for many years as a means of teaching normal child development. Readings and discussions about parenting behaviors that foster optimal child development and adult-child relationships are stressed in the lecture periods. A parallel course for teachers and child-care workers has also been developed for professional applications. Guerney's Parenting Skills Training program also has been used to train professionals in addition to high school and college populations.

Popular now in postsecondary schools (particularly junior colleges) are parent education programs designed for parents currently functioning in the parent role. Among the most widely known are Gordon's, Dinkmeyer's, and Patterson's programs. Courses oriented around film strips and tapes also have proliferated. Some programs are affectively oriented, some reinforcement-oriented, and some (e.g., Guerney's) include elements of both orientations.

Another type of programming permits the schools to serve a normalizing function for students struggling with the building of complex familial relationships beyond those of the nuclear, intact family. Among these are programs for pregnant teenagers or teenage parents. These courses sometimes include content reaching far beyond pregnancy and childcare per se, covering areas such as understanding of self, employment planning, relationships with the baby's father and grandparents, and peer and community relationships for the teenage mothers. Some include skill-training components.

DESIRABLE DIRECTIONS

While it is clear that many schools are moving in appropriate directions, it would serve the cause of family wellness to vastly increase the number of schools that include in the curriculum all of the types of programs described above on a regular basis. New programs also should be added that increase self-discipline, habit control, rational psychosocial thinking, and other new individual and relationship-enhancing skills.

We think it is very important that such programs not merely teach concepts and principles. Better, but still not sufficient, is the type of experiential learning that makes the principles emotionally meaningful through various tasks and exercises. We believe that to be long-lasting in its impact, such instruction needs to concentrate mainly on skill training as such. The concepts and principles taught need to be translated into *behavioral* terms, and the students should perfect and incorporate the skilled behaviors through *practice* with specific corrective and supportive *feedback* from the instructor.

In addition, we believe that in every area of such instruction, the ways in which such skills can be used to improve present and future *family life* should be brought clearly into focus and emphasized. Unfortunately, skills do not generalize readily from one life arena to another. Relationships with peers, superiors, subordinates, and family members need to become the targets of specific training separately as well as jointly. If a program of psychosocial instruction is to reach its full potential, its specific application in social situations, in the world of work, and in family settings, it needs to be separately considered and practiced *in vivo* and/or through role playing. The family— perhaps the most important of the three areas—is probably the area most likely to be overlooked by educators if the principle of attending specifically to each applicable life setting is not followed.

FACILITATING THE CHANGE

In contemplating how increased training of family wellness in schools might be facilitated, a number of factors should be considered. In the realm of traditional subject matter, in the coming decades we think technological aids—particularly audio-visual aids that will be linked to computer terminals making them responsive to the individual needs of each individual student—may release much teacher time for work best done by humans, and that would certainly include psycho-social instruction. Certain others things need also to occur, however, to facilitate a greater emphasis on family-oriented psychosocial instruction.

The first is educating the educators themselves as to the legitimacy and value of psychosocial instruction in facilitating cognition, voca-tional productivity, the welfare of the students, and the welfare of their future families. Second, the educators must in turn show the public that psychosocial education, and especially family-oriented psychosocial education, is an economically sound investment in the welfare of their children, themselves, and the nation. Third, the programs must be further perfected and their vocational and family focus made clearer and stronger. Fourth, teachers themselves need to acquire the attitudes and skills they will be teaching to the students. Finally, teachers will need to be well trained to conduct this special kind of teaching. Teaching appropriate attitudes, skills, and instruc-tional methodology for psychosocial instruction should not be left for teachers' postgraduate instruction. Such attitudes and skills enhance teacher effectiveness in all areas of instruction, not just affective education per se. It should be an important part of basic educational instruction.

Those links in the facilitative chain are interdependent, and their forging must be synchronized. Probably the most difficult link to forge is that of educating the public in order to win its support. We believe this may not be the impossible task that many—particularly many in today's sociopolitical and economic climate—might fear. We believe the task is feasible for the following reason: Over the last decade, following the lead of a colleague, Gary Stollak, we have been studying informally many groups of parents of elementary school students. We have asked these parents simply to write down the attributes they hope the school system will help their children to acquire. In our experience, the great majority of the answers do not stress purely intellectually or vocationally oriented attributes. Rather, they stress adaptability, the ability to get along with others, self-esteem, self-confidence, and other personal and interpersonal qualities. Apparently, parents generally can recognize more readily than many professionals that it is ineffective and costly to wait until something goes wrong before one tries to improve personal functioning.

Recent empirical evidence supports this concentration. Moore and Ishler (1980) researched citizens' views across the state of Pennsylvania and found that a "reordering of priorities within schools is called for to place greater emphasis on training students in skills that will be useful in adult life." The desire was expressed for more training in parenting, budgeting, respect, responsibility, and interpersonal communication. In another study by Love, finished in 1981, parents with children still in school acknowledge the value of teaching human development in the schools. In giving their opinion of the types of things which should be taught in school, parents ranked these questionnaire items first and second: "Students should be taught the skills necessary to be an adult family member," and "Our students should be taught in school how values affect their decisions."

Parents need to be shown that the school is willing to undertake psychosocial instruction and can help their children to achieve such valuable psychosocial attributes and skills. As more parents become convinced of that, what many now fear to be a stormy ocean of public resistance will be revealed instead to be a vast reservoir of public support.

REFERENCES

ANDRONICO, M. P. and B. G. GUERNEY, Jr. (1967) "The potential application of filial therapy to the school situation." J. of School Psychology 6: 2-7.

ASPY, D. N. (1969) "The effects of teacher-offered conditions of empathy, positive regard and congruence upon student achievement." Florida State J. of Educ. Research 11: 39-49.

———(1968) "The effects of the level of facilitative conditions offered by teachers upon student achievement indices." J. of Educ. Research 52: 87-94

———and W. HADLOCK (1967) "The cumulative effects of facilitative conditions upon student performance," in R. R. Carkhuff and B. G. Berenson (eds.) Beyond Counseling and Therapy. New York: Holt, Rinehart and Winston.

AVERY, A. W., K. RIDER, AND L. HAYNES-CLEMENTS (1981) "Communication skills in training for adolescents: A five-month follow-up." Adolescence.

BESSELL, H. and U. PALOMARES (1973) Methods in Human Development. La Mesa, CA: Human Development Training Institute.

BORGEN, W. A. and H. L. RUDNER (1981) Psychoeducation for Children: Theory, Programs, and Research. Springfield, IL: Charles C. Thomas

BROWN, G. (1971) Human Teaching for Human Learning: An introduction to Confluent Education. New York: Viking.

CARKHUFF, R. (1969) Helping and Human Relations, vol. I and II. New York: Holt, Rinehart and Winston.

CASTEEL, J. and P. DOYLE (1979) Valuing exercises for the middle school. Resource Monograph No. 11. Gainesville: Florida University.

DINKMEYER, D. (1973) Developing Understanding of Self and Others (DUSO, D-2). Circle Pines, MN: American Guidance Services.

———(1970) Developing Understanding of Self and Others (DUSO, D-1). Circle Pines, MN: American Guidance Services.

———and E. CALDWELL (1970) Developmental Counseling and Guidance: A Comprehensive School Approach. New York: McGraw-Hill.

———and G. McKAY, (1973) Raising a Responsible Child. New York: Simon & Schuster.

Education for Parenthood. (1974) U.S. Office of Education.

FELNER, R., A. STOLBERG, and E. COWEN (1975) "Crisis events and school mental health referral problems of young children." J. of Consulting and Clinical Psychology 43: 305-310.

Forum on Creativity, White House Conference on Child and Youth. (1972) "Creativity and the learning process." Colloquy 5: 3-7.

GAZDA, G. M. (1971) Group Counseling: A Developmental Approach. Boston: Allyn & Bacon.

GAZDA, G. M., F. R. ASBURY, F. J. BALZER, W. C. CHILDERS, and R. P. WALTERS (1977) Human Relations Development: A Manual for Educators. Boston: Allyn & Bacon.

———and D. K. Brooks (1980) "A comprehensive approach to developmental interventions." J. for Specialists in Group Work: 121-126.

GAZDA, G. M. and M. F. POWELL (in press) "Multiple impact training: A model for teaching/training in life-skills," in G. M. Gazda (ed.) Innovations to Group Psychotherapy. Springfield, IL: Charles C. Thomas.

GLASSER, W. (1969) Schools Without Failure. New York: Harper and Row.

GOLDSTEIN, A. P. (1978) Prescriptions for Child Mental Health and Education. New York: Pergamon.

GOLDSTEIN, A. P., R. P. SPRAKFIN, N. J. GERSHAW, and P. KLEIN (1980) Skill-Streaming the Adolescent. IL: Research Press.

GORDON, T. (1974) Teacher Effectiveness Training. New York: P. H. Wyden.

——(1970) Parent Effectiveness Training. New York: P. H. Wyden.

——[ed.] (1969) Psychotherapeutic Agents: New Roles for Nonprofessionals, Parents, and Teachers. New York: Holt, Rinehart and Winston.

——(1977a) Relationship Enhancement: Skill Training Programs for Therapy, Problem Prevention, and Enrichment. San Francisco: Jossey-Bass.

——(1977b) "Should teachers treat illiteracy, hypocalligraphy, and dysmathe-matica?" Canadian Counsellor 12: 9-14.

——(1979) "The great potential of an educational skill-training model in problem prevention." J. of Clinical Child Psychology 3: 84-86.

GUERNEY, B. G., J. (1981) "Foreword," in W. A. Borgen and H. L. Rudner (eds.) Psychoeducation for Children: Theory, Programs, and Research. Springfield, IL: Charles C. Thomas.

——"Skill training in interpersonal relations." Pennsylvania State University. (mimeo)

——and A. B. FLUMEN (1970) "Teachers as psychotherapeutic agents for withdrawn children." J. of School Psychology 8: 107-113.

GUERNEY, B. G., Jr. and L. F. GUERNEY (in press) "Family life education as intervention. J. of Family Relations.

GUERNEY, B. G., Jr. and M. L. MERRIAM (1972) "Toward a democratic elementary school classroom." Elementary School J. 72: 372-383.

GUERNEY, B. G., Jr. L. STOVER, and M. P. ANDRONICO (1967) "On educating the disadvantaged parent to motivate children for learning: A filial approach." Community Mental Health J. 3: 66-72.

GUERNEY, L. F. (1978) Parenting: A Skills Training Manual. State College, PA: The Institute for the Development of Emotional and Life Skills.

——(1973) What Do You Say Now? University Park: Pennsylvania State University in cooperation with the Pennsylvania Department of Public Welfare. (Film)

——and L. JORDON (1979) "Children of divorce—A community support group." J. of Divorce 2: 283-293.

HATCH, E. (1973) "An empirical study of a teacher training program in empathic responsiveness and democratic decision making." Ph.D. dissertation, Pennsylvania State University. (unpublished)

——and B. G. GUERNEY, Jr. (1975) "A pupil relationship enhancement program." The Personnel and Guidance J. 54: 102-105.

HAUSERMAN, N. J. S. MILLER, and F. T. BOND (1976) "A behavioral approach to changing self-concept in elementary school children." The Psych. Record 26: 111-116.

HAYNES, L. A. and A. W. AVERY (1979) "Training adolescents in self-disclosure and empathy skills." J. of Counseling Psychology 26: 526-530.

Human Relations Laboratory Training Student Notebook, Ed. 018834. (1961) Washington, DC: U.S. Office of Education.

JOHNSON, D. and R. JOHNSON (1980) "Promoting cooperation among pre-school children." Children in Contemporary Society 13: 134-137.

JUDAH, R. and D. B. KEAT, II (1977) "Multimodal assessment: the classroom ecology schedule." Elementary School Guidance and Counseling 12: 97-104.

KING, M. (1980) "Children: Self-concepts and communication skills." Children in Contemporary Society 13: 117-118.

KIRSCHENBAUM, D. S. and A. M. ORDMAN (1981) "Preventive interventions for children: Cognitive-behavioral perspectives," in A. W. Meyers and W. E. Craighead (eds.) Cognitive Behavior Therapy for Children. New York: Plenum.

LEVENSON, P., J. HALE, M. HOLLIER, and C. TIRADO (1978) Parenting Skills: A Curriculum for Teenage Mothers. Harris County: The Authority for Mental Health and Mental Retardation in Harris County, Texas.

Life skills for health: Focus on mental health. (1974) Division of Health, Safety, and Physical Education, North Carolina Department of Public Administration.

MERRIAM, M. L. and B. G. GUERNEY, Jr. (1973) "Creating a democratic elementary school classroom: A pilot training program involving teachers, administrators, and parents." Contemporary Education 14: 34-42.

MICHENBAUM, D. and J. GOODMAN (1971) "Training impulsive children to talk to themselves: A means of developing self-control." J. of Abnormal Psychology 77: 115-126.

MILLER, J. P. (1976) Humanizing the Classroom. New York: Praeger.

MOORE, D. and A. ISHLER (1980) Pennsylvania: The Citizens Viewpoint. University Park, PA: Pennsylvania State University.

PALOMARES, U. H. and T. RUBINI (1973) "Human development in the classroom." Personnel and Guidance J. 51: 653-657.

PATTERSON, G. and E. GULLION (1971) Living with Children: New Methods for Parents and Teachers. Champaign, IL: Research Press.

Project HELP (1979) Rhode Island Department of Education. Bureau of Vocational-Technical Education.

RANDOLPH, N. and W. HOWE (1966) Self-Enhancing Education. Palo Alto, CA: Sanford.

REIF, T. F. and G. E. STOLLAK (1972) Sensitivity to Young Children: Training and its Effects. East Lansing, MI: Michigan State Univ. Press.

ROCKS, T., S. BAKER, and B. G. GUERNEY, Jr. (1981) "Communication training for underachieving, low-communicating secondary school students and their teachers. (unpublished)

SAMUELS, D. (1977) "Dade County's PRIDE Program." J. of Drug Education 7: 29-32.

SEIDENBERG, G. H. (1978) "The sibling interpersonal improvement program and its impact on elementary and junior high school children." Ph.D. dissertation, Pennsylvania State University. (unpublished)

SHAFTEL, F. R. and G. SHAFTEL (1967) Role Playing for Social Values: Decision Making in the Social Studies. Englewood Cliffs, NJ: Prentice-Hall.

SHERIDAN, J. (1981) "Structured group counseling and biblio therapy as in-school strategies for preventing problems in children from changing families." (Includes a "Changing Family Handbook.") Presented at the annual convention of the American Educational Research Association, Los Angeles, CA.

SIMON, S. (1973) I am Lovable and Capable. Niles, IL: Argus.

SIMON, S. B. (1973) "Values clarification: A tool for counselors." The Personnel and Guidance J. 51: 614-619.

———L. W. HOWE and H. KIRSCHENBAUM (1972) Values Clarification: A Handbook of Practical Strategies for Teachers and Students. New York: Hart.

SPIVACK, G. and M. SHURE (1974) Social Adjustment of Young Children. San Francisco: Jossey-Bass.

TIPPETT, J. S. (1936) Schools for a Growing Democracy. Boston: Ginn & Co.

TURNER, M. (1957) The Child Within the Group: An Experiment in Self-Government. Stanford, CA: Stanford Univ. Press.

VALETT, R. E. (1977) Humanistic Education: Developing the Total Person. St. Louis: C. V. Mosby.

VOGELSONG, E. L. (1978) "Relationship enhancement training for children." Elementary School Guidance and Counseling 12: 272-279.

——R. K. MOST and A. YENCHKO (1970) "Relationship enhancement training for pre-adolescents in public schools." J. of Clinical Child Psychology 3: 97-100.

WEINSTEIN, G. and M. D. FANTINI (1970) Toward Humanizing Education: A Curriculum of Affect. New York: Praeger.

18

Growth-Promoting Family Therapy

Claude Guldner

Families are dynamic systems composed of complex patterns of organization and structure. These patterns must continually change in order to accommodate the needs of the individuals in the family system through the various phases of the family life cycle. The patterns must also adapt in order to meet the rapid and vast array of societal changes impinging upon families. In North American society there tends to be a pervading mythology about families, that they can be self-contained and self-sufficient in resources and in expertise in handling changes in ways that are beneficial for all involved. The spirit of rugged individualism of our pioneer past still influences families to want to "do it ourselves and in our own way."

The ability of North American families to use formal support structures, apart from times of crisis, seems relatively low. Many families even experience difficulty in using informal support systems such as the extended family, friends, and neighborhood, or natural groups like the church or school. For a family to live amidst the complexities of the 1980s and to believe that it can function smoothly and adequately through all the stages of a family life cycle is to be either highly optimistic or naive.

For example, there is so much information being rapidly exchanged today that the average family attempting to process it will experience an overload. The family must decide what is important to take in, how to let it in, and how to evaluate and make use of it or this information can get in the way of family functioning. Therapists and other family specialists are increasingly aware that families have difficulty in dealing with all the various and complex aspects of family living. Thus external facilitation as a formal support to the family system becomes vital if we are to enable families to actualize their growth potential rather than have them drift into problems that may make the family dysfunctional.

Salvador Minuchin (Minuchin, 1974) has described the family as society's principal stabilizing influence. Yet the family itself is constantly adapting to shifts from within the family and from outside it. Shirley Luthman expresses a similar faith in the family's adaptability and stability. According to her Growth Model theory,

> to be symptom free, all individuals must feel they are growing, producing, creating. . . . The family must allow this kind of growth and individuality, while maintaining its own stability and self-esteem. The family must also at the same time adapt to the continually changing growth needs of the family [Luthman, 1974].

She goes on to express even more strongly her belief in the individual's and the family's capacity for therapeutic change. In her theory of positive intent she says, "all behavior is somehow related to that intent to grow" (Luthman, 1974).

Virginia Satir (Satir, 1976) makes a similar point when she discusses the idea that a parent validates a child and builds his or her self-esteem by recognizing the child's growth, communicating that it has been recognized, and giving opportunities for the child to exercise the new abilities that are its consequence. The parents' own modeling of self-esteem teaches the child to value self and others. How the parents treat each other is the model for the child's regard for self and other people.

Marital and family enrichment programs have capitalized on the concepts of enhancing the strengths within individuals and systems as a means of promoting growth (Hof and Miller, 1981; L'Abate, 1981; Mace and Mace, 1978).

Growth-promoting family therapy can be understood from at least two perspectives. On the one hand, the concept of growth as the natural inclination of individuals and families can undergird the theory and practice of any family therapist. This therapist is alert to any potential for enhancing or releasing that growth dimension while working with the crisis that has brought a family into therapy. Many growth-oriented family therapists will work with the family to enhance its strengths for growth after having "solved" the problem that brought the family to therapy. During this stage of the therapy, the focus is on maximizing strengths and not on taking the therapy to a "deeper" level, which is often seen as the reason to extend therapy sessions once the presenting concerns have been alleviated.

The second perspective on growth-promoting family therapy is that of a therapeutic prevention service. The term "therapeutic" implies the need for extensively training the person providing the service. Unlike some prevention services that can be easily adapted and learned by paraprofessionals, growth-promoting family therapy should be rendered by a competent professional. More will be said about this later. It is a prevention service in that the families do not begin in a state of crisis. They come because they wish to enhance knowledge and skills that will enrich family functioning.

Most ordinary families have some ideas as to how to function along various stages of the family life cycle. However, when they become attuned to the wide range of possibilities for functioning, or become aware that they can intentionally change their level of functioning, they may seek therapeutic support to change family patterning toward the promotion of optimal growth. Having worked for the past 10 years in a context that provides family enhancement services in tandem with other therapeutic services, it is my belief that the families in a community do utilize these services as they are available and when their intent is clearly communicated. In our context families know they can come to therapy for enhancement purposes and do not have to have a problem or a crisis.

When we combine these two perspectives, growth-promoting family therapy can be provided for clients who come to the family therapist through four basic means.

(1) *Crisis intervention followed by growth-promoting therapy.* Many families come to the family therapist in the midst of a crisis with

which they are unable to cope. They break out of the family boundaries and reach out to someone for help. One way of looking at a crisis relates to growth, for we could state that the more a family system actualizes its growth potential the higher will be its level for coping. Though no family can avoid crises (such as death, by loss or natural consequences) how they deal with each crisis greatly varies. The family therapist working with a family in crisis evaluates the resources present—and those that are not present—in order to help the family to cope. Following the crisis reduction or resolution, the growth-promoting family therapist contracts with the family for a series of sessions aimed at enhancing present competencies and developing their latent strengths.

(2) *Growth promotion following problem focused therapy.* When a family is not in crisis but is seeking therapy, it is usually because of a problem identified as disruptive to positive family functioning. The problem may be focused on a child and involve issues such as failure in school, stealing, lying, conflict with siblings, or sexually acting out. The problem may be focused on a parent: A mother may accuse her husband of being uninvolved with his children and thus causing frustration and depression for her. A father may feel that the mother is too permissive or too strict and so the two fail to accomplish the task of adequate parenting. In these families someone is usually labeled as the scapegoat or symptom bearer. The family comes to therapy so that the designated "patient" will be helped to change. They seldom think there is a need for the entire family to make changes.

The family therapist must challenge their linear way of looking at the problem and help move them to a more circular perspective. As all members of a family are interdependent, anything that affects one individual affects the entire family, and vice versa. The family therapist will work with the family using a variety of models in order to reduce the stress. This may entail elimination of the symptom or problem. It could mean a change of focus within the family so that a shift in the patterns of functioning takes place bringing new levels of satisfaction for all family members. Many therapists may choose to stop at this point.

Growth-promoting therapist, however, continue working with the family at reduced intervals in order to crystalize present changes and to build on those new developments as a means of enhancing family growth. The Robins family's experience is a good example of this approach.

Vicki and Les Robins came to therapy concerned with the constant conflict between 13-year-old Doug and 7-year-old Geoff. Vicki had become depressed and felt helpless to handle the boys. Les commuted 65 miles to work and was home only late night and weekends, which were often spent relaxing or with his friends. The therapist contracted with the Robins for 10 weeks of family therapy. The structural therapy model was used with emphasis upon getting Vicki and Les to deal with their conflicts. It also focused on enabling Les to take more responsibility for setting limits and carrying out his parental control with the boys. At the end of the 10 sessions the family was functioning much better. During the therapy several concerns had been expressed around family goals, life-style, decision making, and use of leisure time. When these were reflected upon with the family a new contract on a biweekly basis was made to do some family enhancement therapy. The family began to define goals such as more fun times, less focus on making money, more cooperation with home duties. Behavioral plans for carrying through with these were made. In order to enhance differences it was decided that the kids would go to separate camps during the summer. During the therapy, tensions within the marital system emerged and four sessions were spent equalizing power and communicating more clearly each partner's needs, especially for affection. This family had a lot of good intentions, but the pressures of time and trying to "keep up with the Joneses" (two brothers in this case) had gotten in the way. The family enhancement therapy was able to slow down their hectic pace and give them a chance to focus on what was really important to them and how to achieve that. After eight growth-oriented sessions the family terminated therapy with an agreement to return in a year for a "well-family" check-up.

(3) *Life cycle changes and growth-promoting therapy.* Life cycle has to do with the natural and unnatural progressions that family systems move through in the course of their existence. Natural cycle events relate to getting married, having children, children going to school, becoming adolescent, their leaving the home, retirement, aging, and so on. Unnatural events refer to such experiences as separation, divorce, death, incapacitating illness, and the like. Life cycle events are the transition points within the family system. Essentially they acknowledge a time when a change in the family patterning is impending or in process. As these changes take place they frequently allow for new growth to occur. However, they can as well produce crisis and dysfunction for the family.

Growth-promoting therapy that takes place at the turning points of the family life cycle is aimed at helping maintain sufficient system stability to allow growth that enhances the functioning of the family rather than hinders it. During the past 10 years I have used and taught a model which focuses on the pre- and neostages of natural life cycle passages. One example is therapy for premarital couples, followed by neomarital therapy six months to a year after marriage. Another is work with prenatal couples to understand their marriage as a system and to see how that will need to change following the birth of a child. This is followed three to six months later by sessions with the "new" family. Another significant time is the transition from small school age children to adolescence. Working with these families at the preadolescent stage helps form a solid base in order to integrate changes necessitated by adolescent needs. This is followed by seeing the family while they are in the stage of raising adolescent children.

Having families available at prestages followed later in the neostage is an ideal arrangement. It is one that I believe could have long range benefits for family growth and health. Many families come for assistance when experiencing some doubt or uncertainty as to how adequately they are handling a developmental cycle. The following case is a good example:

Harry and Bertha Dell brought their family for family enhancement therapy when they felt concern about their parenting roles with adolescent children Tom (16), Greg (14), and Nell (12). Harry and Bertha had been married 18 years, which puts their marriage in a 15-18 year marital cycle. They were experiencing some typical difficulties of that stage. They had been spending so much time on their career developments, raising children, accumulating possessions, and gaining financial security that little time had been given to the maintenance of their marital relationship. Harry was 46 and dealing with concerns usually found in that stage of individual development for men. He was anxious about fulfilling himself at this point rather than about his job success. He was more in touch with his own inner feelings and wanted time for himself—"To be a better father and a more satisfied human being," as he put it. Bertha was also 46. She had reentered the work force 10 years before. She had achieved success. She felt good about her ability to develop herself as well as being an adequate mother. At this point she wanted more involvement with Harry and a reaffirmation of the marriage. There is an overlay of at least three life-stage cycles operating at any one time within the family system: the individual cycle of each family member; the marital stage; and the family cycle. All of these must be recognized and understood when working with any part of the family system.

Although Harry and Bertha and their family had come to gain new awareness and skills for coping as an adolescent stage family, the therapist must not ignore what is happening to individual and marital stages of development within the family system. The Dells will be looked at in more detail later in this chapter. The point to be made now is the recognition that transition points within any of the family life cycles can be a fruitful time for growth-promoting therpy.

(4) *Well-family interviews as a means of promoting family growth.* It will take a lot of time and public relations to enable families in a community to recognize the value of having regular family life check-ups, much as they might have family physical examinations. There are few families that do not ask the question from time to time "How are we doing as a family?" As noted earlier, few families use their informal support systems to talk with friends or other families and get feedback. Even fewer families seek formal therapeutic feedback about their family functioning. However, when it is done families find it a source of strength and comfort; it can create a range of choices for growth.

Well-family interviews may be done as a single session. The family is interviewed as a unit and the therapist highlights its strengths and provides information that reduces confusion. The therapist also enables the family members to see the range of choices they have which enhances differentness. The differences within the family can then be dealt with as strengths. As confusion goes down and choices go up, this produces a process that leads to competency building within the family system. The changes that the family members make through this process of awareness will more likely be growth promoting than growth restricting.

There are times during a well-family session when the family and therapist define an area where the family would like to enhance their attitudinal, behavioral, or communicational repertoire. A maximum of two sessions may be scheduled to focus on this clearly defined task. This is followed by a session three to six months later that enables the therapist to assure that the changes have become integrated and are beneficial to the family rather than creating dysfunction. Each family therapist develops his or her own model for conducting well-family sessions. The model just described has been used in my practice and training center over the past 10 years.

A MODEL FOR GROWTH-PROMOTING FAMILY THERAPY

There are many models of family therapy that could be adapted to conceptualizing and working with families where growth promotion is the goal. The following is a cubistic or four-level model integrating the elements of family systems theory and techniques for change.

LEVELS

The growth-promoting family therapist can enter the family system at any organizational level: individual, the couple, the family, the extended family or even a wider network of people involved. The Dell family again provides a good example:

Following the assessment session with the Dell family a contract for four family enhancement sessions was made for the whole family. It was also agreed that as a family they would join a four week family enrichment workshop. This would provide a context for some subsystem work with the adolescents in groups of their peers and parents with other parents. Harry and Bertha also agreed to participate in a marriage enrichment weekend coming up in the future. Although it was not agreed upon at the start, a fifth session took place in which Bertha's parents were included in order to do some boundary establishment work between the three generations. Since Bertha's parents lived near, it soon became obvious that they were much a part of the dynamics occurring in the Dell family.

Although no formal network therapy took place, the family was encouraged to use their informal network to achieve some of their growth goals. With the Dells, therapy took place at all levels of family organization, although it could just as well have taken place at only one or two. Growth promotion therapy can intervene at any and all organizational levels.

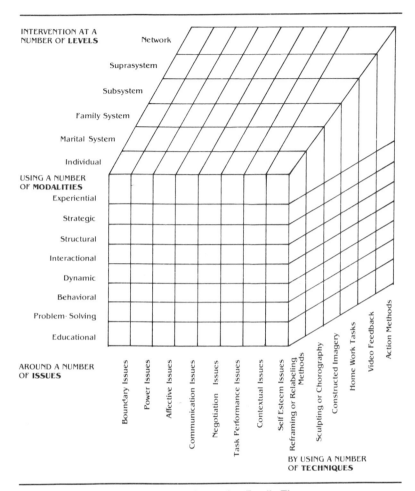

INTERVENTION AT A
NUMBER OF **LEVELS**

Network
Suprasystem
Subsystem
Family System
Marital System
Individual

USING A NUMBER
OF **MODALITIES**

Experiential
Strategic
Structural
Interactional
Dynamic
Behavioral
Problem- Solving
Educational

AROUND A NUMBER
OF **ISSUES**

Boundary Issues
Power Issues
Affective Issues
Communication Issues
Negotiation Issues
Task Performance Issues
Contextual Issues
Self Esteem Issues
Reframing or Relabeling Methods
Sculpting or Chorography
Constructed Imagery
Home Work Tasks
Video Feedback
Action Methods

BY USING A NUMBER
OF **TECHNIQUES**

Diagram 18.1   A Model for Growth-Promoting Family Therapy

MODALITIES

A wide variety of modalities can be used to enhance growth promotion within families. In an attempt to understand how people learn and acquire new behavioral patterns, growth promoting therapy is organized around eight primary modalities:

(1) People learn new ideas and behaviors from new information and instructions for its use from significant others. (Educational)

(2) People learn to function more effectively by acquiring new methods for decision making and problem solving. (Problem-solving skills)

(3) People learn to behave in new ways by imitating or using others as models and through establishing goals and receiving appropriate rewards when goals are achieved. (Behavioral)

(4) People learn to function more effectively by becoming aware of characteristics about themselves, about others, and about their environment. (Dynamics)

(5) People learn to function more effectively through contact with others communicationally, affectively, and cognitively. (Interactive)

(6) People learn through shifts in the organization and structure of one or more of the systems in which they are involved. (Structural)

(7) People learn through a strategic process initiated by another which changes the "set" of the individual within his or her context. This change may occur entirely outside cognitive awareness. It is frequently paradoxical in nature. (Strategic)

(8) People learn from an experience in the "now" which enables some novelty to emerge or risk to be taken and which breaks an impasse. Since it is an "experience" it often defies verbal explanation. (Experiential)

It must be granted that none of these occur in isolation and that there is a lot of overlapping between and among the eight. It is conceptually helpful to divide them for clarity of functioning, as we can see in the case of the Dells.

The Dells were provided with a good deal of new information that was supportive of their present level of functioning. In the therapy sessions, as well as in the marriage and family enrichment contexts, they were given opportunity to carry out exercises which provided new learnings (Educational). In the family enrichment workshop they had a chance to discover and work at new models of problem solving related to the adolescent developmental stage of a family. They also did some exercises related to parent-child conflict resolution (Problem-solving skills). Through the process of observing how other families handled parent-adolescent concerns they expanded their repertoire. They also worked at establishing goals for self and knowing how to reward those when attained (Behavioral). During the family sessions as well as the enrichment sessions each family member gained new insight into himself or herself as well as others in the family. This inlcuded how the extended family (grandparents) and the work context of the parents affected their family functioning

(Dynamic). A family session was spent in learning more constructive means of dealing with anger. Throughout the sessions emphasis was placed on practicing dyadic communication rather than on making global statements that tended not to have any impact or follow-through (Interactive). Enabling the parents to create clear boundaries around their marital subsystem and to form a clear parental alliance changed the structure of the family. This had an effect on how power was handled and this enhanced awareness of distance-closeness regulating patterns that enabled all family members to have clearer levels of autonomy and to enjoy their contact when together (Structural).

Bertha viewed herself as adequate in most of her parenting except in some areas of her relationship with her daughter Nell. There she frequently talked on inadequate feelings and behavior. It also emerged that Nell was the one in the family that had most conflict with her grandmother, Bertha's mother. The grandmother would often bypass Bertha and attempt to deal directly with Nell. It became obvious that Bertha and Nell were recapitulating what Bertha and her mother had gone through. A strategy was decided upon to enhance Bertha's competence as a parent (what she did with her sons could be generalized to her daughter) and not support her sense of inadequacy. Also a strategy was developed in which Bertha would seek out her mother as a support. Rather than be a go-between she would contact her mother directly and discuss her parenting style, being open and direct when she differed with mother and where she was in agreement. This would keep the old and unresolved conflict where it belonged between Bertha and her mother and not being acted out through Nell (Strategic). There were many examples of experiential learning. When the family was discussing patterns for showing affection and what they would like they were encouraged to "show me." Rather than letting the parents discuss how they might work closer on their alliance when it came to decisions around the kids they were asked to "do it now." Frequently the sessions moved into periods of "show me what it would look like if you were at home," as well as "how would you like it to be—do it now" (Experiential).

STRUCTURES

There are structural patterns present within every family which are organized as uniquely as a finger print. An examination of the family theory literature produces a range of terms and descriptions of these patterns. Integrating the findings from other theorists with my own experience I have summarized these structural patterns of family systems within eight broad issue areas:

(1) Boundary issues have to do with several aspects of family functioning. A family needs a distinct boundary between the integral family members and those in the extended family. There need to be clear boundaries between the marital subsystem (H-W) that provide each spouse with companionship, affection, sharing, and sex; and the parental subsystem (F-M) where the couple perform an executive function through nurturance, control, and later the guidance of their children. Boundary issues also reflect the degree of total family bonding. If the boundaries are enmeshed the family is often one with very tight and rigid boundaries around the family and inside it. It may be difficult to know where one person stops and another begins, and the myth is often "We are a close-knit family." Other families are disengaged, which means there is a lot of space between members. They may come together in crisis, but the myth is generally, "We are self-sufficient and really don't need a lot from others." Finally, there are families that are differentiated—there is a rhythm of being separate and autonomous as well as coming together for mutuality and belonging. These differentiated family boundaries provide security for being apart without being ejected or being close without getting stuck.

(2) Power issues have to do with where the focus of power resides within a family and how the rules were formulated that brought this into being. The power base may shift as the family moves through the stages of its life cycle. Power issues also relate to the areas of intimacy, nurturance, guidance and control.

(3) Affective issues relate to the degree of feeling availability within the family and the means of expressing feelings that are acceptable to the family system. In some families only certain feelings are okay. These feelings are generally labeled positive and the negative ones must be suppressed. In other families feelings are unleashed and become destructive. In some families there is a wide range of feelings which can be expressed congruently within the context.

(4) Communication issues concern how the family members communicate with each other; that is, how information exchange takes place. Growth communication is direct, clear, specific, congruent and is generally dyadic in nature—that is, aimed at one person at a time within the family.

(5) Negotiation issues go beyond communication. They have to do with how families resolve issues that relate to individual and family functioning. Conflict resolution, decision making, and problem solving skills are all part of negotiation issues.

(6) Contextual issues have to do with space, time, and energy within individuals and the family. How do people get into and out of each other's space? Do people have enough space for privacy? What are the time sequences within the family? How much time is spent together and in subsystems and individually? Energy relates to the reality that most family members operate on differing energy levels at different times. How the family deals with this difference becomes important to positive functioning.

(7) Task performance issues relate to how the family carries out its function of being a family. It includes the broad issues of enculturation of the children, rearing and nurturance of children and adults in a family context, as well as the everyday process of handling family household tasks such as cooking, cleaning, and washing. Task performance can be flexible, rigid, chaotic, or structured.

(8) Self-esteem issues must acknowledge the reality that individuals and families experience varied levels of esteem. Family members need to feel and experience themselves as self-loving, self-accepting, and self-competent.

Any one or all of the eight structural issues provide material that can become the focus for growth promotion within a family system. For the Dells several structural issues were focused upon.

The boundaries were clarified between the primary and extended family, especially those between Bertha, her mother, and Nell. The boundary protecting and enhancing the marital subsystem within the family context was given a new importance. The parental alliance was given strength. Tom was enabled to see his role more clearly as just one of the kids, and not a substitute boss through power of being oldest. Power issues were focused on through enhancing the parental alliance so that they felt more together and not working at odds much of the time. They also worked at a more democratic process of sharing information and feelings upon which decisions in the family were made. Affective issues came into focus in learning more appropriate and comfortable means of expressing anger and hostility. This also enhanced their ability to share more physical contact. This had been present earlier in the family life cycle but had been dropped out as the kids moved into adolescence. Both parents expressed a need for this contact with the children. When this was understood by the kids they became more relaxed and open to "hugs and kisses." Communication changed in that less exchange took place that was nonspecific and it became more dyadic. Communication thus became more direct, clear, and congruent. This all had an effect on negotiation.

As lines of power became clear, communication direct, and feelings more accepted, negotiating became easier. The family also learned new skills for negotiating. Throughout the sessions, task performance became enhanced as a result of better negotiation, communication, and clear awareness of power structures. Tasks became more flexible and shared around the family as opposed to being male- and female-oriented in performance. The contextual issues of space, time, and energy made significant changes. First of all Harry and Bertha defined more time for themselves individually as well as for themselves as a couple. This often involved being together in their room without interruption. They learned they didn't have to leave the context to get private space. A sense of individual space emerged in the family. Each learned to respect the space needs of the other and to guard his or her own. More time emerged to be together as a family. Meals were eaten together more often rather than in the TV room. More flexibility in time for carrying out task functions was allowed, accounting for individual energy levels at different times in the day.

Although the self-esteem level of this family had been quite good it improved during the sessions. There was an increase of self-acceptance and other types of acceptance. The stress throughout the sessions on levels of competency refocused the awareness of all on the unique contributions of each family member. All this added to a more solid sense of self-love and a feeling that it was "good to be in this family."

TECHNIQUES

The growth-promoting family therapist can use endless techniques provided the operational framework is on growth. Some examples of techniques are described below and some are illustrated through the work with the Dell family.

To look at boundary issues the Dell family was encouraged to use family imagery to construct a fence around them. What would it be made of, how would it look, how high or low, how many gates in it, and who comes in and out of the gates? Is there anyone within the fence that doesn't belong, or anyone the fence needs to keep out? (Nell shared the information about grandmother at this point.) What does each individual fence look like—the couple fence, the fence around the kids? Imagery becomes an excellent technique for seeing what is there, as well as for identifying the potential within family members that can be drawn upon for growth enhancement.

Family sculpting was used with the Dells when looking at power issues. Each was given a chance to sculpt the family, in light of how much or how little power to influence changes in the family each had. Chairs and stools of different heights enhance this process. Each individual first does it as he or she sees it now, and then as each would like it to be if it could be changed to meet his or her own needs. Each person shares verbally what it is like to be where placed by the sculptor.

Video playback or audio playback can be helpful in enabling the family to learn about its communication process. Video can also reflect the affective level of the family or various individual members.

The use of homework tasks based on action plans can be very vital in promoting growth. Bertha had a task to do with her mother. She and Nell also chose to spend more time together. Tom and Greg were to make more independent decisions. Harry was to find time to be more self-indulgent at least three times a week without feeling guilty. These are a few examples related to specific issues of growth.

In growth therapies, the technique of reframing or relabeling what is viewed by a person in regard to self or other family member is very important. Most families fall into patterns of labeling self and other and it becomes very difficult to change the "set" of that thinking. However, when a therapist presents a new "set" for looking at that behavior, it joggles the pattern and can create a new perspective that can stimulate a change process. For example, Harry believed that his desire for more time for himself alone was self-centered and Bertha colluded with him in this belief. The therapist reframed this issue by saying tht Harry was in touch with a normal and vital ingredient for personal satisfaction that frequently reemerges in one's mid-40s. It was important that he indulge himself in this without guilt if he were to provide a model for his adolescent children to move into separateness and yet still feel a strong bond of family mutuality. This new perspective freed Harry to find ways for doing this rather than simply longing for it. It broke Bertha's colluding negatively and enabled her to support his autonomy positively. The therapist's reframed message to both children and parents that individuation, which included separateness as well as belonging, was an important process for everyone.

Finally, the more words that can be changed into action within growth promoting sessions the better. When Bertha talked about being put down by her mother she was encouraged to get down on the floor and get in touch with what that feels like. She could also gain a clearer perspective on how she got herself into that position and what alternatives she had for dealing with it differently in the future. When Harry talked about Tom and Greg being so "tied" together, the two boys were encouraged to tie a rope to each so that they could "experience" how difficult it was to be clearly separate. Action pictures are powerful and send messages for change at feeling levels, as well as bringing cognitive awareness.

This cubistic model provides the growth-promoting family therapist with a range of possible contact points with a family. How the therapist uses such a model will depend upon training and the working context.

THE THERAPIST AND THE CONTEXT

Growth-promoting family therapy is not just another tool in the therapist's repertoire, nor should it be viewed as just another service that an agency provides. Prevention services require new lenses through which to look at community needs, agency policy, and how the therapist functions with families. It is my belief and experience that several factors must be considered if growth-promoting family therapy is to work.

Let's begin with the therapist. It is my experience that beginning therapists do not work well with primary prevention services. Most of their educational and training background and supervision has been to discover pathology, or "what is the presenting problem of the family and how does that fit in with how the therapist sees what the family is experiencing." It is very difficult to change this way of looking at families, to learn instead to bypass many areas within the family that may be problems or potential problems and focus upon the strengths and competencies present in the family. As Louis L'Abate explained in Chapter 4, for many beginning therapists this takes away the excitement and intrigue of working at the family puzzle. When a therapist feels comfortable about his or her problem solving and change skills, then that therapist is ready for a different challenge. That challenge comes through prevention services like growth promoting family therapy in which the therapist enables the family to investigate how they are functioning within the family structural areas, to find and learn to reward competence among its members and for the family as a unit, and to expand its repertoire without having change become the producer of new problems. The fine use of timing—knowing where to intervene and where to provide maintenance—is a very important function. The use of structured homework tasks that augment sessional learning and the ability to create methods by which the therapist and the family have a chance to devise different means of functioning in the here and now are essential. However, it takes skilled therapeutic awareness of family theory, family therapy techniques at a vareity of levels, a high reliance upon intuition or "what feels right for this particular family at this time," and the ability to integrate and implement these in action.

Any agency providing this approach to working with families must establish a policy that is understood and sanctioned at all levels of operation. It is important that the board of directors clearly understand and support prevention as a service that supplements all other services and that can stand alone on its own offerings. I was involved with one agency where the board agreed to preventive services but later kept raising questions about the small amount of revenue these programs were bringing in. This caused the staff to cut back on prevention offerings. The board, or individuals responsible for the on-going direction of an agency, must understand the potential long range consequences to a community (and to the agency itself) of prevention services.

Directors and supervisors must also be committed or the service can easily be sabotaged. I know of one situation where the supervisor kept challenging members of the staff for failing to see how seriously disturbed many of the families were that had been placed in their "well-family" services category. Despite the fact that the families had come for three sessions designed to augment their "wellness," the supervisor felt the therapist was neglecting far too much pathology. Those therapists who were not so committed to the program soon began to "hook" their clients into longer term therapy that was problem focused rather than growth oriented. How this can happen was eloquently described in the L'Abate chapter.

The staff must have a commitment to growth in their orientation. I have consulted with many agencies that were interested in providing prevention services. After being with them for a short time I can now almost predict those where the services will work and those where it will not. The variable is the ability of the staff to talk about the potential for growth within individuals and families. It is especially significant that the staff should see the growth potential in what is labeled a "problem" by the family or the therapist. When staff members view families from this perspective they are already working at a growth promoting style, and it will be easy for them to move into services more directly designated as prevention. The staff must present these growth promoting services at their regular team and case conference meetings, use these cases for research, talk about them with each other, and generally keep them in the foreground. Otherwise the prevention area will gradually find itself pushed into the background and before long subtly phased out of the service.

Finally, it will only be when community awareness is behind this kind of service and when communities have governmental, religious, educational, and industrial support for it that we will see a major change of direction toward prevention. This is a difficult task—it is much easier for most communities to focus on problems rather than prevention. Because of this lack of foresight, the growth-promoting family therapist must become a political activist, prodding the community into awareness and then into providing service.

As Professor Kenneth Boulding, the eminent systems economist, has said, one of the most important ecological resources we have today is the family as a learning center. To maximize that resource we will need to enable families to value their task of learning how to learn. Dr. Boulding believes that we need to learn a good deal more about how families produce competencies among their members. Following that, we need to learn interventions that will be growth promoting of individual competencies within the family context. Growth promoting family therapists are responding to both of these challenges.

REFERENCES

HOF, L. and W. MILLER (1981) Marriage Enrichment: Philosophy, Process, and Program. Bowie, MD: Robert J. Brady Co.

L'ABATE, L. et al. (1975) Manual: Enrichment Programs for the Family Life Cycle. Atlanta: Social Research Laboratories.

LUTHMAN, S. (1974) The Dynamic Family. Palo Alto, CA: Science and Behavior Books.

MACE, D. and V. MACE (1978) "The marriage enrichment movement: its history, its rationale, and its future prospects," in L. Hopkins et al. (eds.) Toward Better Marriages. Winston-Salem: ACME.

MINUCHIN, S. (1974) Families and Family Therapy. Cambridge: Harvard Univ. Press.

SATIR, V. (1976) Making Contact. Millbrae: Celestial Arts.

Epilogue

David R. Mace

In this book we have examined, at many levels and in some detail, the concept of family wellness. We have seen that it is already being promoted, and we have looked at some exciting future possibilities.

The goal is ambitious—to do whatever lies in our power to make possible the full development of their relational potential to all families willing to claim it. As yet we have only a partial concept of what this would mean. But in our midst we have some families that are functioning at very high levels, and we could learn from them what resources they have used in the process of achieving this important objective. In fact, we have already begun to do this.

Nothing stands in the way of our continuing and increasing studies of this kind. The families concerned would be delighted to share their good fortune with other families who are falling far short of their hopes and expectations. The field for a major investigation along these lines is wide open.

By a concerted and enlightened effort, therefore, it should be possible to identify clearly what families need, in their early development, in order to maximize their later chances of achieving high levels of wellness. The marriage and family enrichment movement already knows some of the answers—truly effective interpersonal communication, the necessary skills to resolve conflict creatively, and the criteria for progressive relational growth—these are good examples.

This means that we already are in possession of the resources we need to launch a major campaign to promote family wellness. And once this is in operation, further data necessary to improve the process would be continually becoming available.

If we did in fact launch, on a wide scale, a national program for family wellness, what might we hope to achieve? One obvious result would be a significant reduction in the number of broken families. No one in his senses would seriously suggest that any and every marriage could hope to reach the high level of our present cultural expectations. But it is equally true that no one in his senses could justifiably claim that our present rates of marriage failure are inevitable and unavoidable. I have often said that most of those who resort to divorce today are not failures, but victims—victims of a culture that sees them embark on a difficult enterprise, and provides them with neither a clear sense of direction, nor the tools and skills necessary to make the journey successfully. Much of the same can be said of parents who fail to give their children what they need in order to grow up to be mature, responsible adults.

Supposing we were to begin to change our disastrous laissez-faire policy, and to devote enlightened and sustained efforts to the task of equipping men and women with the necessary resources and the kinds of support systems that could enable them to succeed where so many are now failing. Supposing we could thus begin to increase significantly the number of strong, skilled, and enlightened families in which the conditions exist for warm, caring, creative relationships to develop between husbands and wives and between parents and children. Supposing we could gradually convince the citizens of this country that the qualifications for effective functioning in a family are at least as important as are the qualifications for success in a career, and that we now planned to make it possible for all who wished to gain these qualifications to do so. What might be the results?

Surely the logic is unassailable. From an increasing number of truly happy homes there would begin to come forth growing numbers of mature and fulfilled men and women, their lives enriched by loving relationships that gave them a deep sense of self-worth and a strong sense of purpose. In those homes, sons and daughters would grow up who were emotionally secure, developing their natural abilities in an atmosphere that inspired them with high ideals.

These results would be registered, over time, in falling statistical records for crime, delinquency, personality disorder, physical and mental illness, and other troubles that simply reflect the high proportion of unhappy and maladjusted people who are the inevitable products of malfunctioning families.

Moreover, this would be achieved at greatly reduced cost in terms of the maintenance of legal, medical, and social services that are now rendered necessary to cope with the tragic products of the disordered and conflicted state of so many of our homes.

This is not a new idea. A saying from ancient China, attributed to Confucius and variously rendered, says something like this: "When there is happiness in the home there is order in the community; when there is order in the community there is prosperity in the nation; when there is prosperity in the nation there is peace in the world." Another way of putting it is that the quality of our marriages decides the quality of our families, and the quality of our families decides the quality of our communities. Can anyone seriously question this?

What then stands in the way? One obstacle represents a serious concern on the part of some professionals in service agencies. It has been referred to by two of our authors—L'Abate and Guldner. There is no doubt that, at the present time, most people are not prepared to find money for preventive services, at any rate on a scale comparable with the fees they will pay for therapy. I call this phenomenon the "pain-gain formula." When you are in so much trouble that you are really hurting, you will engage the services, almost regardless of the cost, that can provide treatment that will bring you relief. And this principle has also its public aspect. Money can be raised or granted by local authorities to help people who are really suffering. Prevention may be better than cure; but cure is what brings in the cash. And here I am not speaking in judgment—highly trained professionals deserve to be paid adequately for their services.

There is, however, yet another obstacle in our path. It is the unwillingness of most people to acknowledge that achieving well families calls for highly developed skills which they don't naturally possess. Clark Vincent calls this the "myth of naturalism"—the widespread assumption that we are endowed by nature with all that it takes to achieve successful family relationships, and that to admit that we have anything new to learn is to appear stupid or incompetent. There is no doubt that this myth stubbornly survives. Indeed, it lies at the root of the "pain-gain" formula. It is only when we are in serious trouble that most of us become willing to acknowledge that we need help; so that, added to our hesitation to spend good money on professional assistance, there is the view that it is also humiliating to have to do so. It therefore becomes habitual to us to put off accepting help as long as possible—and sometimes then it is too late.

These are powerful barriers, and it will take skill and determination to overcome them. But the process is already in operation, and I believe time is on our side. My hope is that this book may help to speed up the process.

What we now need is a determined and sustained campaign to convince people of the wisdom of making the shift from our present massive array of remedial services, to a more balanced program which makes preventive services equally available, and convinces people that it makes good sense to plan ahead so as to avoid the kinds of disasters which could otherwise overtake them. We have already done this for life insurance and for dental care. The time has now come to do it for family wellness.

About the
Authors

EDWARD BADER and CAROLE SINCLAIR: Bader is Assistant Professor in the Department of Family and Community Medicine, University of Toronto, Ontario, Canada. He played a leading role in an extensive research project to investigate the effectiveness of premarital and neomarital programs for couples. He works closely with Carole Sinclair, his wife, who is a physician.

TED W. BOWMAN is Family Development Director, Family and Children's Service, Minneapolis, Minnesota. He has played a leading part in helping the Family Service Association of America to develop a national policy in the preventive field.

DAVID and SARAH CATRON are both psychologists with particular focus in the family field. They have served together as Presidents of the Association of Couples for Marriage Enrichment.

ANN ELLWOOD is Founder of MELD, a pioneering program for the preparation of husbands and wives for their first experience of parenthood. The program is supported by a number of foundations and is being established in various cities in the United States.

BARBARA and ROBERT FISHMAN are both family therapists. Barbara is also a teacher and researcher; Robert is Executive Director of Resources for Human Development in Ardmore, Pennsylvania.

THOMAS GORDON: Founder of the Parent Effectiveness Training Course, he is also the author of the well-known book of that title. He is nationally and internationally recognized as a leading authority in the field of parent-child and teacher-student relationships.

BERNARD GUERNEY, Jr., LOUISE F. GUERNEY, and JANET M. SEBES: Bernard Guerney is Professor of Human Development and Head of the Individual and Family Consultation Center at Pennsylvania State University. With his wife Louise Guerney and colleague Janet Sebes, he has done pioneering work in interpersonal communication training. He authored *Relationship Enhancement,* a classic in the field.

CLAUDE GULDNER is a marital therapist and Professor in the Department of Family Studies at Guelph University in Canada. He is a leader in the fields of marriage preparation and marriage enrichment.

LUCIANO L'ABATE: A pyschologist and Professor at Geogia State University, L'Abate is also the author of many books and articles and a recognized authority on training professionals for preventive services to families.

DAVID R. MACE is Professor Emeritus of Family Sociology at Bowman Gray Medical School, North Carolina. Formerly Executive Director of the American Association for Marriage and Family Therapy, he has also served as Vice President of the International Union of Family Organizations.

DAVID H. OLSON: Professor at the University of Minnesota, he has a national and international reputation as a researcher in the field of marriage relationships. He is author of *Treating Relationships* and the developer of many programs for testing the effectiveness of premarital and marital relationships.

MARGARET M. SAWIN is internationally known for advancing the field of whole family enrichment. She is a consultant to churches of all denominations and the author of both *Family Enrichment Through Family Clusters* and *Hope for Families.*

LEON SMITH served as Director of Marriage and Family Ministry for the United Methodist Church in the United States from 1962 to 1982. He has also been actively involved in the National Council of Churches and is known for having been a pioneering force in the development of marriage enrichment.

NICHOLAS STINNETT is Chairman and Professor in the Department of Human Development and Family, University of Nebraska.

He is a recognized figure in the initiation and advancement of national and international studies of family strengths.

ROBERT P. and PATRICIA Y. TRAVIS: Robert, a Professor, and Patricia, an Instructor, are Codirectors of Marital Health Studies, Department of Psychiatry, University of Alabama, Birmingham. They have developed the Pairing Enrichment Program and are coauthors of *Vitalizing Intimacy in Marriage.*

DANIEL WACKMAN: One of the first to work in the field of couple and family communication, he is Professor at the University of Minnesota and a partner in Interpersonal Communication Programs, Inc.